Distinctively American

Distinctively American

The Residential Liberal Arts College

Edited by
Steven Koblik
Stephen R. Graubard

Transaction Publishers
New Brunswick (U.S.A.) and London (U.K.)

Contents

Preface

WE LIVE IN AN AGE OF CELEBRITY. For most individuals, fame's tenure may last a week, a month, perhaps a season. It rarely survives a year, and almost never a decade. Many of yesterday's supposedly significant men and women do not even figure as footnotes in history; they scarcely exist, having lost all their purported importance. Who, for example, recalls even the names of the principal members of former president George Bush's cabinet, individuals once thought to be consequential? The greatest number, denied the perpetual gaze of television and newspaper reporters who are able to make and break reputations, have retired into obscurity. When one considers that most undersecretaries and the small army of assistant secretaries in President Clinton's administration are no better known, inside or outside the Beltway—the president's "friends" having a much better purchase on the mass media's attention—one can only conclude that fame in the last decade of the so-called American century has indeed become evanescent; celebrity is a thing of the moment.

This same condition, interestingly, does not appear to obtain with American institutions. In many instances, having once acquired a certain reputation, they do not quickly lose it. There are exceptions, of course; many of the country's major business corporations that were recognized to be powerful and affluent only a few decades ago have very obviously receded in importance, often to be replaced by others that may not even have existed half a century or longer ago. Yet with intellectual and cultural institutions, decline and demise appear to be appreciably less rapid. One thinks, in this connection, of American institutions as famous and varied as Harvard University, the Metropolitan Museum of Art, and the *New York Times*—to name only three—who today enjoy vastly enhanced reputations. While some may regard their recent fame as the product largely of late-twentieth-century mass media "hype," and others, recognizing America's perpetual fascination with money, may view their renown as a reflection of their vastly expanded financial portfolios, with all the advantages that such wealth brings, no one can seriously doubt that their national and international reputations at the end of the twentieth century greatly exceed any that they enjoyed at the beginning, in Theodore Roosevelt's heyday.

Why should a preface to a book entitled "Distinctively American: The Residential Liberal Arts Colleges" open with a consideration of questions of reputation, celebrity, and fame? In part because these colleges, often small, with only a very few enjoying what can be termed national or international reputations, figure prominently among the insufficiently studied institutions of a society too preoccupied with bigness and increasingly overwhelmed with what the mass media declare to be important. In these circumstances, much that is distinctive to higher education in the United States, those attributes that make the American system very significantly different from any other, are generally lost sight of. The residential liberal arts colleges of the country, while scarcely invisible, do not today figure in the public prints or in television commentary as the country's major private and public research universities do. This is a loss to the nation; it distorts an educational reality that expresses values, practices, and ambitions still unique to the United States.

It may be useful to recall how recent has been the extolling by foreign observers of any segment of America's higher educational complex. Europeans, for example, in the habit of disparaging America's colleges and universities until a hundred or so years ago, began to view these institutions with some modicum of respect only quite recently. Today, when it has become common to speak of "world-class universities"—a term both hyperbolic and vulgar—the United States is acknowledged as standing at the head of the queue. Its most prominent research universities, spread over the continent, are recognized to have only a handful of rivals abroad. While such a claim to American superiority would not have been made even as late as 1914 by Lord Bryce in the third edition of his very popular tome, *The American Commonwealth*—Bryce being one of the first of Europe's men of learning to acknowledge the importance of American higher education—such an attribution might have been made by 1936, the year of Harvard's tercentenary. The claim would have had even greater resonance in 1945, the year when Nazi Germany and Imperial Japan were defeated.

If World War I did much to diminish the principal universities of Europe, even those able to claim distinguished medieval, early modern, and modern origins, and if World War II had even more nefarious effects, revealing the intellectual, economic, and political vulnerabilities of once-proud societies, American universities were not comparably affected. On the contrary, these terrible twentieth-century European civil wars contributed greatly to the aspirations and enhanced reputations of a number of American universities. While a very different judgment would have to be rendered on how the Vietnam conflict affected American higher education—a subject even today more given to rhetoric than to analysis—the society's growing preoccupation with its power and influence has created forms of myopia that bestow significance principally on whatever is recognized to be large and therefore, by definition, important. Optimum size—a classic Greek concept—is not much thought about in late-twentieth-century America. In the circumstances, a handful of higher educational institutions receive an inordinate amount of attention, with others being insufficiently known.

When violence, of the kind rendered famous by pictorially compelling events on Telegraph Avenue, Morningside Heights, and in Harvard Square, is added to the mix, the mass media are in their element. It is much less interesting for them to dwell on the educational practices and philosophies of smaller institutions, to consider how they may be faring in these days of rapid social and cultural change. Yet it is precisely in the study of these institutions—many with proud histories and traditions—that the problems of contemporary America are very obviously illustrated. This, indeed, may be the principal rationale for devoting a book to a segment of American higher education that by definition does not grow and faces very real challenges but persists in believing in its traditional commitments to teaching and learning, accepting the potential need to reconceive both in the context of a society only superficially resembling the one that existed so recently.

These colleges, with their individual and collective enrollments relatively miniscule when compared with those of the great private and state universities of the country, continue to believe that their faith in the advantages of modest size, small classes, and systems of instruction that rely on residential settings are still very much relevant today. Competing for both students and professors—understanding what other institutions are able to offer—they remain committed to educational principles that make the teaching role primary. Knowing that their instructional objectives cannot be realized simply through the provision of more ample classroom space, state-of-the-art libraries, modern scientific laboratories, and a plethora of courses treating every conceivable subject—and yet obliged to address all these needs because so many others do—they seek to demonstrate the virtue of their size and, even more, of their continued commitment to students living together in dormitories that cannot be confused with the skyscrapers of downtown America.

To praise one segment of the American higher educational universe—that of the residential liberal arts colleges—does not call for a disparagement of any other. If the ambition of these colleges is to be viewed as exemplars of certain educational values and ideals, then declaring this to be their sole educational objective is certainly not enough. These colleges, in providing teaching models that merit study by others, in encouraging faculty-student collaboration of a kind not common in other intellectual settings, offer a distinct alternative to the forms of instruction common in larger institutions. If, in addition, they are able to show the self-discipline that allows them to emphasize certain subjects, leaving others to the more specialized universities, they accept the proposition that there is not a single road for all undergraduate colleges to follow. In such policies, they also speak the language of necessity, an idiom wholly acceptable to a society that is not seeking uniformity in its educational offerings.

At a time when new technologies are thought to be rendering irrelevant the teaching practices of yesterday, when distance learning is lauded and private firms offer themselves as certifying bodies to provide the educational credentials that businesses and others will deem satisfactory, the liberal arts colleges of the country are compelled to be explicit in propounding a quite different set of values. Their faith in the liberal arts—not as the nineteenth century chose to define them or as the twentieth century practiced them but as the twenty-first century will be obliged to reconsider them—is being tested. Until there is a keener appreciation of what the natural sciences, the humanities, and the social sciences have become, until candid inquiry into both their successes and their failures as modes of inquiry and as intellectual disciplines prevails, the country will be riven, revealing either a too bombastic triumphalism about its educational accomplishments or an equally unattractive and exaggerated pessimism. Until higher education for the most ambitious youth in American society is seen as something other than credentialing—providing a certificate that the individual will be able to exchange for something called a job—the joys and necessities of learning will be rendered in a debased coinage. The best of America's liberal arts colleges recognize that their so-called product is something other than a negotiable instrument designed to guarantee employment.

In their emphasis on the values of community, and not as utopians of every age since the Renaissance have explicated those virtues but as young men and women living at a time of unprecedented change are invited to consider and experience them, the better liberal arts colleges seek to foster relations among students, faculty, and their communities that rely on continuous discourse, on an ethic of sharing not universally appreciated today. Achieving intellectual purposes—support-

ing the values of criticism and candid inquiry at a time when
many of the major cultural, social, and economic institutions of
the society preach quite other values, emphasizing certainty
and success—cannot be easy. The term "useful" needs to be
given new meaning by those who understand what Alexis de
Tocqueville learned from his travels through the country more
than a century and a half ago: Americans will most ardently
seek those things they believe will offer them concrete advantages. The liberal arts colleges of the country, if they remain
faithful to their declared intentions, can never accept the values
of the mass media, with their somewhat arbitrary and ill-
conceived formulations of what they think to be best, in higher
education as in so many other things. Because present circumstances compel these colleges, predominantly private institutions, to think in market terms—to consider the wishes of their
so-called customers, both parents and students—they can rely
on the principle of *caveat emptor,* refusing to make exaggerated claims for their own wares but knowing that the fatuous
pursuit of the inconsequential and the trivial in higher education can never prove to be a good bargain.

For the liberal arts colleges of the country, the challenge of
the moment is to articulate and realize purposes that extend
well beyond the purely vocational, avoiding the policies once
pursued based largely on ethnic, racial, and religious exclusions, on snobbery and ignorance. The virtues of the learning of
the past can never be despised, but the vulgarity and parochi-
alism of earlier times ought also to be seen, acknowledged, and
avoided. The residential liberal arts colleges of the country,
once predominantly tied to specific religious denominations and
now more frequently secular, once gender-separated and now
more often coeducational, pride themselves on what they perceive to be their newly achieved "diversity." Their efforts in
this regard almost certainly exceed their accomplishments. True
diversity is still an objective to be sought, and it goes beyond
ethnicity, race, gender, and sexual orientation. So, also, there is
a desperate need for a truly international perspective, which is
not simply related to the cliche of the world having become a
"global village." Today it is easy to be beguiled by the "village
pump politics" of a nation that for the moment lacks a military

rival and too frequently acts as if its current economic prosperity is destined to last forever. There is much in American higher education today that is distinctly provincial. It is by no means certain, for example, that without a greater commitment to the study of foreign languages and foreign cultures, of the history and traditions of many, which translates into something more than a mere proliferation of courses, American undergraduates will be able to learn what is necessary for intelligent living, defined as something more than having gained a vocation or profession.

It is a truism to say that we live in a time of rapid change. The more compelling observation is that we are obliged to consider how traditional institutions, including American colleges and universities, are changing, how they ought to change, and why it is not enough for them simply to crave bigness. Their concern with quality ought never to be subordinated to other more superficial goods. America's liberal arts colleges can be an example to other higher educational bodies, but also to other institutions that have no wish to abandon or neglect those human values once greatly prized.

The creation of communities of serious discourse—an invaluable educational experience for young men and women destined to live their lives in the twenty-first century—is not an objective easily achieved in an age so preoccupied by the ephemeral, so unwilling to make the effort to understand complexity. It is not enough to be a "caring and sharing" society. Even the most attentive care provided to individual students, taking into account both their intellectual and psychic needs, can never be sufficient. We live in a time of casual propaganda and calculated insult, where the intelligence and potential of individuals is rarely sufficiently acknowledged. Our preoccupation with celebrity and with what passes for fame makes us see ourselves and the institutions the society has managed to create in much too superficial a way. This book, in seeking to explore both the triumphs and challenges of one segment of the American higher educational universe, is concerned with a larger question: What ought this country be teaching its young, the many millions who now throng its colleges and universities?

Thanks are due to the Annapolis Group—an association of the presidents of 110 small liberal arts colleges—whose initial discussions in New York did so much to define the agenda for this study. Their generous financial benefaction, which helped provide editorial and other support, also made possible a meeting of authors at the House of the Academy in Cambridge, where all the draft essays were criticized and discussed. David Finn, of Ruder·Finn, first brought the editors and the Annapolis Group together, and all of us feel a deep sense of gratitude to him for seeing that such a collaboration was possible.

Stephen R. Graubard

Steven Koblik

Foreword

THE WESTERN UNIVERSITY TRADITION began in the medieval learning centers of Europe. The American university tradition began with the founding of the first residential liberal arts colleges of Harvard in 1636 and William and Mary in 1693. As the country expanded, similar institutions sprang up in nearly every state. Designed to serve religious, intellectual, personal, local, and practical needs, these institutions were the pioneers of American higher education.

By the late nineteenth century, new forms of higher education, especially the land-grant colleges, technical schools, and research universities, had developed. While most of the residential liberal arts colleges chose to remain small and committed to undergraduate education, a few of the most prominent—Harvard, Yale, Princeton—elected to become research universities while retaining an undergraduate liberal arts college or program at their core. The spectacular growth of American higher education after World War II—in terms of both total student enrollment and new schools—occurred primarily at large public institutions. This expansion was driven by public policy, which saw new investments in higher education as crucial to the future of the country. The residential liberal arts colleges became an increasingly smaller part of the educational scene. Today only 4 percent of all American baccalaureate degrees are awarded at these institutions.

Yet these colleges remain remarkably prominent in and vital to American education. They remain the best models of under-

Steven Koblik is President of Reed College and a member of the Annapolis Group.

graduate education in the country. Educators at the large public schools create "honors colleges" or "residential colleges" to try to emulate their values. Whole new institutions, such as the University of California, Santa Cruz, were created in their spirit in a university setting. The small schools continue to produce disproportionate shares of the country's leaders—doctors, lawyers, teachers and professors, politicians and civil servants, and businessmen.

For most Americans, the residential liberal arts colleges lack visibility. They have neither famous athletic programs nor large numbers of alumni. The media tend to ignore them. The colleges themselves have been buffeted by the main cross-currents of American higher education: the dominance of the large public and private universities; increased specialization of the professoriate; the creation of a highly competitive national market for higher education; the economics of the education sector; and a growing public demand for training and certification rather than the preparation of our youth for lives that will be satisfying, professionally and intellectually. Today, small residential liberal arts colleges, even the strongest of them, face an uncertain future.

This book seeks to examine the residential liberal arts colleges—where they have come from, their current condition, and their future prospects. The reader needs to appreciate that the 212 remaining residential liberal arts colleges represent an amazing diversity of institutions: sectarian/nonsectarian, coeducational/single sex/historically black, highly selective/open admissions, local-regional/national, and strongly theoretical/practical. These differences do not undermine their common characteristics: residential, small (five hundred to three thousand students), educationally comprehensive, close interaction between student and teacher, and totally dedicated to undergraduate education. They are distinctively American; no other country has schools committed so clearly to the highest quality of undergraduate education.

Hugh Hawkins

The Making of the
Liberal Arts College Identity

FOUNDED AS A NORMAL SCHOOL and serving later as a teachers college, North Adams State College lobbied successfully in 1997 to be renamed "Massachusetts College of Liberal Arts." The institution's leaders sought inclusion in a well-established category of higher education, one that is peculiarly American. The institutional identity of a "liberal arts college," however, has emerged only after some painful vicissitudes.

In undertaking a survey of those ups and downs I am well aware that educational history, however delightful to its practitioners, gives no close guidance in policy decisions. There is nevertheless comfort in knowing of earlier administrators, teachers, and students who faced uncertainties. This is not to say that their responses will apply today; still, a historically contextualized approach is likely to be healthily tentative, with more respect for alternatives and imponderables and an awareness of the strange interlacings of persistence and change.

NEW VARIETIES IN HIGHER EDUCATION: THE NINETEENTH CENTURY

In the United States of the mid-nineteenth century, no one was deeply concerned about a specific meaning for "college." Every frontier community, it sometimes seemed, wanted one and state legislatures issued charters without asking hard questions. An "academy" and a "college" often competed for the same students and offered the same subjects. Although the name "university" was usually associated with a single institution that

Hugh Hawkins is Professor of History and American Studies at Amherst College.

was the capstone for education in a state and somewhat more of a state obligation than other educational institutions, there were conspicuous exceptions. In spite of the vindication of continuing charter privileges in the Dartmouth College case of 1819, the distinction between "private" and "public" institutions remained hazy. A college with enough influence in the legislature could get not just a charter but supporting grants, often in the form of land.[1]

Observers with European experience might find fault with the untidiness of it all. At England's Oxford and Cambridge, a college was a residential unit that performed teaching functions but lacked degree-granting authority. In Germany, the gymnasium prepared students for entrance into a "university," where they at once chose a specialized "faculty"—philosophy, theology, medicine, or law. French education at all levels still functioned under the highly standardized system instituted by Napoleon I, with ultimate authority assigned to the minister of public instruction.

Though they were to grow much more intense by mid-century, as early as the 1820s calls for a more utilitarian approach questioned the customary required curriculum with its emphasis on ancient languages and mathematics. Nowhere were these challenges as thoughtfully addressed as at Yale, where paired reports drawn up by faculty and trustees defended Yale's "impractical" course of study. The heart of the document declared:

> The two great points to be gained in intellectual culture, are the discipline and the furniture of the mind; expanding its powers, and storing it with knowledge. The former of these is, perhaps, the more important of the two. . . . No one feature in a system of intellectual education, is of greater moment than such an arrangement of duties and motives, as will most effectually throw the student upon the resources of his own mind. . . . The scholar must form himself, by his own exertions. . . . We doubt whether the powers of the mind can be developed, in their fairest proportions, by studying languages alone, or mathematics alone, or natural or political science alone.[2]

Strong, artful words. But this rationale of 1828, though often cited and quoted, did not convince all academic leaders. Colleges began adding "partial" and "parallel" courses that let students avoid classical languages and study more science, though these programs did not lead to the prestigious B.A. degree.

Portentous of things to come, in the 1850s the University of Michigan, under a German-inspired president, offered training to graduate students and gave an earned advanced degree (unlike the familiar, virtually automatic, "in course" M.A.). Further evidence of educational ferment came with the creation of Farmers' High School, which soon gave a bachelor's degree and was renamed the Agricultural College of Pennsylvania. Like Peoples' College in New York, it expressed the irritation of practical folks with the elitist limitations of existing colleges, a dissatisfaction reflected also in the founding of technological schools that took the name "institute."

Even though President James Buchanan had recently justified vetoing a similar bill partly on the grounds that it was prejudicial to existing colleges, passage of the Morrill Act in 1862 brought little reaction from educators. The act provided federal land grants for support in each state of at least one institution where the leading object was "to teach such branches of learning as are related to agriculture and the mechanic arts," but "without excluding other scientific and classical studies." Supporters of the infant agriculture schools might have rejoiced, but presidents of the classical colleges did not at first see the new institutions as serious rivals. By 1890, however, when the Second Morrill Act provided for continuing annual federal support for the "A&Ms," small colleges struggling for adequate enrollment began to think themselves unfairly disadvantaged.[3]

Another alternative institution was well defined by the 1890s. "Universities" now differentiated themselves from "mere colleges." After the granting of the first American Ph.D.'s—by Yale in 1861 and Harvard in 1873—came the opening in 1876 of Johns Hopkins University, with research and graduate study as its central purpose. By 1892, the revived University of Chicago proposed to compete with the most advanced universities of Europe. If universities that included liberal arts programs for the bachelor's degree were to be the academic apex, then the "mere colleges" needed to find a clear rationale for their existence and to reconsider their claims to preeminence in the American educational world.

The colleges' intimate connection with religion seemed for some time to offer a firm bulwark. Besides the Congregational-Presbyterian alliance to christianize the West by (among various means) founding colleges, other denominations sought to sponsor at least one college in each state. Such foundings continued apace in the post–Civil War years. These multiplying institutions maintained that they deserved support as Christian communities. They helped questioning youth find faith, trained ministers and missionaries, and kept the children of believers true to the family's denomination (though welcoming others, since potential students were scarce). Colleges also relied on local or regional loyalties. Often their location traced back to an initial town subsidy. Their presence represented civilization, and supporting them let local elites claim a more elevated social function than just raw economic development.

The heightened self-awareness of colleges helps explain a new stress on their role as preservers and purveyors of something called "the liberal arts." If not unique in this task, at least they could claim to be the institution most deeply dedicated to that ideal. Might there not be a way to define the liberal arts that gave a special role to the colleges? Technology and engineering, studies that emphasized things rather than ideas, had no place in the liberal arts colleges. Though supportive of the study of nature (the work of the Almighty), they subordinated it to religion and ethics. No course was more important than moral philosophy, usually taught by the president to all seniors. Graduates, it was asserted, left college with a Christian worldview and standards to guide them through life.

From the more ambitious "universities" the colleges could distinguish themselves by remaining undistracted by specialized studies, studies alleged to be narrowing, even inhumane. Contributing to the growth of new knowledge was less important than conveying to promising members of the rising generation what Matthew Arnold described as "the best which has been thought and said in the world." The human products of such education would take their places among the "cultured" and be prepared for positions of leadership in civil affairs.

Bruce Kimball's study of the liberal arts idea from antiquity to the present distinguishes between the orator tradition (as in the Ciceronian emphasis on civic duty) and the philosopher tradition (as in the Socratic emphasis on questioning).[4] This contrast, which is immensely useful to intellectual historians and encourages a refreshing skepticism about alleged etymologies, is nevertheless one that college spokesmen skated between or found ways to blend into a list of goals. To the extent that their rhetoric can be pinned down, nineteenth-century college representatives preferred the orator tradition, and increasingly so as college revivals and conversions declined in frequency. Here was a substitute for the religious dedication that had often motivated the founders; here was a counter to both the utilitarianism of the technology schools and the claims of "new truths" made by the universities. One heard more and more about "character," "the well-rounded man," and "social service."

The critique from the universities was sometimes gentle. Daniel C. Gilman, president of Johns Hopkins, declared that colleges' preparation of students through the baccalaureate course was a boon to his institution. Hopkins deemphasized its own undergraduate program and insisted that candidates for the Ph.D. already have their bachelor's degree, setting the same entrance standard for M.D. candidates. The latter requirement was unique in the 1890s, but even universities that demanded two years of college before admission to their medical and law schools helped colleges attract students. Leaders of the professions began to stress the need for collegiate preparation, well aware of the potential gains in status and income if qualifications were made more rigorous.

Harvard's Charles W. Eliot was less charitable than Gilman. Scoffing at colleges' claims to produce "well-rounded" graduates, he recommended analogizing the educated mind with a cutting-tool or a drill. As for the religious claims of colleges, those suggested to him narrowness and prejudice. It was "impossible to found a university on a sect," he announced. He was especially hard on the Jesuit colleges' curriculum, which he extravagantly judged to have "remained almost unchanged for four hundred years." In a sharp exchange with President Charles A. Blanchard of Wheaton College in Illinois, Eliot disparaged church colleges as obstructing students' access to the fullest and most stimulating education. For his part, Blanchard called for "a multitude of Colleges widely dispersed," where instructors "who do not worship God" would not "instruct the children of men and women who do." Blanchard also attacked Harvard's elective system for encouraging premature specialization and spiritual decay. Harvard, of course, prided itself on pioneering this system, which widened from the 1860s on until in 1899 nothing was required but English and a foreign language in the freshman year. This "system of liberty," Eliot claimed, allowed all students but the hopelessly shallow to find an interest that released their greatest potential. Confinement to required courses, even in the first years of college, was stultifying.[5]

Since small colleges could not afford to hire the additional faculty electivism required, they sought to vindicate a more limited curriculum. Here they received help from some professors within the proud new universities. Princeton's Woodrow Wilson warned against "the scientific conception of books and the past." Harvard's Irving Babbitt found the free exercise of student choice a dubious development if one valued, as he did, the humanistic tradition with its allegiance to standards, accumulated wisdom, and balance. But besides claiming to provide "that without which no one can be an educated person," some college spokesmen renewed the case for mental discipline. Latin and mathematics should be required because they had proven ability to strengthen the mental faculties. Perhaps Latin and mathematics were not unique in this capacity, but in any case, the faculty as a body was better positioned than students to declare which studies offered genuine intellectual exercise. Allowed free choice, the argument went, students would select the easy courses, or the entertaining ones, or, if they could find them, those that were both.[6]

But none of these prescriptions—not readying students for graduate study, nor the cultural elevation urged by the humanists, nor the strengthening of mental functions—offered panaceas for ailing colleges. In the early 1880s, the presidents of Dartmouth, Hamilton, and Union, who too vigorously played the patriarchal role, something essential to the early colleges, found themselves labeled as anachronisms and placed on trial by the trustees after student and faculty complaints.[7] It was at about this time that clerical influence among trustees began to shrink, and the boards increasingly included successful lay alumni, most of them with urban careers.[8]

In a perceptive study of four mid-Atlantic institutions, W. Bruce Leslie has shown their gradual development of a collegiate culture that had become dominant by the time of World War I. This culture included eliminating preparatory departments, becoming more age specific, relaxing curricular requirements, downplaying religion, and encouraging a vigorous extracurriculum with sports competition at its center. More often than not, these colleges were coeducational. The new collegiate pattern included loosened denominational, ethnic, and local ties and sought students more widely, though colleges still did not welcome blacks, Catholics, or Jews. The first two groups were assumed to be happier "among their own kind," and the last was reputed to corrupt the collegiate atmosphere by being too aggressively studious. In short, the product of these colleges was to be a Protestant gentleman, economically successful and socially adept, one who could answer with confidence the question "What is your alma mater?"[9]

To a considerable extent the same ideal was set for women students at coeducational institutions, though with less expectation of economic achievement or social leadership. The separate colleges for women, especially those founded after the Civil War, such as Wellesley and Smith, attracted students and benefactors partly because of parental caution and partly because women's colleges could combine intellectual challenge with special attention to female self-assertion. Women's colleges were one of the few places where women could pursue intellectual careers, and the faculty sought to inspire confidence in their students that they were as intelligent as men and more insightful into the evils of industrial society. In the social settlement movement, college women took the lead.[10]

Leslie's chapter title "The Age of the College" points to the largely successful effort to form a new institutional identity between 1880 and 1917, but from the standpoint of academic influence and social power, the era has been properly labeled "The Age of the University." In fact, one of his four selected institutions, Princeton, did become a university during this period in both form and name (though it did not develop a medical or law school). Another, Bucknell, continued to offer under-graduate vocational programs even as it claimed to be a "liberal arts college." This duality of function came to characterize another variant that emerged during these years, especially in the cities—the "comprehensive service university," an institution that gradually increased its attractiveness as an alternative to the small residential college.

DEMONSTRATING THE SPECIALNESS OF
LIBERAL ARTS COLLEGES, 1900-1940

Near the turn of the century, national organizations were forming among self-consciously categorized institutions of higher education, a step liberal arts colleges were slow to take. The Morrill land-grant colleges created a national group in 1887 and began a fruitful career of lobbying Congress. A less-active association of state universities followed in 1895. A third organization, the Association of American Universities (AAU), in 1900 identified its members (originally only fourteen) as those with worthy doctoral programs. It tried with some success to squelch colleges that granted low-quality Ph.D. degrees. Some of these offenders were indeed diploma mills, but others were respectable colleges, stretching a point to enhance the reputation of a faculty member or reward a recent graduate who remained on campus for further study. When the AAU found that European universities were rejecting the undergraduate credits of any student not trained at an AAU member institution, the organization began paternalistically to issue a list of "approved" colleges, those whose alumni were regularly accepted for entrance into graduate work by AAU members. The sternly limited list that initiated the program in 1913 embarrassed the omitted colleges. It was gradually expanded, and for a time inspection of candidate institutions constituted the AAU's major activity.[11]

Even as they moved toward the new collegiate model, colleges had plenty of reason to be worried. Academic leaders like John W. Burgess of Columbia and William Rainey Harper of the University of Chicago had been suggesting that small colleges might do well to shrink to two-year institutions—leaving all advanced work for the B.A. to the universities—or even to disappear, squeezed out between universities and enhanced secondary schools. For several decades denominations had supported their colleges through national boards, with the Methodists being particularly active in such oversight. But by 1915 a group of college presidents, notably Robert L. Kelly of Earlham, decided on a more ambitious undertaking. They formed the Association of American Colleges (AAC), which was an outgrowth of a loose confederation of church boards of education but also included non-church-related institutions. The shift was timely. Various forces were loosening ties between colleges and churches, not least the restriction to "nonsectarian" institutions that was attached to the professorial pensions offered by the new Carnegie Foundation for the Advancement of Teaching.

A clear defensive strategy marked the AAC's effort to regularize the definition of a liberal arts college, with an early AAC committee spelling out the minimum criteria for membership and setting higher preferred standards. The association asked the United States commissioner of education to drop the label "sectarian" and distinguish between "church-controlled" and "church-affiliated," and it urged legislatures to block the creation of "institutions with vastly inferior standards." Still, the AAC's efforts were modest compared to the Carnegie Foundation's push to regularize colleges by issuing lists of those with adequate faculty, endowment, and admission standards. In practice the AAC rarely rejected an applicant for membership; still, its promotion of the liberal arts helped those making the case for the four-year college as a clearly identified stage in the formal pursuit of learning, one that provided the sine qua non for those hoping to become "educated persons."

Among the multiple voices within the AAC those stressing intellectual development were only part of the mix. However, two college leaders who first found an audience shortly before the AAC's emergence gained persisting influence as advocates of intellect. Alexander Meiklejohn, dean at Brown and then president of Amherst, attacked the slogans of "efficiency" and "social service," maintaining that "the primary function of the American college is the arousing of interests." The founding president of Reed, William T. Foster, helped create an institution that abjured intercollegiate sports and fraternities and required all seniors to write a thesis. Both objected to the vapid utterances of some who urged the offering of more "culture courses."[12]

The years between the two world wars saw a widening of the distance between universities and liberal arts colleges. An influx of students made universities even larger (seven thousand in 1920 at the University of Wisconsin, ten thousand a decade later), a development welcomed by university administrators seeking legislative support or gains in tuition income, but one that further opened their institutions to charges of impersonality and a lack of distinctive mission. Colleges reasserted their conviction that small size encouraged a healthy sense of community, that they could attend to a student's all-around development (mind, body, and spirit comprised the usual formula), and that college faculty were dedicated teachers not seduced by the mystique of research. Four years with one's age cohort in a physically attractive setting, usually nonurban, promised a life-enhancing self-development.[13]

In the 1920s "selective" colleges could use the new popularity of higher education to adopt a strategy of recruiting widely while limiting enrollment and raising tuition. Some colleges declared themselves to be "small but national," and admission officers or committees could see to it that only suitable companions for their largely middle-class clientele were admitted. The standard of "character" became a sifting device to keep out the grubby, and regional quotas that produced "geographical diversity" could help limit the proportion of "New Yorkers" (or whatever the euphemism was for Jewish applicants). In time, requesting a photograph or the mother's maiden name aided in selecting the desired "qualified student."[14]

Those admitted could look forward to congenial pastimes and opportunities to meet altogether suitable candidates for matrimony. If they wanted to cross social class lines, then a stint in a college-sponsored settlement house might serve. Whereas once women students had been regarded as the most serious of all, seeking to prove their intellectual equality with men, now jokes abounded, such as the one about seeking not the degree of B.A. but of "M.R.S." The pleasure and the prestige of college attendance figured in different proportions among prospective students and their parents, but the combination of these motives surely helped increase enrollment. Political ambition might be better served by going to the state university, but for other forms of "leadership" the small colleges were increasingly the choice of upper-middle-class youth. Ways of showing advanced literacy had changed, but they still mattered in cultivated company. Where once college graduates had been equipped to insert Latin phrases into their conversation, now they could quote a line of Wordsworth or T. S. Eliot.

Briefly after World War I groups that overlapped the AAC membership hoped to reinvigorate the religious emphasis within colleges. Although the pan-Protestant Interchurch World Movement collapsed, the Council of Church Boards of Education continued to be active. Goshen College and other evangelical institutions maintained a strong religious ethos, as did Catholic men's and women's colleges, the number of the latter rising sharply in the 1920s. Elsewhere, the YMCA and YWCA played useful roles as activity centers (sometimes, indeed, altruistic activity), but the collegiate religious atmosphere bore little resemblance to the revivalism and missionary zeal of the mid-nineteenth century. As for required chapel services, they disappeared at Yale after a student campaign for abolition, and some colleges followed suit. Where chapel survived, it usually became briefer, less frequent, and less overtly religious. Still, the image of the "godless university" continued to enhance the case for attendance at a small college, and the term "church-related" allowed for a religious aura without any implication of coercion or proselytizing.[15]

Novels and magazine stories about taboo-breaking students (*This Side of Paradise* set the trend) and ominous connotations to the new term "flapper" made smaller colleges attractive to worried parents. Colleges' rules for student conduct could be stricter than those of universities, or, if no different, better enforced. But student rebelliousness could surface at the small institutions also. At Fisk in Nashville, then known as a "Negro" college, the students successfully battled rules that banned dating and football and so brought their school closer to the dominant liberal arts college model.[16]

The thirties differed, of course, from the twenties. There was less spending money, less frivolity, more concern about economic issues and the danger of another war. In the early depression years enrollments dropped and endowments lost earning power. Some colleges had to close, but a larger number entered into mergers, a step especially notable among church-related colleges and applauded as a corrective for excessive competition, even within the same denomination. When enrollment figures rose, the colleges did proportionally better than the universities. Paid work through the National Youth Administration helped students stay in school, and with few jobs outside the schools, nothing was lost by prolonging one's education. One ambitious youth who found his way to a small college linked to his denomination was Ronald Reagan (Eureka, class of 1932). Others found it necessary to live at home and attend the closest institution, which for Richard Nixon (Whittier, class of 1934) meant a college suiting his family's Quakerism. In contrast, Alfred Kazin took the subway from his family's Brooklyn home to populous City College, where secularism and radicalism set the tone.[17]

One problem for small colleges was that universities typically included a "college of arts and sciences" devoted to the needs of undergraduates seeking a liberal education. These "university colleges" tended to attract more public attention than most colleges could hope for, and not just by dominating the sports pages. They drew praise in educational circles for curricular innovations, such as concentration-distribution requirements at Harvard and the contemporary civilization course at Columbia (developed out of the war issues course). Although denied the renown of being the originating institutions, colleges could readily imitate such programs; an honors system, including tutorials, comprehensive examinations, and senior theses, gave Swarthmore a lasting reputation for challenging bright students to move beyond traditional "college life." Swarthmore's president, Frank Aydelotte, a former Rhodes scholar who insisted that Swarthmore could be both democratic and elitist, became widely known as a spokesman for new possibilities in undergraduate education.[18]

NEW CONFIDENCE, NEW CHALLENGES, 1940–1970

As during the previous war, higher education joined vigorously in the nation's drive for victory in World War II. The desire for national survival and the defeat of a fascist enemy were leading motivations, but there was also the very practical consideration that government training programs could help compensate for the debilitating loss of regular male students of draft age. The nearly four years of World War II allowed time for postwar planning, and various local and national committees explored how to take advantage of the war-related disruptions. Might language teaching be improved by the immersion techniques used by the military? Should the closed fraternities be allowed to reopen? Was credit for nonacademic experience appropriate? Salient in these explorations was the advocacy of "general-education" programs developed in the 1920s and 1930s, notably one at the University of Chicago. The repeated discussions of how "general education" differed from "liberal education" usually concluded that general education was introductory, preliminary to more specialized studies that still qualified as liberal. Typically, the new programs would include a "core curriculum" requiring distribution across divisions or even specific courses. Among other benefits of general education, defenders cited the creation of a community of shared knowledge, the preservation of the Western cultural tradition, and exposure to scientific thinking. The programs were widely adopted in the postwar years, though they often prompted complaints about the shallowness of survey courses and the coercion involved for both students and teachers. Was this really part of liberal education, or was it remedial work required because of inadequate secondary schools?

Some of the problems of general-education programs sprang from the sharp increase in college attendance after the war. Almost no one had foreseen how many veterans would take advantage of the educational opportunities offered by the GI Bill of Rights, and some academic leaders openly dreaded an influx of ill-prepared students. But for colleges that had suffered from a paucity of applicants the sudden increase in aspiring students with government funds behind them was good news. Besides, the veterans could bring a fresh perspective to some of the staid liberal arts. Although veteran enrollments declined after the peak year of 1947, the percent of college-age students pursuing formal education kept rising at a rate that justified an enlarged physical plant and new faculty hirings even at the sleepier institutions. Although the big federal research grants went to universities, colleges shared in federal housing funds that could be devoted to dormitories. As swelling enrollments inspired the founding of new institutions, branches of state universities, urban comprehensive universities, and community colleges were the usual newcomers. Rarely were new liberal arts colleges established. One that did survive and grow was Evangel College, founded in 1955 by the Assemblies of God. Eisenhower College, which was founded in 1968 with an illustrious name but lacking a church affiliation, a traditional reputation, and organized alumni, eventually met with failure.

One source of the rising enrollment figures was a changing attitude toward who should go to college. The democratic ideology of the war and the horrors of Nazi racism raised doubts about the kind of selectivity practiced in higher education, notably in certain private colleges. The Zook Commission (the President's Commission on Higher Education, appointed by Truman in 1946) declared that higher education should no longer limit itself to "producing an intellectual elite" and that nearly half of the population were intellectually qualified to pursue higher education. It was recommended that economic, ethnic, and geographical barriers be lowered and the curriculum broadened. The report's plea for general education pronounced it "not sharply distinguished from liberal education," even though escaping the "original aristocratic intent" of the latter. Liberal arts colleges were torn between resentment at the implied criticism of undemocratic admission policies and curricula and the hope that a widened source of students would keep up enrollments. AAC debates revealed sharp disagreement over how seriously to take the commission's recommendations. Was community homogeneity likely to be damaged? Did the standards of a liberal education risk deterioration from new students insisting on a more immediate vocational payoff? Such concerns help explain the 1959 change of the stodgy name of the AAC's *Bulletin* to *Liberal Education*.[19]

Though not the slogan it was later to become, "diversity" did increase, even in colleges that retained ethnic or religious identifications. Jewish and Catholic students and faculty were increasingly visible at distinctively Protestant colleges. Less often, but still notably, African American students in token numbers appeared at once–"all white" colleges, and an occasional daring Caucasian would enroll at what (years later) would be known as a "historically black college." But this new openness was far from the most conspicuous characteristic of the postwar colleges. By the 1950s, with no new Great Depression in sight, prosperous times were breeding a student population that saw college as a way to prepare for the good life. Fraternities and sororities returned in full vigor. A familiar institutional rationale persisted: a liberal education prepared one for living, not for making a living. But the practices linked to that ideal multiplied and gained variety. A wider curriculum allowed explorations in the arts, study-abroad programs encouraged foreign travel, and the residential ambience offered models for gracious domesticity. Though their numbers were rising, women undergraduates as a percentage of college enrollment declined. Many married and dropped out, and those who graduated were less likely to seek advanced degrees. Observers worried about student conformity among both sexes and spoke of a silent generation. To some extent students were reflecting faculty attitudes. Cold War tensions, with fear of Soviet ambitions and rising McCarthyism, meant that faculty members were not likely to express their more radical ideas, even if they had not altogether given them up. The small-college setting could not protect from dismissal the Dickinson professor who claimed his Fifth Amendment rights before a Congressional committee. Some dismissed radicals found positions in small colleges for Negroes, but even there they were sometimes hunted down and forced out.[20]

In the numbers game liberal arts colleges were proportionally losing ground. By the mid-1950s they comprised about 40 percent of all institutions of higher education, enrolling about a quarter of all students. By 1970 these colleges were down to roughly one quarter of all institutions, dropping even further in their portion of the student enrollment—to about 8 percent.[21] Still, in the increasingly prosperous academic world of the 1950s, liberal arts colleges found causes for optimism. Four-year colleges in 1964 had an average enrollment of between 1,700 and 1,800, still safely below the university giantism that was said to cause loss of community and allow inferior teaching. Increased numbers of applications for admission enabled the more widely known colleges to become even more selective. Generally they used this opportunity to raise the intellectual level of the entering class and—gradually—to shape an ethnically more inclusive student body. The increasing number of students planning graduate education somewhat demeaned liberal education, identifying it as preparatory to more important professional training, but the trend also motivated students to work harder to earn an impressive transcript. Undeniably, university ideals of research and professional preparation were affecting the colleges. Faculty members were increasingly prone to replicate their graduate training in the courses they taught. Younger faculty who judged college teaching as a stepping stone to a university career were attentive to how they were regarded by their graduate-school mentors and looked for opportunities to present work at professional meetings.

The sixties, many historians maintain, began midway into the decade and ended only in the early 1970s. In any case, such a chronology usefully embraces two disparate developments for college students. First, through direct grants and loans to individual undergraduates, the Higher Education Act of 1965 and the Education Amendments of 1972 circumvented old arguments about the inappropriateness of federal support for private institutions and opened the floodgates to federal aid. Second, students starred in a series of uprisings against racism, against academic bureaucracy, and against the war in Vietnam. The media made much of these actions, and at one point polls found "student unrest" to be the leading issue among the public. The new federal money for students was not particularly conspicuous to the general public in an era of breakthrough legislation, but academic officials were well aware that institutional prospects had brightened. It was henceforth easier for them to increase charges to students, and soon students and parents were dealing routinely with "financial aid officers" to work out a package of aid, loans, and earnings that made higher education seem affordable. Faculty saw their salary scale rise, and the students they taught began to come from a somewhat wider range of economic backgrounds. Federal programs significantly benefited hard-pressed private colleges where salaries had lagged and where it had seemed necessary to admit students who, though untalented, could afford to pay. Of course, neither of these problems disappeared.

As to "student unrest," here a certain time lag affected the collegiate situation. It was Berkeley, Columbia, and other universities that saw the early strikes and building seizures that sometimes paralyzed academic activities. Still, colleges were not immune to student protest, just as their students were not immune to the appeals for racial justice, resistance to institutional regulations, and mobilization against the war. If not the superstars, some memorable student activists came from liberal arts colleges: Mary King from Ohio Wesleyan, Ruby Doris Smith from Spelman, and Bob Zellner from Huntingdon College. William Sloane Coffin, first at Williams and then at Yale, typified the college chaplain who could inspire students to risk challenging the status quo. The oft-claimed community atmosphere did sometimes make a difference, with moratoriums on classes voted by faculty to allow a campuswide discussion of issues. A sit-in in a president's office at a college was more likely to lead to a frank exchange than to arrests. Still, the colleges did not escape trauma. At Oberlin demonstrating students were teargassed, and at Swarthmore the president suffered a fatal heart attack in the midst of a campus protest.

Were there long-range benefits from the protest era? Most colleges would count as positive the widened economic and racial origins of students and the regularized participation of students in decision making. In the curriculum, general-education requirements often dropped away, and programs or departments in black studies set a trend that women and various ethnic groups later followed in search of curricular relevance and recognition. Gone at most colleges were compulsory physical education and chapel attendance, along with strict supervi-

sion of dormitory life. Separate January terms allowed participation in freewheeling courses or time away from campus.
Among the new experimental colleges of the decade, most were
to grow traditional, but the private Hampshire and the public
Evergreen managed to survive and to institutionalize some of
the era's ideals, by using student-created dossiers instead of
transcripts, for instance, or encouraging student-designed courses.
After the notorious sixties ended, however, many of these changes
helped set the themes for external criticism.

AFTER THE SIXTIES: SOBRIETY AND MANAGERIALISM

Although the "selective" colleges had long thought of themselves as easily distinguishable from the "local" or "church"
colleges, a movement set in after 1970 toward clearer classification. When the American Association of University Professors (AAUP) agreed that its published figures on faculty salaries and benefits should not lump four-year colleges with universities, a wave of protest spread through those colleges where
salaries were often close to the higher university levels. Indeed,
the publication of the AAUP statistics had been used by these
faculties to increase salaries. Some colleges claimed that they
could and should compete for students and faculty with even
the leading universities. The AAUP relented and began to report separately on "Liberal Arts Colleges I." Soon thereafter
major studies of higher education sponsored by the Carnegie
Foundation and headed by Clark Kerr sought to categorize the
postsecondary educational institutions, with their "three thousand futures." The result included a slightly euphemistic division of liberal arts colleges into "selective" and "less selective,"
with a careful explanation of the criteria used.

Of course the prestige order was infinitely more complicated,
and colleges weak in one aspect might emphasize another—if
not high average SAT scores among matriculants, then a junior
year abroad program, if not a high proportion of Ph.D.-holders
on the faculty, then a specialty in environmental studies. Was
there institutional snobbery? Yes. Was there a sense of a shared
enterprise in which colleges helped each other? Also yes. Regional groups of institutions, such as the Great Lakes Colleges,

developed many avenues for mutual aid, including cross-enrollments and sharing of library resources. As the AAC expanded its central office and admitted increasing numbers of complex institutions (ultimately changing its name to the "Association of American Colleges and Universities"), various smaller gatherings of college leaders appeared. The so-called Annapolis Group brought together annually the presidents of fifty small residential liberal arts colleges, who purposely avoided organizational apparatus and limited themselves to discussions of shared problems as well as projects to address them.

It is hard to find the right name for what followed the sixties. Backlash, conservative reaction, hard times, times of troubles—none of these quite captures the danger to academic life and the need for sober attention to difficulties old and new. After its enrollment dropped 35 percent in six years, Beloit College in the late 1970s cut its faculty by one-third and instituted courses in "applied liberal arts," such as museum management. Overall, however, the long-predicted decline in student numbers was slow in coming; 1984 was the first year to see a drop in total higher-education enrollments. In part because the lower birthrate had forewarned of such a decline, institutions had undertaken various programs to attract "nontraditional" students. Generally this meant older students, most often women, but the new effort to admit "disadvantaged students" or "students of color," even when motivated by a sense of the social good, also helped fill classrooms. The same can be said of the shift of single-sex colleges to coeducation (a shift more widely seen among men's colleges, since many women's colleges continued to maintain that they filled a special need). The motive might be gender equality, but usually there was the benefit of a rise in the ratio of student tuition-payers to fixed costs. Fears that the "Reagan Revolution" would decimate federal aid programs proved exaggerated. The higher-education lobbyists in Washington, once rather ineffectual, had learned the ropes.

Slowly the solemn truth dawned that along with government aid went government regulations, and academic officials adapted to setting affirmative-action goals and equalizing salaries across gender lines. Although both racial and gender discrimination were subjects of court cases, the latter made more of the headlines.

After the Supreme Court ruled in the Grove City College case that federal aid to one program at a college did not entail bringing the entire institution under civil-rights regulation, Congress passed a new law to reverse the effects of the decision. Federal involvement was here to stay, and academic bureaucracy expanded to deal with it.

Administrative elaboration was an old story at universities, and part of the colleges' claim to specialness was that they escaped the bureaucratic octopus and could concentrate on the teacher-student encounter. Now, however, colleges found that they needed new officers for both external relations and internal order. Sometimes faculty members were happy to have a dean replace a committee. More often they complained about coercive application of rules and the swelling of the administrative part of the budget. Administrators were increasingly likely to be imported professionals with relevant advanced degrees rather than colleagues taking up deanly duties. Painfully for the presidents, faculty members increasingly regarded them as the head administrator rather than as *primus inter pares*. The cross-pressures on presidents from the colleges' various constituencies, which had always made for difficulties, now intensified. The length of presidential tenures declined; the thirty-four-year presidency of the beloved "Casey" Sills of Bowdoin now seemed like something from another age.[22] Managerial practices and language of the sort derided by Thorstein Veblen impaired the college's vaunted communal atmosphere. One heard of "cost accounting," "waste management," "mailouts," and even "throughput." Should admissions officers speak of "yield" and "pools"? Rhetoric professors might shake their heads, but as computers and computerese spread across campus, it seemed clear that the battle against jargon was lost.

Among the changes in which administrators, backed by trustees, took the lead was a higher bar to winning tenure. Whereas once a young faculty member who got along with colleagues and was liked by students had not needed to worry much about being "kept on," in the 1970s era of stagflation, with returns on endowment dropping and heating costs rising, junior faculty submitted to a sterner inspection. In the next decade, after a new federal law forbade forced retirement because of age, worries about institutions being overtenured deepened. The resulting tensions for younger faculty mocked claims to warm communality. Money was saved by turning to part-time and visiting faculty who had no claim to tenure consideration; for them, too, it was difficult to feel part of an academic "family" (as the term had once been).

Did evangelical colleges escape some of these problems? Did shared religious faith bind administrators, faculty, and students in a special way? It is hard to be sure. The big evangelical academic successes of the late twentieth century have been Oral Roberts University in Oklahoma and Liberty University in Virginia, large institutions created by fundamentalist charismatic leaders and enriched by television audiences. In 1988 only 1 percent of the operating costs of colleges claiming church connections came from churches. Calvin College survives, but the 167 private four-year colleges that disappeared between 1967 and 1990 included some that had once been the hopeful offspring of a denomination. Catholic women's colleges were especially undercut by rising costs and the declining appeal of single-sex institutions. Some simply closed, others merged with a nearby Catholic men's college. Among institutions of higher education, both the proportion of four-year colleges and the proportion of undergraduates attending them declined during the 1990s.

Amid new crises colleges could be surprisingly resilient. Alumni loyalties proved strong in fund drives, private foundations continued to judge education a deserving object of philanthropy, and gifts from business corporations did not always have strings attached. The more "private" an institution appeared, the more generously these three sources gave, sometimes because of a conviction that government influence in education was a dangerous thing. Perhaps, too, memories of college years were especially warm in a mobile nation where neighborhoods, hometowns, and corporate employers were increasingly seen as temporary, or perhaps the colleges had truly opened paths to a better life for which graduates were expressing thanks. At any rate, one branch of the expanded bureaucracy, increasingly expert, was dedicated to fund-raising. Whatever euphemistic name this branch operated under, it still entailed a bigger administration. But faculty members could hardly resent the resulting benefits to scholarship funds, salaries, research support, and classroom buildings.

Part of the post-sixties reaction focused on the curriculum, on increased electivism and course proliferation. Among the more publicized documents were an AAC committee report that deplored the "supermarket curriculum" and a study by Secretary of Education William Bennett that praised the loyalty to core courses in three distinctly "less selective" colleges.[23] A portent of many future books, Russell Kirk's *Decadence and Renewal in the Higher Learning* assailed "Behemoth State University" and suggested small liberal arts colleges as a hope for restoring timeless values. He praised the approach of two Catholic colleges, Thomas Aquinas in California and Cardinal Newman in Missouri, as well as Gordon in Massachusetts, a Protestant institution.[24] But later, more widely read assaults on academe's student radicals and faculty relativists, notably Allan Bloom's *The Closing of the American Mind*, denounced "the university" without suggesting that small colleges might provide a healthy alternative. In truth, the most selective colleges generally shared the offending openness to curricular and behavioral freedom, but some did begin asking if curricular exfoliation and student choice might have gone too far. In one case, every course at Gustavus Adolphus College was challenged in a quo warranto proceeding in 1981. Some disappeared, and a required core was instituted.

For all the turmoil they had caused, it was hard not to recall the more idealistic young protesters with some favor, especially as later student generations turned sharply to self-interested and economically focused goals. Stagflation had raised questions about whether they would attain even the level of security and comfort of their parents, much less live out the American dream of generational upward mobility. But the glittering prizes of law firms and corporations had an appeal independent of hard-times worries. As enrollments in humanities departments declined, undergraduate business majors outstripped all others, reaching 16 percent by 1980. Elite colleges that did not offer such a major still found more and more corporate recruiters scheduling meetings on campus and telling those interested that the skills developed in a liberal arts education would prove highly useful in a business career—in fact, it was just those skills they were looking for. If after a stint at the firm the student wanted to go on to earn an M.B.A., there might be help with that. No one could recall when careerism had been so powerful in liberal arts colleges. "My folks want to know what I can do if I major in your department?" was a question often heard. Between 1970 and 1987, the proportion of entering students who embraced the goal of "being very well-off financially" rose from 39 to 76 percent. The trend thereafter reversed, however, and increasing numbers of new freshmen cited their desire to develop "a meaningful philosophy of life."[25]

* * *

Like any institution, liberal arts colleges in the United States have changed under the influence of their changing social environment. Like any academic institution, they have responded to alterations in accepted knowledge—more slowly than research institutes and universities, more rapidly than lower schools. Given weak central control, governmental or nongovernmental, liberal arts colleges have been able to vary from a standard model. A few have innovated rather adventurously, some have altered themselves in order to adapt to a particular setting or clientele, most have only grudgingly departed from inherited prescriptions. By the early 1900s and continuing through the century, the interested public has accepted a relatively firm meaning for "liberal arts college"—namely, a four-year institution of higher education, focusing its attention on candidates for the B.A. degree who are generally between the ages of eighteen and twenty-one, an institution resistant to highly specific vocational preparation and insisting on a considerable breadth of studies. Motives for adherence to this ideal have included an understandable wish to justify institutional survival by claiming a unique identity. The most generous motive, however, has been the hope that liberal arts colleges will develop interests and capabilities that will enrich both the individual learner and future communities.

ENDNOTES

[1]Readers seeking a survey of all of American higher education over a longer period can consult John S. Brubacher and Willis Rudy, *Higher Education in Transition: A History of American Colleges and Universities, 1636–1968* (New York: Harper & Row, 1968); Christopher J. Lucas, *American Higher Education: A History* (New York: St. Martin's, 1994); or Frederick Rudolph, *The American College and University: A History* (New York: Alfred A. Knopf, 1962). Two valuable recent works, more narrowly focused, are Richard M. Freeland, *Academia's Golden Age: Universities in Massachusetts, 1945–1970* (New York: Oxford University Press, 1992) and Philip Gleason, *Contending with Modernity: Catholic Higher Education in the Twentieth Century* (New York: Oxford University Press, 1995).

[2]"The Yale Report of 1828," in *American Higher Education: A Documentary History,* ed. Richard Hofstadter and Wilson Smith (Chicago: The University of Chicago Press, 1961), 1:278–279.

[3]Edward Danforth Eddy, Jr., *Colleges for Our Land and Time: The Land-Grant Idea in American Education* (New York: Harper & Brothers, 1957), esp. 32–33.

[4]Bruce A. Kimball, *Orators & Philosophers: A History of the Idea of Liberal Education* (New York and London: Teachers College Press, 1986).

[5]Hugh Hawkins, *Between Harvard and America: The Educational Leadership of Charles W. Eliot* (New York: Oxford University Press, 1972), esp. 88–91, 125–127, 187.

[6]Laurence R. Veysey, *The Emergence of the American University* (Chicago and London: The University of Chicago Press, 1965), esp. 194–206.

[7]George E. Peterson, *The New England College in the Age of the University* (Amherst, Mass.: Amherst College Press, 1964), chap. 4.

[8]For an exemplary exploration of the shifting composition of boards of trustees, see David B. Potts, *Wesleyan University, 1831–1910: Collegiate Enterprise in New England* (New Haven and London: Yale University Press, 1992).

[9]W. Bruce Leslie, *Gentlemen and Scholars: College and Community in the "Age of the University," 1865–1917* (University Park, Pa.: The Pennsylvania State University Press, 1992).

[10]Barbara Miller Solomon, *In the Company of Educated Women: A History of Women and Higher Education in America* (New Haven and London: Yale University Press, 1985), 189–192. See also Lynn D. Gordon, *Gender and Higher Education in the Progressive Era* (New Haven and London: Yale University Press, 1990).

[11]This paragraph and the following two draw on Hugh Hawkins, *Banding Together: The Rise of National Associations in American Higher Education, 1887–1950* (Baltimore and London: The Johns Hopkins University Press, 1992).

[12]Veysey, *Emergence of the American University,* 210–212.

[13]This paragraph and the next two draw on David O. Levine, *The American College and the Culture of Aspiration, 1915–1940* (Ithaca and London: Cornell University Press, 1986). On the "collegiate syndrome" at universities, see Roger L. Geiger, *To Advance Knowledge: The Growth of American Research Universities, 1900–1940* (New York: Oxford University Press, 1986), 115–139.

[14]Marcia Graham Synnott, *The Half-Opened Door: Discrimination and Admissions at Harvard, Yale, and Princeton, 1900–1970* (Westport, Conn: Greenwood Press, 1979); Harold S. Wechsler, *The Qualified Student: A History of Selective College Admission in America* (New York: John Wiley & Sons, 1977).

[15]Here I draw broadly on *The Secularization of the Academy*, ed. George M. Marsden and Bradley J. Longfield (New York: Oxford University Press, 1992) and William C. Ringenberg, *The Christian College: A History of Protestant Higher Education in America* (Grand Rapids, Mich.: William B. Eerdmans, 1984).

[16]Paula S. Fass, *The Damned and the Beautiful: American Youth in the 1920s* (New York: Oxford University Press, 1977) is usefully supplemented by Raymond Wolters, *The New Negro on Campus: Black College Rebellions of the 1920s* (Princeton, N.J.: Princeton University Press, 1975).

[17]Levine, *American College*, chap. 9.

[18]Frederick Rudolph, *Curriculum: A History of the American Undergraduate Course of Study Since 1636* (San Francisco: Jossey-Bass, 1977), esp. 230–231.

[19]Hawkins, *Banding Together*, chap. 8.

[20]Ellen W. Schrecker, *No Ivory Tower: McCarthyism and the Universities* (New York: Oxford University Press, 1986).

[21]For the difficulties of statistical exactitude regarding liberal arts colleges, see the essays in this issue by Alexander W. Astin and by Michael S. McPherson and Morton Owen Schapiro. See also Charles J. Anderson et al., comps., *Fact Book on Higher Education* (New York: Macmillan, 1989), 138.

[22]On presidential challenges see Clark Kerr and Marian L. Gade, *The Many Lives of Academic Presidents: Time, Place and Character* (Washington, D.C.: Association of Governing Boards of Universities and Colleges, 1986).

[23]*Integrity in the College Curriculum: A Report to the Academic Community* (Washington, D.C.: Association of American Colleges, 1985); William J. Bennett, *To Reclaim a Legacy: A Report on the Humanities in Higher Education* (Washington, D.C.: National Endowment for the Humanities, 1984).

[24]Russell Kirk, *Decadence and Renewal in the Higher Learning: An Episodic History of American University and College since 1953* (South Bend, Ind.: Gateway Editions, 1978).

[25]Eric L. Dey, Alexander W. Astin, and William S. Korn, *The American Freshman: Twenty-Five Year Trends, 1966–1990* (Los Angeles: Higher Education Research Institute, 1991), 23.

Overall, I think the future will see more differentiation among institutions of higher education, for some of the reasons noted above. The need to reexamine missions, to focus and adapt to these changing forces and circumstances, is imminent. This could be a very healthy scenario for the nation and for higher education as an enterprise. Certainly, having more institutions with differing missions, goals, and educational experiences will offer students of various backgrounds and ages more options for their education, and technology will allow a greater degree of commonality and uniformity across institutions. These positive outcomes will be enhanced if differences among institutions are not automatically translated into differences in quality and if excellence is accepted and judged in different ways for different institutions. Along similar lines, a healthy differentiation among institutions could be inhibited by attempts to apply a uniform set of criteria to measure institutions, as is happening in the growing number of such popular rankings of colleges and universities as *US News and World Report* and others.

Periods of great change can be unsettling and may be seen as threats or opportunities; higher education is not immune to these feelings. However, we have reason to be optimistic about the future of American higher education. One of the great strengths of our system of higher education has been its great diversity, not in terms of students on campuses, but in terms of the different types of institutions. As with any organism, the ability to adapt to change and evolve is proportionate to the complexity of the organism. American higher education is certainly diverse and also complex.

—Walter E. Massey
"Uncertainties in the
Changing Academic Profession"

from *Dædalus*, Fall 1997
"The American Academic Profession"

Paul Neely

The Threats to Liberal Arts Colleges

IN 1998, A POLL OF UNIVERSITY OFFICIALS conducted by *U.S. News & World Report* ranked the University of Arkansas fifty-third in academic reputation among the fifty-four schools of the nation's five major athletic conferences. Also in 1998, the University of Arkansas increased the number of first-year students scoring in the ninety-fifth percentile on standardized entrance tests by 42 percent. It used a heavy marketing campaign, but the key difference was an increase in the scholarship budget from $1.8 million to about $4.4 million. Approximately $1.5 million of the increase came from the family of the late Sam Walton, founder of Wal-Mart Stores Inc., with headquarters in Bentonville, Arkansas. The funds were earmarked for full scholarships targeted specifically at academically superior, not economically poorer, students. University officials have reported success. Many students who would have gone to out-of-state schools are now staying in Arkansas. And the quality of these students has added new vitality to academic life at the university. There is little doubt that the university's academic reputation will rise, since at heart it depends most heavily not on history, faculty, or facilities but on the quality of the students.[1]

The University of Arkansas is a long way from most of the schools that are referred to as "prestigious" or "selective" liberal arts colleges. But the trends showing up in Fayetteville reflect the many pulls that threaten to undermine the status, role, and maybe even existence of those liberal arts colleges. Among the growing trends evident in this example are competi-

Paul Neely is publisher of The Chattanooga Times *and a trustee of Williams College.*

27

tive marketing, merit-based aid, private support for state schools, and student choice being heavily influenced by price. Underneath those trends are implicit assumptions that the reputation of a school will not diminish or enhance the generic credential it grants and that enough money will provide a critical mass of high-caliber students anywhere. Is there a university today that does not have some elite honors college or scholarship designation, worth $20,000 or more over four years and granted with some pomposity to a select group of eighteen-year-olds four months before they sit down in their first college class? Considering the high correlations between family income and academic performance, a large portion of that money will go to students whose families could easily manage the full tuition. Around schools like Arkansas, there have always been jokes about recruiting the best football team that money can buy. Now the joke has been turned on the student body at large.

Merit scholarships alone will not undermine the rich history of the nation's more selective liberal arts colleges, but the issues behind them reflect the risky economics, aggressive competition, and eroding purpose that threaten the future of those schools. As a trustee of Williams College, I am at the tail of a long line of thoughtful, devoted board members. They have had many concerns over the years, but surely none had to worry about competition from the University of Arkansas. We worry about such things now.

There are other trends commonly cited as threats to the liberal arts colleges, including culture wars and identity politics. But those are winds that buffet every shore. There is not much reason to think that they affect liberal arts colleges more than the largest research universities. Indeed, the small residential community, where students actually know vast numbers of their peers on a personal basis, mitigates trends based on division.

But some of those issues raise real concerns. For instance, the culture wars include sharp critiques of curriculum, usually along the lines that we have fallen away from some golden age of a core that taught the verities of Western civilization. In fact, the supposed core has always evolved, the golden age was not really that golden, and there are parts of Western civ that fall short of pure *veritas*. There are, however, serious problems in today's curriculum. Not every course in the catalog should discuss every permutation of race, gender, and sexual preference. Not every professor specializing in an obscure corner of scholarly life needs to teach a course reflecting his singular interest, as if to replicate the thickest university catalog. Again, though, these are widespread issues, clearly not restricted to selective liberal arts colleges.

Likewise for the impending doom threatened by various forms of electronic teaching. In terms of convenience and cost, but probably not effectiveness, the prospect of going to class by television or computer is an attractive one. If such teaching is to displace the traditional forums, though, it is likely to follow a clear order: first, professional and vocational courses that are required as part of employment, thus addressing the many motivational problems of distance teaching; second, the colleges and universities where teaching modes most closely resemble television watching, namely, large lectures before passive students; and third, and only then, the colleges where the educational process *and* campus life are heavily based on the personal interaction of students and faculty.

TO MARKET, TO MARKET

The most serious threats to liberal arts colleges are not the battles of ideology or the shifts of technology, although the latter will have some indirect effects. In a market-driven world, the primary threat to liberal arts colleges is found in the marketplace. Many of the market forces are beyond the influence of individual schools or even whole categories of schools. They include demographic, economic, and geographic shifts; cultural trends, including materialism and utilitarianism; and the dominance of market economics as a determining force. In addition, there is probably an overcapacity in higher education in general, and liberal arts colleges share in that problem. There may simply be more pure liberal arts colleges than we need, at least as the market defines need.

Within the category of liberal arts colleges, there are special market forces. Specifically, those schools may be slowly undermined by the economics of their business and the marketing of their product, and the results may challenge the very purpose for which those schools exist. Competition within the liberal arts sector leads colleges into high spending. Like the modified winner-take-all aspects of sports teams, the best colleges spend a lot to attract the best students, with great success. Their competition makes perfect sense within their own realm. The same competition, however, drives up costs and price (both full or discounted). It complicates the issue of access, for it scares away many diverse and able students. And it causes liberal arts colleges in general to suffer in comparison to other sectors of higher education—at least to the extent that higher education is regarded as a credential with a price.

The first thought about the higher-education marketplace that comes to almost anyone's mind these days is price. The most selective schools are pushing beyond the previously unthinkable limit of $30,000 a year—a figure that does not cover many of the costs of actually attending college, from computers to travel to an occasional movie, and that amazingly may represent less than half of the college's per-pupil total expenses. Many schools below that top tier are into the $20,000 range. Charges for public colleges have gone up too, and one can make various arguments about percentages, but the absolute dollar spread shows the high price of the selective schools.[2] In context, it should be noted that almost three-quarters of all full-time undergraduates attend four-year colleges and universities that charge less than $8,000 a year. That figure hides the substantial subsidy from private and public sources, but it also dramatizes just how much more the selective colleges are asking.

Couple that with other trends. Twenty years ago, the major part of student aid was in outright grants; now it is in loans. Over the same time, the income distribution of the nation has been slowly shifting. The rising tide of prosperity has raised the front end of the boat more than the back. The result is that net tuition (after student aid) as a proportion of family income at private institutions is three times greater for low-income students than it is for high-income students. Increases in financial aid have not kept pace with increases in tuition, and, sure enough, all this has had an effect.

The probability that a student from the highest income group (over $100,000 annually) attended a selective institution increased from one in five in 1981 to one in four in 1997. Colleges sometimes claim that tuition is not increasing any faster than the incomes of the families from which their full-paying students come, but just as important is the fact that this highest-income group may be declining as a proportion of all families with children attending college. The most respected analysts of these movements suggest that "taken to their logical conclusion, these trends suggest that a restratification of American higher education may be under way."[3]

That would be a particularly ironic result, for in the past few years the better liberal arts colleges have gone to exceptional efforts—using everything but the maximum charge, the so-called sticker price—to escape their old elitist images and broaden their student base. In part this is a matter of modern social conscience, but it is also basic marketing. In general, the highest performing students want to go to a college where the other students are equally bright but different in as many ways as possible. Today's top students welcome diversity and, usually having grown up in more homogenous suburbs and schools, will actively seek it out as part of their college selection. The better a college assembles a diverse student body—in race, ethnicity, geography, and the like, but also in the full range of talents from athletics to performing arts—the more likely it is to draw the best, most open, and most creative students to its academic pool.

Then why does tuition keep going up? The simple answer is that selective colleges are also competitive colleges. They raise tuition because every extra dollar will go towards better faculty, facilities, and financial aid, thus attracting the best student body, which is the ultimate source of a school's quality. Beyond that, they compare themselves to a Mercedes in an educational market of mostly Fords and Chevys, and their price makes a statement. Indeed, to lower the price would send a signal of lesser quality, and at the upper end of these schools there is a clear correlation between tuition and selectivity or reputation.

In that odd market sense, there is no incentive for any school to reduce its price. Doing so would be a self-inflicted injury. A particular school can attract better students and thus is a better school by raising its price, within reasonable peer comparisons. Unfortunately, there is also a tragedy of the commons at work here. The rational decision for the single school works against long-term survivability for all the schools as a group.

Furthermore, costs are increasing and are doing so faster than familiar indices, largely because education is still a labor-intensive business. But further costs have been added over the years. Curriculum has been expanded: Thirty years ago, some of the best liberal arts colleges did not offer much, if anything, in certain familiar subjects, including anthropology, religion, and theater, let alone the more "modern" subjects now filling the catalog, such as environmental science, biochemistry, or Asian studies. Faculty have come to expect that research will be a large part of their roles, which means colleges must provide relief from teaching, which means more faculty need to be hired. Technology is adding a new element to overhead expense. And the creep of social problems into campus life requires greater spending on student health services, security, counseling and other support services, especially with the customer expectation that the college should address social problems therapeutically. High-end liberal arts colleges, which pride themselves on ignoring economies of scale on their academic side, often face a difficult time with these new added costs, for they are imposed on a small base.

FOLLOW THE MONEY

The resources of selective liberal arts colleges do not depend solely on the tuition of current students, of course. As in the past, many of them continue to benefit from extraordinary generosity, and here a discussion of the economic model begins to overlap with marketing. Colleges have two sales departments, admissions and development. The former is creating some problems for the latter, which already faces difficulties from outside forces. Suppose, for instance, that the lofty admission goals at the better schools were met. Each incoming class would be geographically and racially diverse. Most students would go on to a graduate school (or two). The academic quality would be so high that many graduates would pursue careers in research and teaching. This would mean that their alumni would include fewer members of families with substantial net worth, the surest course to having capital wealth to contribute in the future. Fewer would wind up living near the college, the easiest way to maintain alumni involvement. More would enter the job market with high debt, delaying for many crucial years any established habit of contributing to the college. More would hold dual loyalties, with a strong tug at their pockets from their professional graduate schools, which would often be geographically closer to their chosen homes, especially in fields like law or medicine. On the face of it, the alumni of the future would then be less able and less likely to support the college and its students than were the alumni who supported past undergraduate years. That is not to say that admission offices should not go ahead and pursue their current goals. They should, but there may be some unintended consequences.

This concern might be overdrawn. Perhaps the experiment is already being run. After all, colleges that began to broaden their base a generation or two ago are still raising lots of money. Even so, it takes some faith in social and economic mobility and in personal attachment to the college to assume that today's admission trends will not bring their own financial drawbacks later. Maybe that faith is justified, but like many issues based on faith, there is at least enough doubt to cause some worry. As if that were not enough concern for the development office, though, there are also erosions of current outside support. A higher proportion of private money is going to public higher education. The University of Tennessee, not known as a national academic center, recently raised more than $430 million in a capital campaign for private funds. Even in the face of stagnant state support, that is a lot of money, and this is not an unusual example.

There are other reasons behind this shift. First, more businesses now fall into the categories of national or multinational (rather than regional) and public (rather than private). Corporate centers are more widely scattered, especially away from the New England–Ohio–Virginia triangle that holds so many of the selective liberal arts colleges. Great fortunes have been built in the Southeast and the West, where private liberal arts colleges are relatively scarce. All these changes fit the example of the Walton family gift mentioned earlier. In many other cases, the largest owners of corporations are now pension funds and mutual funds, rather than single families with strong ties to old schools. More importantly, both corporate and foundation giving has gone through a wave of accountability focused on words like outcomes, results, and effectiveness. That trend produces strong biases favoring the specific over the general, research over teaching, and the quantifiable over the abstract. For business, this often relates to specific payoffs for the donor—newspapers give to journalism schools, drug companies give to chemistry departments.

All this reflects a marked movement toward integrating all corporate charity into the corporate business plan, a philosophy that leaves little room for general support of the liberal arts. At its logical conclusion, businesses and some foundations will regard liberal arts colleges the way they previously regarded secondary education—as general preparation with no direct link to measurable corporate purpose, and thus outside their charitable strategy. The more that graduates of liberal arts colleges go on to graduate school, the easier it is to place the colleges in that lower preparatory tier.

MISSION IMPOSSIBLE

The temptation, then, is to change the college's mission to get in on the funding. These selective liberal arts schools will never be research universities, but now one hears the phrase "research college," a ratcheting up of status to aim for the best of both. In the abstract, the concept makes some sense. Certainly, better teachers pursue scholarly activity outside the classroom, even if it does not involve the artificial and stretched concept of original research. Artfully done, by professors with a strong interest in teaching, research integrated into the student curriculum can be productive pedagogy.[4] But the concept of a research college bears considerable risk. It may attract faculty whose primary interest is not in teaching, who resist leading the general courses that are an important part of undergraduate studies, and who think that a university model of exploited teaching assistants, specialized courses, and obscure, almost frivolous research topics is perfectly appropriate at a college of fifteen hundred students. Academic specialization itself can separate faculty from students, which is contrary to the mission of the liberal arts colleges.

Indeed, faculty recruitment is often the justification for the tilt toward research. A new faculty member, after all, has usually just spent six years or so at a research university, doing what she really wants to do. It may take some semblance of the old research site to lure the young scholar into a new teaching orientation, especially for the schools that aim to be just as selective in seeking top faculty as they are in seeking top students. At least, so the rationalization goes. In fact, it is hard to draw the line between the faculty's desire for a diverse and intellectually challenging curriculum and its desire for courses meant largely to indulge scholars with their own specialized interests. In a four-year regimen, students can "vote" by course registration in only a limited way. Besides, the design of the curriculum still rests heavily with the faculty itself.

In the broader market context, the risk involves what business would call product differentiation. If the college is to be just a smaller version of a research university, then why not go to the bigger university? Chances are it will offer more and charge less. This leads then to a general critique of higher education, which might challenge the whole idea that institutions built on undergraduate enrollments should subsidize the scholarly life of the faculty, in some ways at the expense of undergraduates, state and federal governments and private donors. We will not go down that path here, but it is useful to keep in mind, since the liberal arts college is supposed to be a quite different model.

The top-tier liberal arts colleges largely stick to that different role. In many ways, they can do so because most of their students will go on to graduate school or into certain premium jobs, such as investment banking, that do not yet put great weight on an advanced degree and which still favor the better

liberal arts colleges. The next tiers, however, present an immediate problem of definition. At many liberal arts colleges, more
than 60 percent of degrees are awarded in professional fields.
Granted, there is usually a heavy component of liberal arts
courses outside of one's major, but they frequently become
accessories to the professional course rather than freestanding
intellectual interests. Why then even call them liberal arts colleges at all? This question leads to the purpose of the pure form
and the threats to that purpose.

In the last century, colleges were quite explicit about their
purpose. As an 1829 faculty report at Amherst put it, "Our
colleges are designed to give youth a general education, classical, literary, and scientific, as comprehensive as an education
can well be, which is professedly preparatory alike for all the
professions." Many went beyond that curricular view. The
Yale Report of 1828 said that the study was "especially adopted
to form the taste, and discipline the mind, both in thought and
diction, to the relish of what is elevated, chaste and simple."[5]
Those purposes stood well when education was meant to produce a good Christian, and then when it was meant to produce
a gentleman, to use the categories of Williams historian Fred
Rudolph.[6] For the third time period, defined by the student who
enters and leaves as a consumerist, the purpose becomes more
problematical. In that time, since World War II, college education has moved strongly away from the general and surely
away from the chaste and simple. Hundreds of colleges still
place the name liberal arts upon themselves, but in fact they
graduate thousands of students in nursing, journalism, criminal
justice, business, and almost any undergraduate degree to match
a job that one can imagine. At many of the hundreds of schools
that call themselves liberal arts colleges, the term represents
nostalgia more than curriculum.

PRESSURE OF PURPOSE

There is another side of student consumerism. Call it
vocationalism, credentialism, or even dollarizing—students and
their families have defined undergraduate education in starkly
utilitarian terms. Young people do not go to college to become

fuller persons, better citizens, or more lively intellects. In postwar America, college education is justified by the additional lifetime income it will produce.

Some of this has reflected the booming economy and competitive market orientation of the postwar years. Some of it has reflected the outright materialism that came with growing affluence. Some of it, perversely, was created by higher education itself. Pushing forward to attract and satisfy those consumers/ students also pushed up costs, and whether the price was borne in cash or prolonged loan payments, the resulting second thoughts of the payers leaned strongly to the economics of life. Those who paid had grown up in the depression, when security became intertwined with employment, and this echoed into the years as a demand that their children pursue "something better," especially better than a manual skill, but still "something you can use," which meant use to economic benefit.

Materialism brought a parallel development—narcissism, to choose the blunt term. Colleges espoused old images of opening up broad new worlds for students. The students, it turns out, began to focus on themselves instead. College was their chance to discover their career and other personal interests, and maybe to dabble in some self-exploration as well, both in class and out. Women's studies and black studies are the clearest examples, but so are the rise of current-events and pop-culture courses and earning academic credit for everything from nutrition to physical education (once considered an academic oxymoron). In many programs, credit is given for career-related outside employment, which turns the pure concept of a liberal arts education absolutely on its head.

There are clear measurements of these abstractions in the American Freshman Survey. In 1966, more than 80 percent of respondents checked off "Develop a meaningful philosophy of life" as the purpose of college, but by 1990, that figure had dropped below 50 percent. Conversely, some 45 percent listed "Be very well off financially" as the purpose in 1966 (and it dropped even further by 1970), but by 1996 the number had risen to more than 70 percent.[7] (This would seem to imply that the greatest increase in personal wealth in the world's history has also increased personal economic insecurity. In fact, it may merely reflect the fact that more wealth produces more desires, the very basis of modern materialism. This is a somewhat philosophical point, but it has direct effects on how the nation regards higher education, and thus on the marketplace for those services.)

The several dozen liberal arts colleges in the most selective ranks have managed to resist these trends best. It is easier for them to do so, since so many of their students will go on to graduate school, thus reducing the need for a "useful," career-based undergraduate major. Oddly enough, however, so have some of the schools at the lowest economic tier of liberal arts colleges. They have not had the resources to develop an additional, career-oriented curriculum. Their funding rests on a restricted base. Their appeals for both students and support are often focused by religion, race, or proximity, and secularism, desegregation, and mobility have taken their toll. Some have closed, and this remains the most vulnerable category of higher education.

In the middle are several hundred nominally liberal arts schools. Some have strayed farther from the traditional liberal arts concept; some remain more true to it. All face escalating costs, increasing competition, and relatively meager capital resources. Many are quite locally based, relying on part-time, nontraditional, nonresidential students, all far from the higher model of liberal arts colleges. These schools suffer the greatest ambiguity about their mission, for they see economic salvation in meeting student demands for specialized training. Without large endowments, economics forces them toward a larger scale, undermining the smallness that is part of their social and pedagogical (but not curricular) attraction.

In sum, schools in this middle category suffer most in comparison to public colleges and universities. They are likely to cost more, offer less, shortchange faculty, defer maintenance, and scrape for full-fare students. The more that the broad, middle-performing cohort of prospective students regards higher education as a generic credential, the more these middle-level schools will suffer competitively. The more that this same public sees higher education as a vocational credential, the more these schools will suffer as well. In other words, credentialism in general will have to loosen its grip for these schools to reverse their current steady decline, and that seems an unlikely prospect. The trend only increases when such schools get into a downward spiral, in which declining enrollment forces cost-cutting, which visibly harms quality, which sends enrollment lower, and so on.

WAVING TO THE LIMITED

Even if the greatest threat is aimed at mid-level colleges, there is a danger for the top-tier schools too. The danger is that they will go the way of high-end American passenger trains in the late 1940s: they performed exceptionally well, but people began to use automobiles and planes more often. Eventually, the best passenger trains suffered not just because of direct competition for their passengers but because they were isolated. It did not mean as much to be the best when they were almost the only trains, and the decline was inevitable as their infrastructure disappeared. When people wanted to travel, their first thoughts turned to the car or plane. The full range of train options had narrowed too far to keep the best trains viable.

This analogy cannot be followed forever; after all, planes were faster than trains. There is a danger, though, if upper-tier liberal arts colleges become more isolated than they are today. They might no longer be seen as the premier example of liberal arts colleges, which is still a legitimate alternative form of education for almost anyone. In many ways, they might be perceived the way secondary boarding schools widely are today, as remnant centers of economic privilege—once central and powerful, now mostly a social holdover.

The governance of these schools adds to the antiquated image. At its best, the faculty is the soul of the institution and the heart of its excellence. At its worst, it closely resembles a bad legislature, a council of self-absorbed egos that puts process above substance and personal prerogatives above group adaptation. The administration may be considered no better. Any president who can claim to be the intellectual head of a college is probably failing as its funding and administrative head. Deans and academic vice presidents often preside in a proud amateurism. Actual training or experience in financial management, personnel, counseling, or almost any other field directly relevant to their work is usually a serendipitous coincidence. The colleges in turn, then, look like small hospitals of the past, in which doctors ran everything (usually by committee) in ways that left them perfectly unprepared for the rapid shifts in medical care that modern technology and government finance engendered.

The image of the liberal arts colleges as elite remnants of the past will be even more difficult to shake if the colleges cannot control their escalating tuitions. In theory, the competition of liberal arts colleges with schools like the University of Arkansas should force them to hold the line. Suppose that with enough money the UAs of the world can manage to draw students, even if it is only a core of students, from the high-performing ranks and that they can offer an education in the midst of those high performers for free rather than for $30,000 a year. Then the elitist image will become self-fulfilling, for the liberal arts colleges will draw most heavily from those for whom $30,000 is only a minor concern.

Such a difference will have its greatest impact on students from poorer economic backgrounds, for even with good financial aid, the burden of attending the selective liberal arts schools will weigh disproportionately on them. There is not much evidence, though, that the children of high-income families want to attend a college composed almost exclusively of their own demographic sector. Indeed, children of the affluent are less likely now to favor private schools. The proportion of college freshmen from families earning more than $200,000 who attended public institutions rose from 31 percent in 1980 to 38 percent in 1994.[8] These families clearly maintain their ability to pay a premium price. What seems to be weakening is their willingness to pay it.

Relatively low, flat-rate tuitions at the public schools are obviously part of the draw, and the class snobbery that used to lead some to private schools has diminished greatly. Special honors colleges within the university, set up as if to say a student can be part of a school like Swarthmore but stay in Fayetteville, pretend to offer the best of both worlds. Merit scholarships can drive the tuition savings up to $25,000 a year or more, and at that level the price of prestige has reached the limit for many affluent families. These merit designations function like a Lexus does in the luxury car market. They allow top students to forget the Mercedes, overcome the obstacles of both quality and status, and settle for a car that is actually made by Toyota.

The competition of those same liberal arts colleges with each other, however, leads in the opposite direction. That competition—for the biggest market share of the best and brightest students—pushes costs ever higher. Rising prices at the top colleges and universities exceed estimates of the rising operating costs facing the schools, and one economist measuring the spread attributes much of it to "unbounded aspirations."[9] Colleges are marketers, and fresh new facilities, expanded programs, sought-after teachers, and generous financial aid are the marketers' tools. Unfortunately, they also require more and more from both tuition and donor support, which leads us back to the insidious trap: increasing quality decreases access. As long as liberal arts colleges are perceived as the way to go for many of the best students, financial aid provides the main avenue around this trap. As more of the best students come to believe they can find an equally good education and experience in other places, though, the liberal arts colleges will increasingly have to seek a different avenue. Already there are signs that financial-aid departments may turn to discounting practices that make airline fares look simple and equitable by comparison.

During the postwar years, higher-education institutions grew because of larger populations and increased college attendance rates. They could look successful just by capturing a portion of that growth, so they had little incentive to wonder what students they were getting. Now, as participation rates are leveling off and as state governments face demands that restrict support, the need to look good has been extended to the quality of the school, which has to include the quality of the students. In many instances, pressure in that direction also comes from public officials concerned about economic development. In many cases, restricting the student body pays off by increasing the per-pupil subsidy.[10]

Add to that the broad merit scholarships that are primarily aimed at keeping students from migrating. Georgia's Hope Scholarships, given for rather average high-school performance, are rapidly becoming a middle-class entitlement rather than aid to the poor. Like Medicare and various other government programs, the broad base of political support for these scholarships has derived from the very fact that they are *not* meant just for the poor.

All this leads universities to raise standards and to compete for better students, and in recent years that competition has extended to the very best students—the ones who might otherwise go to Harvard or Yale, Williams or Amherst.

THE ENEMY WITHIN

The marketplace threats to liberal arts colleges, in sum, are from within and without. So-called merit aid, which is actually a host of discounting techniques, is a stark effort to buy market share of high-quality students. It may, however, turn out to be a powerful force, swamping the economics of need-based aid in its wake. Outside sources of support have growing weaknesses, and in the worst scenario, the high-quality liberal arts colleges could be left with no one but the children of the wealthy, who then turn out to be unwilling to attend if no one else is.

Many of these schools have great endowments, so an early demise cannot be predicted. They already rely heavily on those endowments to compete with one another and may have to draw on them more heavily in the future, since their competition for students and for quality is broader than they have ever encountered. Competition will present special problems for maintaining need-blind/full-need aid policies, now remaining in just a few schools, and for the high-price/high-aid strategies behind them.

The entire category of liberal arts colleges coasts forward with a certain vulnerability, however. All spend to the hilt. Indeed, they feel an almost fiduciary duty to maximize the quality of the education they offer to those currently enrolled.

But what if things were to go bad? These are not swiftly adaptable institutions, and they have high overhead. Because no student pays the full cost, the schools could not simply increase enrollment to cover their basic costs. High financial aid is the only way around the quality/access trap, but a real economic crunch could escalate financial aid into untenable levels. In a rather short time, all but a handful of colleges could find the drain on endowment unbearable.

There are mitigating factors to these glum scenarios, of course. There are no particular signs that the states will all suddenly return to the largess of old, and public schools may face cost pressures that will undermine their other great advantages of size. If the insistent critiques of higher education in general ever turn into action, liberal arts colleges might find new favor, but there is now heavy inertia within the business-supported, government-run universities of the nation. If the job market becomes so disjointed that employers see more benefit in a general degree, followed by continuing education and retraining as years progress, then the emphasis on specialization might weaken—but that is unlikely.

This last point bears its own irony. If one asks the chief executive officers of business corporations and nonprofit organizations what they prize most in an employee, the list resembles the mission statement of a liberal arts college—critical thinking, oral and written communication abilities, conceptual application of quantitative skills, a commitment to lifelong learning, and the like. The list seems to be little noticed in the CEO's own personnel departments, however, for more and more jobs go first to those with specific vocational credentials. Given the choice, a newspaper publisher is likely to favor the history major from Middlebury to fill a beginning reporter's slot, but a cautious director of human resources, or even a cautious managing editor, is likely to hire the journalism-school graduate from Kansas. Somehow, the professional certificate seems to assure safety, and hiring is now a risk-averse activity.

Liberal arts colleges face many threats, including rising costs (and price), problematic access, weak governance, and a changing status in the marketplace of higher education. Yet the threats present no obvious remedies, for many of the possible adaptations for the modern market would wreck the model itself. That would be a particularly perverse result at a time when larger universities are copying the model in honors colleges within the larger institutions—accepting by imitation that the liberal arts model remains the ideal form of undergraduate education.

If the nation places even greater emphasis on higher education as a fungible commodity and a generic credential, however, liberal arts colleges will be at a continuing disadvantage. A small band of the faithful will see a greater good in the liberal arts, but if the brilliant biology researcher of the future sees no more widely than his own future prizes, he is likely to begin that career as a freshman at a research university. If the lawyer figures it will be the law-school record that determines her first job, and thus her future happiness, then she will likely aim to save her family thousands of dollars for the four years of undergraduate prep work.

If results are increasingly measured in dollars, liberal arts colleges will suffer—unless they are seen even more clearly as the precise antidote to that way of measuring the world. As scholar and social critic Todd Gitlin wrote recently, "Little attention has been paid to the strongest reason to cultivate knowledge that is relatively enduring: to anchor a high-velocity, reckless, and lightweight culture whose main value is marketability."[11] The real threat to the best of the liberal arts colleges is that Gitlin's exhortation is ignored, that as a culture we choose trends over permanence, image over substance, money over values, and the market over meaning. It is the liberal arts that can spare us from that world; if that fails, however, the colleges that hold the ideals of liberal arts in the highest esteem will be threatened themselves.

ENDNOTES

[1]Jennifer Pinkerton, "UA Scholarships Attract More Bright Freshmen," *Arkansas Democrat-Gazette*, 27 September 1998.

[2]See, for instance, The College Board, *Trends in College Pricing 1998* (New York: The College Board, 1998).

[3]The National Center for Postsecondary Improvement, "The Choice-Income Squeeze: How Do Costs and Discounts Affect Institutional Choice," *Change* (September/October 1998): 53–56 (based on research by Michael McPherson and Morton Schapiro).

[4]The qualifier "artfully done" may explain contradictory conclusions about whether research bears any correlation to good teaching. See, for instance, a positive conclusion in Zachary Karabell, *What's College For?* (New York: Basic Books, 1998), 134, and the contrary assertion in Christopher J. Lucas, *Crisis in the Academy* (New York: St. Martin's Press, 1996), 193.

[5]Lucas, *Crisis in the Academy*, 52–53.

[6]Frederick Rudolph, *Mark Hopkins and the Log*, 2d ed. (Williamstown: Williams College, 1996), appendix.

[7]"The American Freshman: Twenty-five Year Trends," cited in David W. Breneman, *Liberal Arts Colleges: Thriving, Surviving or Endangered* (Washington, D.C.: The Brookings Institution, 1994), 141.

[8]Peter Passell, "Affluent Turning to Public Colleges, Threatening a Squeeze for Others," *New York Times*, 13 August 1997, p. A16.

[9]Joyce Mercer, "Expensive Ambitions," *Chronicle of Higher Education*, 26 April 1996, p. A33–35, describes Charles T. Clotfelter, *Buying the Best: Cost Escalation in Elite Higher Education* (Princeton, N.J.: Princeton University Press, 1996).

[10]For a fuller discussion of this economic model, see discussion papers published by the Williams Project on the Economics of Higher Education. A useful beginning would be Gordon C. Winston, "The Economic Structure of Higher Education: Subsidies, Customer-Inputs and Hierarchy," Williams College, 1996.

[11]Todd Gitlin, "The Liberal Arts in an Age of Info-Glut," *Chronicle of Higher Education*, 1 May 1998, p. B4.

A measure of further disaggregation, then, is clearly called for if one is to come to terms adequately with the changing nature of professional life even in the tiny, liberal arts college sector of the American academic universe. A century ago, the great *condottieri* of the university "revolution" in America were notably condescending towards the institutions characteristic of this sector—what one of them dismissed as "a regime of petty sectarian colleges." Thus David Starr Jordan, president of Stanford, confidently predicted that with time "the college will disappear, in fact, if not in name. The best will *become* universities, the others will return to their place as academies." A century later, however, his prediction has proved to be incorrect. While they no longer dominate the American higher educational scene, they are far from having been nudged into the world of secondary education—from which, in any case and *pace* Jordan, they had not emerged in the first place. Nor have they *become* universities—or, at least, not universities as he understood that term. They remain instead what they have always been, direct lineal descendants of the single-college universities that, in the fifteenth and sixteenth centuries, had emerged in Spain, Scotland, and Ireland. They remain, that is to say, small universities devoting themselves exclusively to undergraduate instruction, representing a distinctive strand in American higher education and constituting the institutional arena where about 8 percent of American academics now pursue their professional careers.

—Francis Oakley
"The Elusive Academic Profession:
Complexity and Change"

from *Dædalus*, Fall 1997
"The American Academic Profession"

Michael S. McPherson and Morton Owen Schapiro

The Future Economic Challenges for the Liberal Arts Colleges

O
VER THE LAST TWENTY-FIVE YEARS, America's liberal arts colleges have endured a steady shrinkage of their traditional market. The number of high-school graduates declined by 21 percent, from 3.2 million in 1976 to 2.5 million in 1993, promoting a ferocious competition for applicants. More recently, a rising tide of competition from alternative providers of education services—beginning with the vigorous expansion of public colleges and universities in the 1960s and continuing now with the abrupt entry of venture capitalists into the world of for-profit education—has put a squeeze on the market for private liberal arts colleges. Schools that once subsisted on a combination of genteel poverty among the faculty, tweedy relationships between admissions deans and prep school headmasters, and "old school" ties with the alumni now depend on four-color brochures, marketing directors, meticulously planned capital campaigns, and elaborate pricing and discount policies that make airline pricing look straightforward by comparison.

It is not surprising that during this period of dramatic change the number of schools that could by any plausible measure be called "liberal arts colleges" dropped sharply (although the number that found it useful to hang onto that sobriquet held steady). The two hundred or so such institutions that remain (of a total of more than three thousand colleges and universities in the United States) can look forward to some promising opportunities, including the reversal of the decline in the population

Michael S. McPherson is President of Macalester College.

Morton Owen Schapiro is Dean of the College of Letters, Arts and Sciences and Professor of Economics at the University of Southern California.

47

of young people; a continued strong market demand for educated workers; and a higher-education marketplace in which
their commitment to residential education and personal attention to students makes their offerings increasingly distinctive.
Yet in realizing those opportunities, the liberal arts colleges
continue to struggle on several fronts. They face a public that
is skeptical about rising college costs and pricing policies that
are seen as unfairly "redistributive"; an education economy in
which new information technologies are transforming how and
why people need schooling; and a competitive environment that
favors resource-wasting maneuvers for tactical advantage over
strategic investments in quality.

HOW DID WE GET HERE?

Immediately after World War II, private colleges and universities educated about half of all U.S. students, and probably 40
percent of these students were in liberal arts colleges. Moreover, before the Cold War upsurge in federal support for research, the undergraduate programs of leading private universities had much more in common with those of liberal arts
colleges than is true today.

Beginning with the World War II– and Korean War–era G.I.
Bills and continuing through the baby-boom years of the 1960s,
the notion that a college education was a natural aspiration for
middle-class families took hold. College enrollments, which
totaled only about 2.3 million in 1950, rose to 8.6 million by
1970. Most of that increase was absorbed in a rapidly expanding public higher-education sector, so that by the time the last
of the baby boomers entered college, fewer than a quarter of all
college students were in private colleges and universities.

During the 1970s, the economic returns to college education
ebbed as the huge cohorts of baby-boom college graduates
flooded the labor market. That decline in returns, coupled with
the near cessation of overall college population growth as the
baby boomers reached adulthood, led to a fearsome scramble
for college students throughout the disco era. Private colleges
found themselves unable to raise tuitions fast enough to keep up

with rising inflation, and the salaries of college professors fell by 17 percent in real terms from their peak in 1972 to a low in 1980.

Liberal education suffered notably in market popularity as stories of English majors driving cabs made the rounds and students sought the seemingly greater security of professional and vocational majors. The percentage of America's college graduates majoring in a traditional liberal arts discipline fell from 38 percent in 1970–1971 to 25 percent in 1994–1995.[1] Faced with this change in student interests, public and private universities shifted their commitments rapidly, though hardly painlessly, toward undergraduate professional programs.

Perhaps more surprisingly, the liberal arts colleges followed suit. The Carnegie Foundation publishes an elaborate classification of America's colleges and universities, sorted by their programs and degree levels. The economist David Breneman looked at the curricular offerings of the 540 colleges classified by Carnegie in 1987 as "liberal arts colleges." He proposed a rather modest criterion for regarding a college as committed to liberal education: at least 40 percent of its students should major in a liberal discipline.[2] And the result of Breneman's inquiry? Only 212 of these so-called liberal arts colleges passed that test.

The remainder—the majority—had transformed themselves, some quietly, some with fanfare, into schools specializing in business, computing, nursing, and the like, often equipping themselves with large populations of adult and part-time students. It is no accident that in its latest published classification, the Carnegie Foundation has dropped the term "liberal arts colleges" altogether and simply refers to these schools as "baccalaureate" institutions.

The result is that today, in a vastly expanded higher education marketplace, fewer than 250,000 students out of more than 14 million experience education in a small residential college without graduate students, where a substantial fraction of their colleagues major in a liberal discipline. If one made the definition of a "liberal arts college" more stringent, focusing on places where the majority of students major in the liberal arts and live on campus, and where admission is moderately selective (turning down, say, more than a third of those who apply), the numbers would drop further. Indeed, by this standard, the nation's liberal arts college students would almost certainly fit easily inside a Big Ten football stadium: fewer than 100,000 students out of more than 14 million. The question of whether anybody should care if this dwindling segment of American postsecondary education were to shrink further is one to which we will return.

THE FINANCING OF LIBERAL ARTS COLLEGES

Liberal arts colleges are, with rather few exceptions, part of the private nonprofit sector in American higher education. Table 1 provides data on how various types of colleges and universities in both sectors raised and dispersed their revenues.[3] (These data rely on the expansive definition of liberal arts colleges built into the Carnegie classification system.) Public institutions generally receive half or more of their operating revenues from state government appropriations, allowing them to charge tuitions that are markedly below true costs. As a result, public-college tuition revenues, net of the institutional spending on

Table 1. Breakdown of Expenditures and Revenues, 1994 (percent)

| | Research & Doctoral | | Comprehensive | | Liberal Arts | | Two-Year |
	Public	Private	Public	Private	Public	Private	Public
Expenditures							
Instruction and self-supported research	39.53	43.29	48.48	43.85	46.46	40.12	51.70
Funded research	21.82	18.79	3.02	2.91	1.56	1.03	0.18
Public service	8.48	3.35	4.26	1.76	4.67	0.92	2.37
Academic support	6.63	5.27	6.55	5.49	6.49	5.10	6.21
Library	3.32	3.50	3.99	3.71	3.86	4.34	2.68
Student services	4.27	4.88	8.60	12.70	9.36	14.45	10.32
Institutional support	8.25	12.81	13.97	19.39	15.60	22.24	15.86
Operations and maintenance	7.70	8.12	11.13	10.19	12.01	11.80	10.69
Revenues							
Federal grants and contracts	18.79	27.09	5.96	4.92	5.31	2.66	5.73
State and local grants and contracts	3.42	3.87	3.62	4.35	5.06	4.74	4.86
State and local appropriations	49.98	0.86	56.90	0.69	56.64	0.37	66.50
Endowment income	1.65	12.84	0.00	5.28	0.00	16.13	0.00
Net tuition revenue	26.15	55.34	33.51	84.75	32.99	76.09	22.91

Source: McPherson and Schapiro, *The Student Aid Game.*

student aid, provide generally between a quarter and a third of operating revenues.

In private higher education, tuition plays a much bigger role. Major research universities and other doctoral-granting universities get more than a quarter of their revenues from federal research grants and contracts, helping to hold their reliance on net tuition to around 55 percent of revenues. Liberal arts colleges, by contrast, get more than three-quarters of their revenues from tuition, net of the revenues they rebate to students in the form of student-aid grants. Much of the rest of their revenues, about 16 percent in 1994, derive from income on endowment. However, that resource is very unevenly distributed among liberal arts colleges, with the twenty richest colleges accounting for more than half of all endowments in that sector and the forty richest colleges accounting for three-quarters of the total.

Liberal arts colleges are distinctive in their expenditure patterns as well. Although their spending on instruction is comparable to that at other types of private colleges, their spending on student services and "institutional support"—the administrative infrastructure—accounts for well over a third (37 percent) of all spending, compared to just 18 percent at private research and doctoral universities. This reflects in part the strong attention to student needs that is characteristic of liberal arts colleges, but perhaps as important is the small scale of these places: the much larger research and doctoral universities (average enrollment: 8,439) can spread the overhead of deans and vice presidents over a lot more students than can the liberal arts colleges (average enrollment: 1,316). This problem of scale—the other face of the greater personal attention liberal arts colleges provide—may be important to the future of the sector, a point we return to later.

The management of tuition and student aid is a key factor in the finances of liberal arts colleges. In 1993–1994, the average liberal arts college received $10,823 in tuition revenues per student, but immediately rebated $2,882 to students in the form of institutionally financed aid grants. The percentage of tuition dollars rebated in this way has grown from 18.5 percent in 1986–1987 to 26.6 percent in 1993–1994. For a sector that is so dependent on tuition from students and their families to finance the educational effort, this trend is problematic.

Why are these colleges handing back their precious tuition dollars in the form of aid? The data in table 2 shed significant light on this trend. This table shows how the college destinations of first-time, full-time college freshmen vary with family income at two different points in time, 1981 and 1997. The group of private four-year colleges in this table is considerably broader than the category of liberal arts colleges as classified by Carnegie, for it includes a number of schools with extensive master's-level programs. Still, the numbers are suggestive of important trends, and the subgroup of "highly selective" four-year colleges consists almost wholly of liberal arts colleges.

Examination of the data for 1997 makes clear that income is a major determinant of where Americans begin college. Just over half of the students from the richest families enroll at private institutions, while only 19 percent of students from the poorest families do. The likelihood of attending a private four-year college also rises with income, although not as sharply as the likelihood of attending a private university. Among highly selective institutions, the relation of attendance to income is even more pronounced, in part because the academic qualifications of high-school graduates are correlated closely with income. Fewer than one in a hundred students from families with incomes below $60,000 begin their undergraduate work at a highly selective four-year college, while students from the richest group are more than six times as likely to do so.

What is of special interest from the standpoint of the financing of liberal arts colleges is the comparison of the 1981 and 1997 data. What does not appear in these data is the often-alleged phenomenon of "middle-class melt"—the speculation, often presented as fact, that rising tuitions are driving middle-income students from private into public colleges and universities. In fact, a slightly larger percentage of students from middle- and upper-middle-income families began their college careers at private universities and private four-year colleges in 1997 than was true in 1981. Although middle-income parents complain about the price tag, they continue to find ways to send

Table 2: Distribution of Freshman Enrollment by Income Background across Institutional Types, Fall of 1981 versus Fall of 1997

1997	Lower <$20	Lower Middle $20-$30	Middle $30-$60	Upper Middle $60-$100	Upper $100-$200	Richest >$200	All Groups
Private							
University	2.5%	3.1%	3.8%	6.2%	11.9%	21.1%	5.8%
Low Select	(1.0)	(1.3)	(1.6)	(2.3)	(3.4)	(4.5)	(2.0)
Medium Select	(0.6)	(0.7)	(0.9)	(1.5)	(3.1)	(5.7)	(1.5)
High Select	(0.9)	(1.1)	(1.4)	(2.3)	(5.4)	(10.9)	(2.4)
4-Year Colleges	12.6%	14.9%	16.5%	17.8%	21.1%	26.6%	17.1%
Low Select	(10.1)	(11.8)	(12.3)	(12.1)	(12.2)	(12.2)	(11.9)
Medium Select	(2.0)	(2.4)	(3.2)	(4.2)	(5.9)	(8.5)	(3.8)
High Select	(0.6)	(0.7)	(0.9)	(1.4)	(3.1)	(6.0)	(1.4)
2-Year Colleges	3.9%	2.7%	2.5%	1.8%	2.3%	3.3%	2.5%
All Private	18.9%	20.7%	22.8%	25.8%	35.3%	51.0%	25.4%
Public							
University	11.9%	14.2%	17.5%	23.5%	27.9%	24.5%	19.4%
Low Select	(5.0)	(5.4)	(6.7)	(8.6)	(8.9)	(8.2)	(7.2)
Medium Select	(4.2)	(6.1)	(7.7)	(9.6)	(10.4)	(7.6)	(7.9)
High Select	(2.7)	(2.7)	(3.1)	(5.3)	(8.6)	(8.6)	(4.4)
4-Year Colleges	22.0%	24.4%	24.5%	24.8%	20.5%	12.6%	23.3%
Low Select	(20.7)	(22.4)	(21.2)	(20.6)	(15.9)	(9.7)	(20.1)
Medium Select	(1.3)	(2.0)	(3.3)	(4.1)	(4.6)	(3.0)	(3.2)
2-Year Colleges	47.1%	40.7%	35.2%	26.0%	16.3%	12.0%	31.8%
All Public	81.1%	79.3%	77.2%	74.2%	64.7%	49.0%	74.6%
	100%	100%	100%	100%	100%	100%	100%

1981	Lower <$10	Lower Middle $10-$15	Middle $15-$30	Upper Middle $30-$50	Upper $50-$100	Richest >$100	All Groups
Private							
University	2.2%	2.7%	3.2%	5.4%	11.3%	18.6%	4.8%
Low Select	(1.3)	(1.4)	(1.5)	(1.8)	(3.0)	(4.6)	(1.7)
Medium Select	(0.5)	(0.7)	(0.9)	(1.6)	(3.1)	(4.4)	(1.3)
High Select	(0.4)	(0.6)	(0.9)	(2.0)	(5.1)	(9.6)	(1.7)
4-Year Colleges	13.6%	15.0%	14.9%	16.3%	21.9%	32.4%	16.2%
Low Select	(11.6)	(12.2)	(11.3)	(10.8)	(12.6)	(17.1)	(11.7)
Medium Select	(1.6)	(2.3)	(3.0)	(4.2)	(5.8)	(9.5)	(3.5)
High Select	(0.4)	(0.5)	(0.6)	(1.3)	(3.4)	(5.8)	(1.1)
2-Year Colleges	6.2%	5.5%	4.2%	3.6%	3.5%	3.0%	4.3%
All Private	22.0%	23.2%	22.3%	25.3%	36.7%	54.0%	25.3%
Public							
University	10.1%	12.9%	16.1%	22.0%	25.9%	22.8%	17.7%
Low Select	(4.2)	(5.0)	(6.2)	(8.2)	(9.7)	(9.2)	(6.8)
Medium Select	(3.7)	(5.4)	(6.5)	(8.9)	(10.0)	(8.4)	(7.1)
High Select	(2.2)	(2.6)	(3.3)	(4.8)	(6.3)	(5.1)	(3.8)
4-Year Colleges	23.4%	22.5%	22.2%	21.6%	16.9%	10.0%	21.4%
Low Select	(22.2)	(20.8)	(18.9)	(17.9)	(13.7)	(8.5)	(18.5)
Medium Select	(1.2)	(1.7)	(3.3)	(3.7)	(3.2)	(1.5)	(2.9)
2-Year Colleges	44.6%	41.4%	39.3%	31.2%	20.4%	13.2%	35.6%
All Public	78.0%	76.8%	77.7%	74.7%	63.3%	46.0%	74.7%
	100%	100%	100%	100%	100%	100%	100%

Source: Calculated from results from The American Freshman Survey.[4] McPherson and Schapiro, *The Student Aid Game.*

their children to private colleges. One reason they have done so is undoubtedly the increase in tuition discounting noted above.

The picture is very different for students from more affluent backgrounds. While private universities have managed to increase their share of students from the upper-income and richest backgrounds, this is emphatically not the case for the private four-year colleges. These schools captured almost a third of the richest students in 1981, and they get just over a quarter today. These are the students who can pay their own way at the expensive private colleges, and the private four-year colleges loss of their share of these students is linked to increasing pressures to provide non-need-based price discounting. The fact is that while the presidents of four-year colleges have been bemoaning mythical "middle-income melt," they have actually been experiencing the much more painful phenomenon of "upper-income melt"—a phenomenon that it would not be politically prudent to complain about too loudly.

Looking at subgroups of the private four-year colleges adds an important dimension to this analysis. The highly selective four-year colleges—of which the flagships are leading liberal arts colleges like Swarthmore and Wellesley—have not experienced much loss of share among affluent families. Although they enroll a slightly smaller share of the students in the $100,000 to $200,000 range (3.1 percent in 1997 versus 3.4 percent in 1981), they have managed to increase slightly their share of students from the richest families (6.0 percent in 1997 versus 5.8 percent in 1981). This is in marked contrast to the least-selective private four-year colleges, where the loss in share of the richest students is concentrated (12.2 percent in 1997 versus 17.1 percent in 1981). This development points to an increasing stratification among more- and less-selective liberal arts colleges, which is a key element in their future. The fact is that the well-endowed, highly selective liberal arts colleges with strong brand-name identification are at least holding their own in the market for students, while the less well known and less affluent are losing ground.

This picture of student enrollment destinations by income also provides a first lesson in understanding the phenomenon of tuition discounting that we have noted. Many observers speak of a "high tuition/high aid" strategy in private higher education in a way that suggests private colleges and universities are voluntarily giving up much-needed tuition revenue in order to aid students. The natural question would be, if you want more net tuition revenue, why not just cut back on the aid you offer? There are indeed a handful of private colleges and universities in the United States where student aid is for the most part a discretionary expenditure—where the college offers aid in order to promote such social and educational goals as greater economic and racial diversity in the entering class and more opportunity for students with poor economic backgrounds.

For most private colleges, however, a major motive for offering student aid is that they cannot find enough qualified students who will pay the full price. These schools have to offer aid to middle-income students in order to keep tuition charges within reach. And increasingly, as these schools find themselves losing the battle to recruit students from high-income families, they are extending financial aid into that realm as well, often in the form of merit scholarships. The principle here is the same one the airlines follow in charging more to business travelers than to leisure travelers who are willing to stay over the weekend to get a lower fare: the colleges try to charge the full price to students who can afford it, and who are not in danger of being enticed away by other schools, while offering discounts to those who cannot or will not pay the full fare. The economics is the same for airlines as it is for colleges: just as a passenger flying at a discount fare provides more net revenue than an empty seat, so a student providing some tuition revenue is doing more for the bottom line than an empty dormitory bed and classroom seat.[5]

Here lies a huge financial challenge for many less-prominent liberal arts colleges. A relative handful of highly selective, well-endowed liberal arts colleges use their substantial resources both to subsidize their educational program and to help finance the cost of student-aid discounts. These powerhouses have considerable discretion over whom they admit, what they charge, and how they distribute their student aid. Less affluent, less prestigious colleges lack the resources to give deep subsidies to their educational efforts or to finance substantial tuition discounting from sources other than current revenues. At the same time, they lack the brand-name recognition to recruit qualified full-paying students without offers of merit aid or other discounting strategies.

The fundamental problem here is the lack of a customer base that is willing and able to cover the costs of the enterprise. In times past, many of these colleges were able to rely on a strong regional or local appeal, often linked to a religious denomination. In many cases they could also recruit faculty from nearby graduate institutions at relatively modest salaries. Increasingly, however, the markets both for students and for college faculty have become national in scope, and loyalty to a religious denomination has become less important. It is not uncommon these days to find regional liberal arts colleges where virtually no one is paying the full posted price. At these schools, announcing an across-the-board tuition cut as opposed to continuing to pump money into student aid has little cost—since nobody was paying that price anyway—and may give some short-term publicity benefits. Such a step, however, does little to address the underlying problem that many are less interested in the product than they used to be.

FINANCIAL-AID MANAGEMENT AND THE
ENGINEERING OF ENROLLMENT

Decisions about pricing, discounting, and admissions have grown so much in importance to liberal arts colleges—and to higher education generally—that they deserve a closer look.[6]

It is useful to think in stylized terms of three "ideal types" of student-aid operations. The first, which we might call the "need-blind, full-need" approach, is a fair description of reality at a handful of the best-endowed and most-selective private colleges and universities in the nation. These are schools with long waiting lists of highly qualified full-paying customers. They could easily fill their freshman classes with little or no spending on student aid. For these schools, student aid is a real cost, reflecting a choice by the institution to give up revenue from full-paying students to change the profile of the freshman class, aiming perhaps at socioeconomic or racial diversity, or honoring a more abstract principle of admitting students without the ability to pay.[7] The very few institutions in this happy situation can afford to say, and to mean, that they admit students without regard to financial need and that they fund all such students to the extent of their need.

A second ideal type of student-aid operation, which might be called the "budget stretch" approach, would have fit a goodly number of private colleges and universities ten or fifteen years ago. These were institutions that had roughly the same aims as the elite institutions with the "need-blind, full-need" approach, but lacked the endowment resources and the affluent applicant pool to operate as these elite places did. These schools would budget what they felt they could for student aid and try to stretch those funds to fill their freshman class with the best students they could, taking as little account as possible of a student's ability to pay.

The third approach might be described as "strategic maximization." This outlook also fits schools that lack the resources of the most-selective and well-endowed institutions. But now, instead of aiming to "stretch" a fixed student-aid budget as far as possible, the school sets out deliberately to shape a financial-aid strategy that maximally advances the combined (and conflicting) goals of admitting the best students and gaining as much revenue from them as possible.

In its full glory, strategic maximization can be a pretty ruthless business. If a student is willing to travel a long distance to be interviewed on campus, that can be a signal that she is eager to attend, so it may mean a smaller financial-aid offer to such a student while throwing more dollars at the young person who is somewhat indifferent about attending one place or another. Students with an interest in a popular major may get smaller student-aid offers than those interested in a more obscure and hence more underenrolled subject. And, of course, students with higher SATs or a better jump shot, because they may attract applications from other full-paying students or may fill the stands at the stadium, are likely to get better aid offers than their less-qualified peers.

Few schools have gone all the way down the road to this strategic maximization strategy. But it is fair to say that the number of institutions following the "need-blind, full-need" strategy—always a small number—has shrunk in the last decade, and that most institutions have moved their financial-aid operations from the direction of the "budget-stretch" approach significantly toward strategic maximization.

The colleges' increased focus on the strategic significance of aid and pricing decisions has changed the institutional structures through which aid is managed. When aid was seen as a charitable sideline, most institutions were content to leave the details to the professionals in the student-aid office, with the main high-level concern being that of keeping the aid operation within budget. Student-aid officers, who had collaborated on developing the elaborate needs-analysis apparatus that governed the allocation of need-based student aid, formed strong professional and ethical bonds and developed both a rather inaccessible professional jargon and something of a tradition of holding their operation aloof from institutional goals.

These days, financial-aid policy and practice at private and public institutions alike is frequently the province of high-level consultants and close presidential attention. Following on the heels of their colleagues in the admissions office, financial-aid officers have come to find their duty hazardous, with a high level of accountability for results in terms of meeting institutional goals and limited patience for qualms based on professional ethics.

There are several key decision points in shaping financial-aid strategies. The first broad choice is whether to confine aid offers to students with demonstrated financial need and, if so, to limit those offers to the extent of the need. So-called no-need or merit aid involves awarding aid to students that the school finds attractive, even if they have no need, or awarding aid to such students in excess of their demonstrated need. As shown in table 3, this form of aid has become increasingly important in U.S. higher education generally, growing at a rate of some 13 percent annually faster than inflation between 1983–1984 and 1991–1992, compared to a growth rate of 10 percent in need-based aid. At the more-selective liberal arts colleges (Liberal Arts I in the Carnegie classification), merit aid accounted for only 14 percent of all grant aid in 1991–1992, but growth was

Table 3: Non-need Aid per Freshman, by Institution Type and Carnegie
Classification, 1983–1984 and 1991–1992

| Carnegie Class | Non-need aid per freshman (in 1991$) | | Non-need share of inst.-based aid | | Real growth rate in aid per freshman (%) | | Freshmen enrolled |
	83–84	91–92	83–84	91–92	non-need	need	91–92
Publics							
Research I	71	296	0.32	0.46	18	11	33,056
Research II	112	525	0.62	0.64	19	19	4,957
Doctorate I	90	185	0.44	0.55	9	2	10,874
Doctorate II	43	108	0.14	0.63	11	-17	1,359
Comp I	101	193	0.51	0.67	8	-1	52,488
Comp II	269	507	0.75	0.63	8	15	4,251
LA II	225	852	0.46	0.60	17	10	977
All publics	96	252	0.44	0.56	12	6	110,003
Privates							
Research I	201	474	0.08	0.10	11	8	14,361
Research II	205	1051	0.10	0.19	20	11	4,757
Doctorate I	46	399	0.08	0.18	27	15	6,322
Doctorate II	379	1442	0.29	0.44	17	7	2,515
Comp I	328	790	0.32	0.28	11	13	24,808
Comp II	244	768	0.22	0.24	14	12	11,462
LA I	203	660	0.10	0.14	15	9	27,156
LA II	383	1040	0.30	0.33	13	11	19,123
All privates	253	742	0.17	0.21	13	10	117,262
All institutions	177	505	0.21	0.24	13	10	227,265

Note: Carnegie classification as of 1987. Certain categories of schools are not listed separately (for example, public art and design colleges and private religious schools).

Source: Peterson's institutional and financial aid data bases. McPherson and Schapiro, *The Student Aid Game.*

rapid: 15 percent annually after accounting for inflation. At the less-selective liberal arts colleges, merit aid grew a bit slower—13 percent per year—but it accounted for fully a third of all aid awarded, compared with just 21 percent at the average private institution.

Merit aid, however, is only the tip of the iceberg, because colleges can and do vary the quality of the aid packages they offer to needy students according to how eager they are to attract the student. A typical student-aid "package" includes a financial-aid grant, a loan, and a work-study job. It is not uncommon for two students enrolling at the same school with an equivalent ability to pay to receive very different packages. One might, for example, have $9,000 in grants, $4,000 in loans, and an expectation of earning $1,500 through work during the school year; the other might have $14,500 grant with no loans or expectation of earnings during the year. The difference can be accounted for through the fact that the second student had a higher SAT score or some other attribute that made him more attractive to the college. Such "merit within need" is a major factor in student-aid practice at a great many institutions that have no explicit merit or no-need aid. Schools also must decide whether to take financial need into account in deciding which students to admit and whether to meet the full need of all the students they do admit. Variations and combinations of these strategies are almost endless and provide employment for a growing army of consultants.

The current market situation poses a particularly vexing problem for the less affluent and less selective among private institutions. In the United States a handful of highly selective, highly successful, and very rich private colleges and universities set a standard on class size, research reputation of faculty, course load, scientific facilities, and gymnasium equipment. Less-affluent schools try to emulate the product of the leading institutions while lacking the endowment resources and deep applicant pools that the market leaders enjoy. These less-affluent institutions find themselves judged not only on the basis of their ability to deploy these costly resources but also on their ability to recruit a student body with impressive qualifications. Needing every dollar of revenue they can get, and needing to attract every high-quality student they can find, these institutions are under enormous pressure to use their financial-aid resources effectively, through aggressive packaging policies and increasingly through explicit merit aid.

In this context it is hard not to notice a touch of self-righteousness in the insistence of the most affluent and selective schools on the principles of need-blind admissions, full-need financing of admitted students, and no merit aid. In one sense, because the elite institutions use their large endowments to subsidize the education of all their students, they offer a substantial merit scholarship to every student they admit. Competing schools with fewer resources can with some justification claim that they are merely using their targeted merit scholarships to try to keep up. Moreover, even for very well endowed institutions, their ability to fund fully their needy students depends heavily on having a great many high-quality applicants who are willing and able to pay the sticker price. Or, more bluntly, what mostly differentiates schools that use merit aid or other strategically oriented aid strategies from those that do not is not their moral fiber but the number of top quality full-paying students they are able to attract without such devices.

So, how does this actually work? How does a college that wants to manage its enrollment strategically go about that work? A stylized example drawn from *The Student Aid Game* may help make things more concrete.[8] The top panel of table 4 provides admissions and aid statistics for the class of 2000 at mythical "Conjectural University," a moderately selective private institution that practices need-blind admissions and full-need funding of enrolled students. The table crossclassifies the applicant pool according to ability to pay and academic promise (measured here for convenience simply by combined SAT scores). Within each academic ability/financial need group, the table reports the number of applicants, the number accepted, and the number enrolling. The table gives a rather rich picture of how the combined policies of the admissions and aid offices wind up producing the freshman class.

As the summary data for the first section show, Conjectural University enrolls a freshman class of 1,011 students by admitting 2,565 out of an applicant pool of 4,785. The selectivity of the place is evidenced in the fact that the average SAT score of the freshman class (1,006) is substantially above that of the applicant pool (864). Although the data are pure fiction, they reflect some realistic features of profiles of actual schools. Thus, for example, higher-ability students are generally more likely to be admitted and less likely to enroll than lower-ability students. High-need students are more likely to enroll if admitted and, at a need-blind place, are no less likely to be admitted, given ability levels.

The strategic usefulness of a table like this lies in examining the consequences of potential changes in admissions/aid policy. Suppose, for example, that Conjectural University had formulated a goal of raising the number of high-ability students in the class (perhaps because the current situation reflected a fall from a more glorious past), and that a board member stood

Table 4: Admissions Profile, Conjectural University

| | Combined SAT Score | | | | | | |
	1300+	1100–1300	900–1100	700–900	Below 700	Total	Average SAT
No Need							
Apply	75	125	300	300	400	1,200	866
Accept	75	110	250	200	10	645	1018
Enroll	20	40	75	80	9	224	988
Low Need							
Apply	75	125	300	300	400	1,200	866
Accept	75	110	250	200	10	645	1018
Enroll	25	45	80	80	9	239	1003
Medium Need							
Apply	75	125	300	300	400	1,200	866
Accept	75	110	250	200	10	645	1018
Enroll	30	50	90	80	9	259	1015
High Need							
Apply	60	125	300	300	400	1,185	858
Accept	60	110	250	200	10	630	1008
Enroll	30	60	100	90	9	289	1013
Total							
Apply	285	500	1,200	1,200	1,600	4,785	864
Accept	285	440	1,000	800	40	2,565	1016
Enroll	105	195	345	330	36	1,011	1006

Revised Admissions Policy, Conjectural University

| | Combined SAT Score | | | | | | |
	1300+	1100–1300	900–1100	700–900	Below 700	Total	Average SAT
No Need							
Apply	75	125	300	300	400	1,200	866
Accept	75	125	300	250	75	825	974
Enroll	20	45	90	100	68	323	910
Low Need							
Apply	75	125	300	300	400	1,200	866
Accept	75	110	250	200	10	645	1018
Enroll	25	45	80	80	9	239	1003
Medium Need							
Apply	75	125	300	300	400	1,200	866
Accept	75	110	250	200	10	645	1018
Enroll	30	50	90	80	9	259	1015
High Need							
Apply	60	125	300	300	400	1,185	858
Accept	60	110	250	0	0	420	1117
Enroll	30	60	100	0	0	190	1134
Total							
Apply	285	500	1,200	1,200	1,600	4,785	864
Accept	285	455	1,050	650	95	2,535	1020
Enroll	105	200	360	260	86	1,011	1001

Note: In this example, low need is considered to require a grant of 0–$5,000; medium need, $5,000–$12,500; high need, $12,500–$25,000.

Source: McPherson and Schapiro, *The Student Aid Game.*

ready to put up enough cash to support a big investment in this effort. An obvious thing to try would be raising the "yield" of high-ability/low- or no-need students by offering merit scholarships. Suppose that Conjectural were to offer $10,000 merit scholarships to no-need students in the applicant pool from the 1300+ SAT group. This might yield, say, ten new students. Notice that the cost of the program in the first year would be not only the $100,000 going to the newly attracted students but an additional $200,000 to the students who would have enrolled anyway (since there is no way to figure out in advance which ones they are). If this program were sustained for each new class through its four years at Conjectural, its cost when fully implemented would be $1.2 million per year.

But there is an obvious way to offset some of that cost. With ten more high-ability students added to the class, the college could reduce its admission of other students by ten, and the obvious place to look would be in the low-ability/high-need group. If the college simply rejected the ten students it now accepts from that group, it would avoid financial-aid expenditures on them of about $17,500 per student for nine students, or $157,500. Over four classes, this would amount to annual savings of $630,000, offsetting just about half the cost of the merit-aid program. The net effect on average SATs of replacing these low-ability/high-need students with high-ability/no-need students would be a gain of about eight points.

Whether this would be a prudent, clever, or fair thing to do is a matter we will address shortly, but first consider another possible policy change. Suppose the institution, rather than looking for higher-quality students, instead was in a bind that compelled it to look for savings in its financial-aid operation. Again, the obvious strategy would be to deny admission to low-ability/high-need students and replace them with students of lower need. For concreteness, imagine a dramatic change. Suppose Conjectural simply stopped admitting high-need applicants with SATs below 900—a more dramatic step than a real college would likely take. This would cut enrollment by 99. Suppose, for simplicity, that the college replaced those 99 by admitting more no-need students. In particular, suppose they admitted all no-need students with SATs above 900, admitted another 50 from the 700–900 range, and admitted enough with SATs below 700 to make up the remainder of the enrollment shortfall produced by denying admission to the low-ability/high-need students. Assuming constant yield rates for these applicant groups, the results of this policy shift are shown in the Revised Admissions Policy section of table 4.

Notice that the average SAT scores of enrolled no-need students fall sharply, from 988 to 910, but that this drop is partially offset by a rise from 1013 to 1134 in the average SATs of high-need students. On balance, the effect on average SATs for the entering class is a drop of 5 points—achieved however by more than doubling the number of students in the class with very low SATs. The financial savings are spectacular—a saving of about $1.75 million in the first year, $7 million per year once the effects work through the four years.

Such a policy is too draconian to be realistic, but a milder version of the policy might be plausible. Suppose, for example, that the college rejected the ten lowest-ranking students among its high-need applicants and replaced them with the highest-ranking students among the no-need students it would otherwise reject. The effect on the quality of the class might be minimal, and the first year's financial savings would be $175,000.

Policies of this kind—making admission need-aware, or introducing merit aid—obviously have great appeal to hard-pressed colleges. An analysis like that in table 4 makes the options and the trade-offs they imply relatively clear. Real-world admission and aid strategies differ from this stylized example mainly in increasing the dimensionality of the problem, adding to the number of ways in which the prospects presented to different students are manipulated.

It is difficult to generalize about the effectiveness of these various financial-aid strategies in promoting individual institutions' goals. A great deal will obviously depend on the circumstances of the individual institution. However, one broad generalization will stand up: the consequences for any one school of following these kinds of aid strategies will differ greatly depending on how their fellow institutions respond. This is most obviously true of merit aid and differential aid-package strategies. Consider an individual school with four or five close competitors with overlapping admissions pools. If this institution offers selective price cuts in the form of merit aid or "sweetened" aid packages to its most promising students while its competitors do not, the impact on the institution's yield of these desirable students is likely to be quite strong. But if the school's price cuts have this effect, it is likely that they will provoke a response from the competing institutions. In terms of the example discussed earlier, if Conjectural University recruits ten top students through merit aid, there is a good chance that it is recruiting them away from one or a few close competitors. If the College of the Imagination, just down the street from Conjectural, notices the loss and figures out the reason, it is very likely to respond with an equally or more aggressive merit-aid program. It is easy to picture a chain reaction that winds up with all the schools in the area enrolling basically the same students they would enroll without their merit-aid programs, but forgoing a lot of tuition revenue from them.

A different but equally potent dynamic can result from a single school adopting a need-aware admissions strategy or becoming more stingy with grants to high-need students who are in the lower part of their admitted group. Competitor schools who do not follow suit will encounter an abrupt increase in the fraction of relatively high need, low-quality admitted students who choose to enroll, for suddenly the admissions/aid offers will have become relatively more attractive. Thus, the decision by any one school to worsen the offers it makes to high-need students will increase the pressure on competing schools to do the same. There is, however, an important difference between this case and the case of merit aid or differential packaging. Here, while there is clearly harm to the interests of the students whose aid offers are being worsened or withdrawn, there is no harm to the collective financial interests of the schools involved, as there is in the case of a merit-aid price war.

Yet this kind of analysis also brings to the fore questions about the long-run financial wisdom as well as the ethical propriety of such policies. The right answers for particular institutions depend very much on local circumstances and options, but we believe the following general points should be kept in mind when contemplating such policies.

First, colleges should not think themselves obliged to meet goals that are simply beyond their financial capacity. The handful of schools that practice both need-blind admission and full-need funding of aid for enrolled students are in a highly favorable position to honor such claims. They are very well endowed places with the added benefit of having large numbers of affluent full-paying students. There is no more fundamental constraint on ethical principles than "ought implies can"—no one can be morally obliged to do what is beyond her powers. It is our sense that colleges and universities should view the effort to extend opportunities for access to their educational offerings as an important goal, but not one that must override all other goals, including offering a high-quality education to those who do attend.

In this context it is important to recognize that simply being "need-blind" in admission, absent the resources required to meet the need of all who enroll, is an empty goal. Once a college finds that it must ration student-aid funds, the question of how this is best done becomes a matter of strategy and judgment. A school might admit without regard to need but then deny financial aid to the lower ranked and needier among the admitted students. Or it might offer the less attractive among the needy admits financial-aid packages that fall short of meeting need (a "gapping" strategy). Or they might, as in the examples discussed above, make the admission decision itself need-aware. There is no obvious principle that makes one of these strategies more moral than another.

Indeed, there are times when being self-consciously need-aware may be more effective for a school that is trying to promote greater economic diversity among its student body than is a need-blind strategy. This is obviously the case if a school wants to use information about financial need to admit a more economically needy class than need-blindness would yield. But it is also quite plausible to imagine that a school in particular circumstances could find that being purely need-blind is not producing the income profile it desires, and that it could produce a better result by "tilting" in favor of middle-income students or in favor of high-need students.

Although the moral choices facing colleges are clearly complex, there is, in our view, one moral principle that should be widely respected in schools' admissions policies—the principle of honesty. Schools should inform applicants and high-school guidance counselors of how they make their decisions. There is a good deal of pressure on schools to maintain a claim to being need-blind when the reality of their policies is more complicated. Many schools, for example, are need-blind for freshman admits but not for transfers, and others are need-blind for the first round of admits but are need-aware for those on the wait list. Schools should be explicit about such policies.

THE FUTURE VALUE OF THE LIBERAL ARTS

Liberal education is expensive, and the means of its financing are increasingly controversial. Is the game worth the candle? Much of the value of liberal education may lie outside the economist's "nicely calculated less and more," but as economists we would like to take note of compelling reasons for regarding the future economic value of liberal education as strong.

Considerable evidence exists that the economic returns on educational investments of all kinds have risen in the last twenty years. At the college level this is reflected in a widening gap between the earnings of those with high-school educations and those with higher levels of education. Regrettably, most of the growth in the gap comes from the declining real wages of high-school graduates, rather than stronger earnings from those who attend college. Still, it is clear that the economic incentive to attend college is larger now than in past eras. These high returns appear to apply at all levels of postsecondary education—the earnings gap has widened between those with some college and those with none as well as between college graduates and those with some college.

What accounts for these higher returns? Are they likely to prove a transient phenomenon? One source of the higher returns is temporary—a result of changing demographics. As we noted earlier, returns on higher education were depressed in the late 1960s and early 1970s as a result of the very large cohorts of college-educated workers who appeared in the labor force at that time, as the baby boomers matured. Since then, the decline in the number of young persons entering the labor force has produced something of a shortage of young college-level workers, and this has contributed to increased returns. The impact of this force can be expected to diminish as the "echo" of the baby boom leads to larger cohorts of young people in the decades ahead.

This supply-side effect, however, does not appear to be the main explanation for higher returns. Rather, most of the action has been on the side of the demand for labor, and appears to be a result of the rapid pace of technical change. Two economists, Larry Katz and Kevin Murphy, have shown that rising demand for better-educated workers has been driven by the relative expansion of industries that have higher demands for educated labor.[9] That is, those parts of the economy that rely less on college-educated labor (farming, heavy industry) have declined in importance, while industries that use more college-educated workers (financial services, high-tech manufacturing) have grown.

Ongoing rapid technical change implies that this trend is likely to continue, and thus the economic payoff to higher levels of education is likely to be high for the foreseeable future. The stunning developments over the last decades in areas from microcomputers to biological engineering are only beginning to reveal their consequences. Not only will many of these developments continue to generate significant technical changes, but they also provide a powerful engine for the further acquisition of new knowledge. Hence, from the standpoint of economic efficiency and growth, the nation is likely to require high and rising levels of investment in human skills. But should this investment take the form of liberal education, or does the importance of technical change call instead for greater investments in narrowly technical education?

How does one prepare for a world in which the content of one's job may change dramatically five or more times in the course of a career? Keeping pace in a world of rapid technological change puts a premium on learning how to learn, on becoming flexible. Even the very best training in today's technology will quickly become obsolete in the world into which we are moving. All those computer programmers who learned COBOL and FORTRAN in the 1970s have had to learn this lesson. Indeed, it is not implausible that advances in computer technology will render the very profession of computer programming as we have known it obsolete in the next twenty years: computers are increasingly capable of writing their own programs (and even designing their own successor machines) on the basis of more general instructions provided by users of what the computer needs to do.

In the face of the rapid obsolescence of detailed technical skills, it becomes clear that what is needed is not more training in today's technology—indeed not training at all—but education. Education includes being prepared to respond to new situations and challenges. It means cultivating the ability for independent thought, for expanding the capacity to cope with new ideas and new outlooks. These are precisely the strengths of liberal education. Liberal education in this sense is of course by no means a monopoly of the liberal arts colleges, nor is it necessarily a matter only of teaching the traditional liberal disciplines. As Alfred North Whitehead argued many years ago, business can be taught in a liberal spirit and, equally, classics can be taught in a narrow and technical way.[10] Still, as we suggest below, liberal arts colleges are likely to play a critical role in preserving a social understanding of what liberal arts teaching really is.

Perhaps as important as technical change to the future of the economy and the future of liberal education is the growing internationalization of the economy and society. Abetted by rapid advances in communication technology, it is clear that future citizens will need to be comfortable with a much broader range of languages and cultures than has been traditionally required to live their daily lives. Even for relatively narrow business purposes, when dealing with citizens of another country it is an obvious advantage not only to speak the language but to have some understanding of cultural expectations and norms. And there is every reason to expect that cross-national communication and interaction will extend well beyond narrow business purposes. Economic and social issues from pollution to the spread of AIDS are inherently global and will increasingly require a search for common understanding and common values. The capacity to transcend one's own parochial point of view and join in a larger understanding is certainly one that liberal education aims to promote. Higher education, in an extension of its traditional role in liberal and general education, will be expected in the future to help promote both respect for difference and this search for common values.

Although seemingly not an economist's kind of topic, we believe it is of first-rate importance in thinking about social needs for higher education to keep in sight the role of colleges and universities in education about values. Both globalization and rapid technical change pose challenging problems for American values and traditions. A key example is our growing technical ability to prolong life. We will, individually and collectively, be forced in the future to decide matters of life and death that historically have been out of our hands. It is not an exaggeration to say that we have barely a clue about how to do this responsibly, humanely, and morally. Problems of similar depth arise as we as a nation increasingly come to recognize ourselves as part of a world of communities. Both understanding and valuing other cultures (and diverse communities within our own borders) and finding legitimate grounds for criticizing or reforming cultural practices that violate certain core values are huge challenges facing us.

Colleges and universities in the United States, both more than in other countries and more than in our own past, are now the places where systematic and open-minded reflection on these matters happens. There are few social needs more important than maintaining, or sometimes creating, traditions of searching critique and civil discourse about these fundamental issues.

PRODUCING EDUCATION IN THE LIBERAL ARTS COLLEGE SETTING

Viewed as producers of higher-education services, liberal arts colleges have several distinctive features. First, they are small in scale, with enrollments averaging only about 15 percent of those at private universities and 8 percent of those at public. Second, liberal arts colleges are unusually reliant on fully qualified faculty to teach their courses, lacking the ranks of graduate teaching assistants that carry a good part of the undergraduate load at most universities. And third, they are residential enterprises, housing most of their students on campus and emphasizing the educational importance of the residential experience. This is clearly an expensive package, and likely to become more so. It also bucks up against some major trends in U.S. higher education, including the increasing specialization and subdivision of the university curriculum and the increasingly part-time and nonresidential character of the undergraduate experience for more and more students. Can liberal arts colleges overcome these challenges? Should we, as a society, care if they do?

Putting professors in contact with manageable numbers of students in a setting that is on a human scale is the essence of the liberal arts college, as embodied in the metaphor of Mark Hopkins and the log: when President James A. Garfield, a Williams graduate, was asked to define the ideal education, he responded that it was a student on one end of a log and longtime Williams president and professor Mark Hopkins on the other.[11] Yet that way of producing education imposes some limitations. No college with two thousand students and two hundred faculty members can produce the range of majors and interdisciplinary programs offered by a major university (the University of Minnesota had at last count more than 125 undergraduate major subjects, a number that, mapped onto the Macalester College faculty, would yield an average department size of between one and two). A major challenge facing small colleges is therefore that of finding a way for a limited number of faculty to offer a range of topics and subject matters in its curriculum that suitably reflects the range of modern learning. It is fair to say that nobody at this point has a really satisfactory solution to this problem. The intellectual and political arguments for adding new programs—in various foreign languages, in ethnic and area studies, in new scientific subdisciplines—are all plausible, and they add up to an unbearable load. That is true especially when tradition requires each such study to be instantiated in its own space, with its own bureaucratic apparatus and support staff. The solution, if there is one, must be found in articulating persuasively the case that the strength of the liberal arts college lies not in the range of its offerings but in the depth of the understanding it induces, the general intellectual and human capacities it fosters, and the ways it finds to make its organizational structures more flexible.

Scale matters, too, in managing the support services a college needs to provide. Halving the number of students does not halve the number of books the library needs. The number of football coaches at a college of two thousand is not much different from the number at a university of ten thousand, and the swimming pool needs the same amount of water. As mentioned earlier, the administrative infrastructure absorbs a substantially larger share of expenditures at small colleges than at larger universities. The economies of scale in delivering various services argues in favor of consortial arrangements that spread costs over more schools, an opportunity more available to urban than to rural colleges, and an opportunity that may be enhanced for some kinds of services by new developments in electronic communications such as the World Wide Web.

The importance of high-priced faculty in the economy of the small college presents a major challenge. Faculty at small colleges tend to run their own shops to a greater extent than at universities. Activities such as preparing laboratories, organizing slides in art history, typing up syllabi, or grading exams can often be passed off to graduate students or paid professionals in universities but wind up being faculty chores in colleges. Although faculty sometimes find this frustrating, they also take satisfaction in a manner of work that may have more in common with a medieval craftsman than a modern corporate worker.

Yet faculty are very expensive. A big challenge facing colleges is to find ways to relieve faculty of "low-value added" activities while encouraging them to maintain and even increase their immediate engagement with students in the business of learning. A good example is the advising of students. At its best, the work of helping students plan their undergraduate careers is of enormous importance, and many colleges pride themselves on keeping that function with the faculty. In plain fact, though, much advising time at most colleges is consumed with checking paperwork, signing forms, and shuffling paper— tasks for whose skillful performance a Ph.D. is often a disqualification. Here and elsewhere the prospect of using modern information technology to release faculty from purely routine functions so they can give more attention to the creative aspects of their jobs may be considerable.

CONCLUSION: WHO CARES?

Liberal arts colleges have big problems to solve, both in terms of how they produce their product and how they price and market it. Should anyone, besides their presidents and employees, care how well they do in solving these problems? Many universities offer degrees in liberal subjects. Perhaps we should regard the liberal arts colleges as leftovers from an earlier era—the educational equivalent of the British roadster.

There are, we think, important reasons to resist that conclusion. The residential liberal arts college, at its best, remains almost a unique embodiment of a certain ideal of educational excellence. These are institutions that have eschewed most of the enormous variety of activities that define the modern university—from graduate and professional schools to large research establishments to semiprofessional sports. We look to them when we want to know what it means to focus single-mindedly on the education of young minds. This focus extends not only to the classroom environment but to the conscious effort to fashion a framework for residential living that will foster both the intellectual and personal development of students. When Stanford University declared several years ago that it was going to work harder on giving a good undergraduate education, that meant in practice that Stanford, in its collegiate manifestation, was going to try to be more like Bryn Mawr or Carleton—smaller classes, more faculty in the classroom, more faculty attention to students outside of class, and the like.

There are, of course, a handful of liberal arts colleges that are not on anybody's endangered species list. Schools like Amherst and Williams have the financial power and the reputation to remain in control of their own destiny through almost any plausible future. But there are not even fifty colleges about which one could say that with confidence.

The question then arises, how many good liberal arts colleges must thrive in order for the sector to continue to play a meaningful role in defining excellence in American higher education? That number needs to be high enough that the option of attending a liberal arts college gets serious attention from a substantial fraction of talented high-school seniors. Our own best guess is that right now the United States may well have more liberal arts colleges (at least in name) than it really needs or is willing to support. Yet we also judge that if the sector is allowed to dwindle to the fewer than fifty colleges that currently face a secure financial future, it will cease to count for much, and American higher education will be the worse for it. What we need are policies from foundations and governments that seek to sustain the viability of that sector without guaranteeing the survival of every school that calls itself a liberal arts college.

ACKNOWLEDGMENTS

The authors thank Pat McPherson and this volume's editor and contributors for many helpful comments.

ENDNOTES

[1]Traditional liberal arts disciplines here include mathematics, the physical and biological sciences, social sciences and history, English, and the modern foreign languages. These numbers are calculated from data in the National Center for Education Statistics, *Digest of Education Statistics* (Washington, D.C.: U.S. Department of Education, 1997), 261, 307, 311, 313, 315.

[2]David W. Breneman, *Liberal Arts Colleges: Thriving, Surviving, or Endangered?* (Washington, D.C.: The Brookings Institution, 1994).

[3]Expenditure and revenue patterns are discussed in greater detail in Chapter 7 of Michael S. McPherson and Morton Owen Schapiro, *The Student Aid Game: Meeting Need and Rewarding Talent in American Higher Education* (Princeton, N.J.: Princeton University Press, 1998).

[4]The survey of freshmen in 1997 reflected family income in the 1996 calendar year while the survey of freshmen in 1981 reflected family income in the 1980 calendar year. Inflation between 1980 and 1996 equaled 90.4 percent. Inflation-adjusted income brackets for the 1981 survey would be as follows: <$10.5, $10.5–$15.8, $15.8–$31.5, $31.5–$52.5, $52.5–$105.0, and >$105.0. The selectivity definitions vary somewhat across institutional cat-

egories. We define low selectivity as having the following SAT ranges: <1050 for private universities, <1025 for private nonsectarian 4-yr. colleges, <1050 for Protestant 4-yr. colleges, <1025 for Catholic 4-yr. colleges, <1000 for public universities, and <1025 for public 4-yr. colleges. We define medium selectivity as having the following SAT ranges: 1050–1174 for private universities, 1025–1174 for private nonsectarian 4-yr. colleges, >1049 for Protestant 4-yr. colleges, >1024 for Catholic 4-yr. colleges, 1000–1099 for public universities, and >1024 for public 4-yr. colleges. We define high selectivity as having the following SAT ranges: >1174 for private universities, >1174 for private nonsectarian 4-yr. colleges, and >1099 for public universities.

[5]But there is an important difference between colleges and airlines: everyone at a college receives a subsidy, even those who pay the sticker price. According to Gordon C. Winston, Jared C. Carbone, and Ethan G. Lewis, spending (educational and general expenditures plus an allowance for capital costs) at the average liberal arts college in 1994–1995 amounted to $16,000, compared with a sticker price of $10,500. So even students with no financial aid received a subsidy of $5,500. Winston, Carbone, and Lewis, "What's Been Happening to Higher Education? Facts, Trends, and Data: 1986–87 to 1994–95," Williams Project on the Economics of Higher Education Discussion Paper #47, March 1998.

[6]Need-based and merit aid are discussed in great deal in McPherson and Schapiro, *The Student Aid Game,* on which the following account relies.

[7]William G. Bowen and David W. Breneman refer to this type of financial aid as an "educational investment"—as opposed to a tuition discount. They suggest that a good way to distinguish between student aid as a price discount versus student aid as an educational investment is to ask whether the provision of student aid increases or decreases the net resources available to the college to spend on other purposes. A tuition discount seeks to do the former while an educational investment does the latter. Bowen and Breneman, "Student Aid: Price Discounting or Educational Investment?" *Brookings Review* (Winter 1993): 28–31.

[8]An excellent analysis of these strategic dimensions of aid and admissions policy is contained in James Scannell, *The Effects of Financial Aid Policies on Admission and Enrollment* (New York: College Entrance Examination Board, 1992), which contains an example similar to the one presented here.

[9]Lawrence F. Katz and Kevin M. Murphy, "Changes in Relative Wages, 1963–1987: Supply and Demand Factors," *Quarterly Journal of Economics* 107 (February 1992): 35–78.

[10]Truman Schwartz, an award-winning and revered professor of chemistry at Macalester College, said recently, "I don't teach chemistry; I teach students, and the medium is chemistry."

[11]The Nobel Prize–winning economist George Stigler was known to comment that in his experience you might as well sit on the student and talk to the log. He was obviously not employed at a liberal arts college.

Some fifteen years after the publication of *A Nation at Risk*—despite the end of the cold war and the recent upturn in the economy—the country is still gripped by concern for its education system. Responding to the public mood, governors and mayors, like Congress and the president, are declaring education to be a priority. Everywhere, the rhetoric of higher standards for education is heard. And in some places there are at least halting steps toward making the rhetoric a reality, whether by adopting tougher graduation requirements, investing in developing the teaching force, pouring technology into the schools, or creating new forms of governance.

Why is education reform still alive? One reason is the fundamentally changed nature of the economy in the information age. Although U.S. business is booming and productivity is rising, growing numbers of employers continue to call for better educated, more highly skilled workers, claiming that there are good jobs with career prospects going unfilled because of a lack of adequately prepared young people. As intelligent machines take over a growing array of routine business functions, the work left for humans is increasingly the nonprogrammable tasks: those in which surprise and variability must be accommodated, where only adaptive human intelligence can make the evaluations and decisions needed. These economic and technological factors are visibly changing the job market, creating a broad awareness among Americans that their children need more and better education.

—Lauren B. Resnick and Megan Williams Hall
"Learning Organizations for
Sustainable Education Reform"

from *Dædalus*, Fall 1998
"Education Yesterday, Education Tomorrow"

Alexander W. Astin

How the Liberal Arts College Affects Students

THE QUESTION OF EDUCATIONAL EFFICACY is probably more important to the private liberal arts college than to any other type of institution. Indeed, the fact that so many of these institutions have been able to survive and even prosper during several decades of massive expansion of low-cost public higher education can only be attributed to the fact that many parents and students believe they offer special educational benefits not likely to be found either in the more prestigious private universities or in the various types of public institutions with whom they often compete for students. How justified are these beliefs?

The short answer to this question is that residential liberal arts colleges in general, and highly selective liberal arts colleges in particular, produce a pattern of consistently positive student outcomes not found in any other type of American higher-education institution. Moreover, the selective liberal arts colleges, more than any other type of institution, have managed not only to effect a reasonable balance between undergraduate teaching and scholarly research, but also to incorporate a wide range of exemplary educational practices in their educational programs.

In this essay I will review some of the empirical evidence concerning these unique educational benefits and then discuss the implications of this research for the larger higher-education system. However, in order to make sense out of this rather

Alexander W. Astin is Allan M. Cartter Professor of Higher Education at the University of California, Los Angeles.

extensive body of evidence, it is important first to be clear about what we mean when we talk about "the private liberal arts college."

VARIETIES OF LIBERAL ARTS COLLEGES

There are nearly one thousand private colleges in the United States.[1] Since most of these colleges are relatively small, residential, and devoted primarily to providing a liberal arts education for undergraduates, people tend to think of them as a homogeneous group. The fact is that private liberal arts colleges are in certain respects more diverse than any other type of higher-education institution. A few of the most affluent liberal arts colleges, for example, spend *five* times more money per student than do the less affluent ones.[2] And while many liberal arts colleges are closely tied to a particular religious denomination and place a great deal of emphasis in the curriculum and cocurriculum on the student's spiritual development, many others are completely independent of any church. Liberal arts colleges also vary widely in their educational programs, with curricula that range from a highly structured "common core" to a completely idiosyncratic approach where students design their own programs, and with pedagogies that vary from the traditional classroom lecture and discussion approach to a heavy emphasis on independent study or contract learning. Finally, while most of these institutions put little or no emphasis on graduate or professional education, a substantial minority have sizable postbaccalaureate programs in business, education, law, and other professional fields.

Perhaps the most important aspect of diversity is the great variation among private liberal arts colleges in the average level of academic preparation of the students they admit, an institutional quality that has come to be known popularly as "selectivity." Residential liberal arts colleges include some of the most selective institutions in the country, together with a larger number of moderately selective colleges and an even larger number of colleges that operate what amounts to open admission. Selectivity is, among other things, probably the most commonly used yardstick of an institution's degree of prestige or "eliteness."[3]

This diversity contributes to a certain fuzziness in our thinking about this unique and interesting institution. Given that the American liberal arts college was modeled after an elite form of undergraduate education exemplified by the colleges of England's ancient Oxford and Cambridge universities, and given that many of our most elite or selective liberal arts colleges today were among the first such colleges to be founded in the United States, it is understandable that many of us are inclined to equate a "residential liberal arts education" with an *elite* form of higher education. Yet the fact of the matter is that most residential liberal arts colleges today are *not* highly selective or elite. Under these conditions, to limit any discussion of the effects of a residential liberal arts education to that relatively small subset of prestigious or very selective colleges would be highly presumptuous if not misleading. Moreover, contrasting the characteristics of the elite and nonelite liberal arts colleges could prove to be a very interesting and informative exercise in itself. Accordingly, in this essay the research on student outcomes will be examined from several perspectives: effects of liberal arts colleges in general, comparative effects of Roman Catholic, Protestant, and independent colleges, and the effects of highly selective or elite colleges.

INTERPRETING THE RESEARCH EVIDENCE

To review and synthesize the research evidence concerning how the residential liberal arts college affects student development turns out to be a somewhat problematic task, primarily because very few studies have been designed to be both comparative and longitudinal. If we are to have any hope of saying something definitive about the unique effects of the residential liberal arts college, it is obviously necessary to compare student outcomes at these institutions with student outcomes at other types of institutions. One serious limitation of the earliest research evidence is that much of it dealt with individual liberal arts colleges rather than with *samples* of such colleges that are more representative of this highly diverse population.[4] And if we are to have any confidence in the findings, it is also necessary to study how students change and develop over time, rather than simply to take a snapshot of them at a single point in time (a simplistic method that may tell us more about the types of students who enroll than about how they are actually affected by their undergraduate experience).[5]

Still another limitation of this literature is that while some studies examine general institutional characteristics such as private control[6] or religious affiliation,[7] the issue of how such characteristics relate specifically to liberal arts colleges (as distinct from universities) is usually not addressed.[8]

In summarizing what we know about the effects of liberal arts colleges on students we also need to be clear about what is meant by "outcomes." In discussing this question I have found it convenient to differentiate among three types of outcomes: 1) *educational* outcomes as reflected in relatively long-lasting changes in the student that can be attributed to the educational experience—What did the student learn? How was the student changed? 2) *existential* outcomes reflecting the quality of the educational experience itself—Did the student find the experience challenging and meaningful? Did the student feel that the time and energy invested was well spent? and 3) *fringe* benefits, which have to do with the practical value of the degree itself—What further educational, social, and career advantages are associated with having a degree from this particular institution (the so-called sheepskin effect)?[9] While this essay will focus on the first two types of benefits, the question of fringe benefits highlights one of the most critical distinctions between the selective or elite liberal arts college and liberal arts colleges in general. There is good reason to believe that the fringe benefits associated with attending a highly selective liberal arts college are substantially greater than they would be at a less selective college.[10] Thus, while the small size and relative "invisibility" of many private liberal arts colleges probably puts their graduates at somewhat of a disadvantage in competing with graduates of larger and better-known institutions for jobs or admission to postgraduate study, the same is not true (as will be discussed) of the highly selective or elite liberal arts college, given its greater prestige.[11]

The studies to be reviewed here focus primarily on educational benefits, but they also include some measures of existential outcomes, usually in the form of various measures of student satisfaction with their college experience. While none of these studies looked specifically at fringe benefits, it seems safe to assume that such benefits are proportional to the college's degree of selectivity or eliteness.[12] Most of the findings summarized here are based either on a comprehensive review of the literature through 1990 or on a more recent national longitudinal study of student development in 135 private liberal arts colleges.[13] These studies have examined close to a hundred different aspects of the student's personal development, including academic outcomes (academic performance, skill development, and performance on standardized tests), career development (choice of a major field of study and of a career), patterns of behavior, personality, self-concept, attitudes, values, and beliefs. However, rather than simply reporting the particular student outcomes that are associated with each type of liberal arts college, I will also discuss some of the environmental factors that appear to account for the liberal arts colleges' unique effects on students. In this manner we can avoid the "black box" approach to student outcomes where one simply notes that "private liberal arts colleges have such and such an effect . . ." without any real understanding of the institutional-student dynamics that mediate such effects. I shall thus attempt, to the extent permitted by the research evidence, to discuss student outcomes in more explanatory terms: "Liberal arts colleges have such and such an effect *because* they are characterized by this kind of peer group, this kind of faculty, this kind of academic program."

For the methodologically inclined reader, I should point out that these explanatory summaries are made possible by the fact that one major national study was able to examine institutional effects in two stages. First, the comparative effects of institutional type (e.g., private liberal arts colleges versus other types of institutions) were examined after controlling for the characteristics of the entering student, but without reference to any particular explanatory (environmental) variables. Next, the effects of the possible explanatory variables (e.g., institutional size, peer-group characteristics, faculty characteristics) were controlled in order to determine whether they could account for the unique effect of institutional type (i.e., liberal arts colleges).[14] The first stage of the analysis revealed that liberal arts colleges do differ from other types of institutions in their effects on a number of student outcomes. However, virtually all these effects disappear once the environmental or explanatory variables are taken into account in the second stage. In other words, we are able to explain most of the effects of residential liberal arts colleges and the differential effects of different types of liberal arts colleges on the basis of other measurable characteristics of their environments. In the jargon of path analysis, this means that most of the effects of the private liberal arts college (and of the different types of private liberal arts colleges) are "indirect."

It is also important to mention that these analyses included a third stage, designed to identify the mechanisms that *mediate* the effects of environmental attributes such as size, peer-group characteristics, and faculty characteristics. In brief, we found that the environmental attributes that were most likely to be associated with positive student outcomes were those that tended to enhance student "involvement." Involvement, in turn, was defined primarily in terms of student-faculty contact, student-student contact, and time spent on academic work. In other words, a typical causal chain of events might go something like this: the positive effect of attending a liberal arts college on, say, student retention (stage one analysis) is largely attributable to the fact that these colleges are heavily residential (stage two analysis), and the residential experience, in turn, increases retention because it serves to engage the student more deeply in the academic experience (stage three analysis).

Findings will be summarized first for private liberal arts colleges in general, and then for three specific subtypes: independent, Protestant, and Roman Catholic. Since these are all comparative findings based on an analysis of student development in many types of institutions studied simultaneously, when I state that liberal arts colleges "have a positive effect on . . .", I mean "relative to nonliberal arts colleges." And given that most findings can be attributed to particular *characteristics* of private liberal arts colleges that distinguish them from most other types of institutions (small size or residential status, for example), rather than to the effects of being a private liberal arts college per se, as I report the effects associated with a particular type of liberal arts college I will also mention the special characteristics of those colleges that appear to account for their effects.

Private Liberal Arts Colleges in General

All three subtypes of private liberal arts colleges—independent, Protestant, and Roman Catholic—produce similar patterns of effects on several student developmental outcomes. The strongest and most consistent effects are on existential outcomes— the student's satisfaction with faculty, the quality of instruction, and general education requirements, and on the student's perception that the institution is student-oriented. In other words, students attending private liberal arts colleges, compared to students attending other types of institutions, are more satisfied with the faculty, the quality of teaching, and the general education program, and are more likely to view the institution as student-oriented. Attending a private liberal arts college also enhances the student's odds of completing the bachelor's degree, being elected to a student office, trusting the administration, and seeing the institution as being focused on social change.

Since the findings reported here are relatively short-term (covering the four or five years between freshman entry and baccalaureate completion), it is reasonable to ask whether there is any evidence concerning longer-term effects. While there has been disappointingly little longer-term research conducted in recent years, several such studies were done during the 1950s and 1960s.[15] While the outcome measures used were limited in scope, the results are consistent with the more recent shorter-term studies: liberal arts colleges, more than other types of institutions, enhance the student's chances of enrolling in graduate study, winning graduate fellowships, and eventually earning the doctorate degree.[16] These conclusions appear to be especially applicable to the highly selective liberal arts college.

Most of the effects summarized above appear to be attributable to the private liberal arts college's small size, its residential nature, and the strong student orientation of its faculty. These three qualities, in turn, lead to positive outcomes because they enhance student involvement in academic work and increase the amount of student-student and student-faculty contact.[17] In other words, once differences in institutional size, residential status, and the relative strength of the faculty's student orientation are taken into account, the private liberal arts college does not differ much from other institutions in its effects on these student outcomes. Student orientation, an environmental "climate" measure derived from a comprehensive survey completed by members of the faculties of 221 colleges and universities, is defined in terms of the following variables:

• Faculty here are interested in students' academic problems.
• Faculty here are interested in students' personal problems.
• Faculty here are committed to the welfare of the institution.
• Many faculty are sensitive to the issues of minorities.
• Faculty are easy to see outside of office hours.
• There are many opportunities for student-faculty interaction.
• Students are treated like numbers in a book (scored negatively).[18]

A strong student orientation, characteristic of most private liberal arts colleges (especially the Protestant colleges), means that most of the faculty tends to agree that these seven statements are descriptive of the institution's climate. A weak student orientation, by contrast, would mean that most of the faculty believe that these statements are not descriptive of the climate. Not surprisingly, the weakest student orientations tend to be found at the public research universities. Public four-year colleges and private universities also have relatively weak student orientations. As would be expected, the student orientation of the faculty shows a strong negative correlation (-.72) with institutional size.

Although small size, residential status, and a strong student orientation are the most important explanatory factors in assessing the unique effects of private liberal arts colleges, several other characteristics of these institutions also contribute to some of the effects summarized above. These principally include a high percentage of expenditures devoted to student services, positive relationships between students and administrators, and a positive faculty attitude toward students' abilities and preparation. In short, the private liberal arts college's positive effects on the student's chances of completing the bachelor's degree and on student satisfaction with the faculty and the quality of instruction would appear to be attributable primarily to the following qualities:

- small size
- a residential program
- a strong faculty commitment to student development
- trust between students and administrators
- generous expenditures on student services

Although the larger study from which most of these findings have been abstracted concluded that the student peer group constitutes the most potent source of influence on the undergraduate, the peer group did not prove to be a major factor in the findings just discussed.[19] The reason for this seeming contradiction is that private liberal arts college students—considered as a group—do not differ much from students enrolling at other types of baccalaureate-granting institutions. This is not to say that there is not great diversity in peer-group characteristics *among* different types of private liberal arts colleges; as we shall see, peer-group differences do indeed play a significant role in accounting for the comparative effects of different types of liberal arts colleges.

Independent Colleges

This is by far the largest and most diverse subgrouping of private liberal arts colleges. It includes most of the highly selective and elite colleges, together with a much larger number of moderately selective and nonselective colleges. During the past thirty years the size of this subcategory has increased, largely because many institutions founded with religious affiliations have become officially nonsectarian.

In addition to the general effects of private liberal arts colleges already noted, the independent colleges have positive effects on writing skills, cultural awareness, scores on the Medical College Admissions Test (MCAT), and choosing a major in the physical or social sciences. They also have positive effects on the student's degree of satisfaction with individual support services (counseling, health services, and the like), with opportunities to take interdisciplinary courses, and with the student's perception that the institution values diversity. Independent colleges also show positive effects on cultural awareness, participation in protests, and attending recitals or concerts, while showing a negative effect on the student's materialistic views (that is, their likelihood of agreeing that "The principal purpose of college is to increase one's earning power"). This last finding is especially significant, in light of the fact that one of the most dramatic changes in college students during the past three decades has been an increase in their materialistic values.[20]

Independent colleges possess a pattern of unique environmental characteristics that appear to explain most of these effects. For example, the decline in materialism and the positive effects on cultural awareness, attendance at recitals or concerts, interest in social science, or participation in protests are mostly accounted for by the fact that these institutions tend to have student peer groups that are liberal, permissive, and artistically inclined, faculties that are also politically liberal, "progressive" course offerings (for example, women's and ethnic studies), and a strong diversity emphasis. At the same time, growth in writing skills and excellent performance on the MCAT are largely attributable to the strong humanities orientation at these institutions, and to the fact that their student bodies tend to be academically competitive and of high socioeconomic status (SES). It is particularly interesting to note that attending an independent college enhances student performance on the MCAT, despite the fact that the professors in these colleges seldom use multiple-choice exams in their courses.[21]

Roman Catholic Colleges

In addition to the general effects of residential liberal arts colleges already noted, Roman Catholic colleges show negative effects on "libertarianism," an attitudinal outcome defined as the tendency to support legalized abortion and the legalization of marijuana, and to oppose the idea that college officials have the right to regulate student behavior off campus or to ban persons with extreme views from speaking on campus. The second stage of the analysis shows that this effect is primarily attributable to the peer group at the typical Catholic college, which is not only predominantly of the Roman Catholic faith but which also scores relatively low on "permissiveness" (a peer-group factor defined by infrequent attendance at religious services and permissive attitudes toward sex, divorce, abortion, and drug use). In other words, Catholic colleges reinforce the individual student's support for institutional authority and discourage the formation of social libertarian views primarily because the student peer group is heavily populated by practicing Roman Catholics and nonpermissive in its views on sex, divorce, abortion, and drug use.

Catholic colleges also show negative effects on joining social fraternities or sororities and positive effects on college grades. In effect, this means that attending a Catholic college will increase the students' chances of getting good grades and reduce their chances of becoming members of social fraternities or sororities. The negative effect on the student's chances of joining a social fraternity or sorority may simply be an artifact of the relative lack of such student organizations on the typical Roman Catholic college campus. But the positive effect on the students' college grades is more difficult to interpret: does it suggest that the grading standards at the Catholic colleges are more lax, or does it reflect a higher level of actual academic achievement?

Protestant Colleges

This is a highly heterogeneous group of institutions that encompasses colleges affiliated with the mainline Protestant denominations (Presbyterian, Methodist, Lutheran, Baptist, etc.) as well as a substantial number of non-Catholic institutions affiliated with a variety of other Christian churches (some of which probably do not consider themselves to be "Protestant").

In contrast to the Roman Catholic colleges, attending a Protestant college *increases* the likelihood that the student will join a social fraternity or sorority. Again, this finding may simply be an artifact of the greater availability of such social organizations on the Protestant college campus. Attending Protestant colleges also increases the student's likelihood of attending a recital or concert and has negative effects on satisfaction with facilities and on performance on the MCAT. While the second stage of the analysis did not reveal any clear-cut explanations for each of these effects, it is worth noting some of the distinguishing features of the typical Protestant college environment: A peer group that includes a high proportion of born-again or evangelical Christians and very few Roman Catholics, that scores low on permissiveness, and that is politically conservative; a faculty that is also politically conservative and that expresses positive attitudes toward the general education program, but which is not research-oriented and has relatively low morale.

In concluding this discussion of the effects of different types of private liberal arts colleges on student development, it is important to remind ourselves that there are substantial peer-group differences among the three major types that help to explain their differential impacts. For example, both major types of religiously affiliated colleges—Roman Catholic and Protestant—tend to attract peer groups that are very low in permissiveness (i.e., conservative in their views on sexual behavior, drug use, abortion rights, and divorce). However, while the student peer groups at the Roman Catholic colleges are relatively strong in social activism and below average in intellectual self-esteem, the students attending Protestant colleges are below average in feminism, scientific orientation, and materialism and status.

By contrast, the peer environments of the independent liberal arts colleges show an entirely different pattern: they tend to be very strong in permissiveness, artistic interests, and feminism and slightly above average in artistic interests and intellectual self-esteem.

There is one other subgroup of liberal arts colleges that should be noted in this discussion of student outcomes: the historically black college (HBC). HBCs include institutions that fit within one or another of all three types of liberal arts colleges examined above. Evidence from two sources suggests that attending an HBC has positive effects on the African–American student's grade-point average (GPA), intellectual self-esteem, satisfaction with college, and chances of attending musical events, participating in protests, tutoring other students, choosing a career in science, and graduating with honors.[22] As with the Roman Catholic colleges, it is difficult to interpret the findings with respect to GPA and honors: are grading standards in the HBCs more lax, or do students actually achieve at a higher level? Most of these effects appear to be attributable to the HBCs' small size, residential program, peer group (which is very low in SES), faculty (which emphasizes diversity, is heavily involved in administrative work, and *frequently* uses multiple-choice exams), and very low selectivity. Notably, when compared to other small institutions of comparably low selectivity, the HBCs also show a *positive* effect on student retention.

THE ROLE OF RESEARCH

One of the most intractable problems in American higher education is the issue of "research versus teaching." Since residential liberal arts colleges, considered as a group, tend to put a much greater emphasis on their teaching function than on their research, the question naturally arises: does research have a significant place in the American liberal arts college? More specifically, one might ask: Does a significant emphasis on research and scholarship necessarily come at the expense of student development? Is it possible to emphasize the research function without sacrificing student development? Can research in the liberal arts college actually be used to *enhance* the educational process?

Recently my colleague Mitchell Chang and I sought to examine this question using a national sample of 212 baccalaureate-granting institutions of all types (including liberal arts colleges and universities, public and private). For each institution we calculated two measures, its "student orientation" (as defined earlier) and its "research orientation." For any individual institution, the research orientation is defined by a combination of the following items derived from surveying the faculty at each institution:

- Number of publications (journal articles and book chapters, with additional weight being given to recent publications)
- Hours per week spent on research and scholarly writing
- Subjective value assigned to doing research (versus teaching)
- Receipt of outside funds to support research
- Research-oriented values (professional recognition, becoming an authority in one's field)
- Time spent off campus in professional activities

The student orientation of the faculty, it will be recalled, is based on the faculty's expressed interest in and commitment to working with students on a personal basis.

As would be expected, the scores of the 212 institutions on these two environmental measures were strongly negatively correlated ($r = -.69$). In effect, this means that institutions that are strongly research-oriented *tend* to have weak student orientations, and that institutions that are strongly student-oriented *tend* to have weak research orientations.

Considering that research and teaching are *both* regarded as fundamental parts of the mission of American higher education, Chang and I were naturally interested in the possibility that there may be a few institutions that defy the trend, that is, that are strong in *both* their research and student orientations.[23] The initial search for such institutions within our sample of 212 proved to be disappointing; not a single institution turned out to be among the top 10 percent in both student and research orientation. As a matter of fact, among the twenty-one institutions that make up the top 10 percent in research orientation, *there are no institutions that are even average in their student orientations.* Even if we were to relax our definition of a "strong" research orientation to include the forty-two institutions constituting the top 20 percent of this measure, we can find only one that is also in the top 10 percent in student orientation.

These findings convinced us that it was necessary to relax our definition of "strong" in *both* measures. Thus, if we define "strong" as being in the top 35 percent, we do find eight of the 212 institutions that are strong in both orientations. If we further relax the definition of a "strong" student orientation to include the top 40 percent, we are able to add three more to the list that "emphasize" both values. What is most important, however, is that all eleven of these "high-high" institutions are residential liberal arts colleges! Each of the eleven is also *highly* selective, placing it in the Carnegie classification of Liberal Arts I colleges. As a matter of fact, if we relax the "high" cutting points on research and student orientation to include the top 45 percent on each, virtually every institution that we would add to the "high-high" group is also a selective liberal arts college. In short, these results suggest that the selective liberal arts college comes closer than any other type of institution in the American higher-education system to achieving a balance between research and teaching.

THE SELECTIVE LIBERAL ARTS COLLEGE

What was especially intriguing about this study was that it had, in effect, "rediscovered" the selective liberal arts college by conducting a purely statistical search for institutions that are best able to emphasize both teaching and research. The next obvious question is: Are there any other unique characteristics of the selective liberal arts college that distinguish it from *both* the research university (the "high-lows") and the nonselective liberal arts colleges (the "low-highs")? (Small size, for example, would not be an "unique" characteristic because the nonselective colleges are also small.) In particular, are there unique qualities that have implications for student outcomes?

To explore this question Chang and I compared the three groups with each other across a wide range of characteristics. We did indeed find many differences in finances, students, faculty, and curriculum, but the most relevant findings have to do with the *educational practices* that distinguish these selective liberal arts colleges simultaneously from their nonselective counterparts *and* the research universities.[24] More to the point, each of the practices identified has been shown in a separate study to be associated with positive student outcomes.[25] These practices are:

- Frequent student-faculty interaction
- Frequent student-student interaction
- Generous expenditures on student services

- A strong faculty emphasis on diversity
- Frequent use of interdisciplinary and humanities courses (especially history and foreign languages)
- Frequent use of courses that emphasize writing
- Frequent use of narrative evaluations
- *Infrequent* use of multiple-choice exams
- Frequent involvement of students in independent research
- Frequent involvement of students in faculty research

It is important to keep in mind that the selective liberal arts colleges surveyed differ from the other types of institutions only in the *degree* to which they exemplify these characteristics. For example, while there is also frequent student-student interaction in the nonselective liberal arts colleges, it is somewhat more frequent in the selective liberal arts colleges. Also, it should be pointed out that we are considering *average* differences here, and that not all of the selective liberal arts colleges surpass all of the nonselective colleges and research universities on every attribute shown above.

These findings make it clear that the selective private liberal arts college, perhaps more than any other institution of American higher education, exemplifies much of what has come to be known as best educational practice in undergraduate education.[26] "Best," in this context, refers to practices shown to have a favorable impact on student learning and development. Why then should such practices be more common among the selective liberal arts colleges than among their nonselective counterparts or, for that matter, among the research universities as well? Since the elite liberal arts colleges are able to spend at least 50 percent more for instructional purposes than most other types of institutions, could it be that these practices are "resource-intensive," and therefore more difficult to fund in the less affluent institutions?[27] Interacting frequently with students, emphasizing essay examinations, and using narrative evaluations clearly require more faculty time and effort. (The same might be true of interdisciplinary courses, depending upon how they are structured and taught.) While one could argue that "generous" expenditures on student services is not necessarily resource-intensive—it is a relative measure reflecting the proportion (rather than the absolute amount) of educational expenditures invested in student services—it could also be argued that it would be easier to spend a higher proportion of a college's resources for student services if the absolute amount of money available for other purposes were also greater.

It should be emphasized here that many of the less selective liberal arts colleges do, in fact, employ many of the "best practices" listed above, in spite of their relatively limited financial resources. Also, when it comes to course content, the less selective liberal arts colleges may put less emphasis on the humanities simply because, in comparison to the selective liberal arts colleges, many more of their students are majoring in education, business, or other professional fields. In fact, most of the selective liberal arts colleges do not even offer majors in such fields.[28]

A more subtle factor affecting the educational practices of the selective liberal arts colleges may be the student *peer group*. The fact that the typical student entering the selective liberal arts college is well prepared academically may make it easier to employ practices such as independent research and involvement in faculty research projects. The better-prepared student may also be more inclined to interact frequently with faculty members. And even if the less well prepared student who frequents the nonselective liberal arts college and the public college would benefit equally from research involvement and frequent interaction with faculty, there is mounting evidence to suggest that faculty who teach such students frequently *assume* that they need a more traditional, didactic kind of pedagogy.[29]

An even more subtle aspect of the student peer group in the selective liberal arts college is its very high socioeconomic status (SES). In a recent longitudinal study of more than eighty-four student outcomes, the average SES of the student peer group was associated with more positive outcomes than virtually any other environmental attribute of the institution, its program, or its faculty.[30] Although the reasons why students seem to benefit from attending institutions where their peers generally come from high-SES backgrounds are not well understood, the fact remains that this is an attribute of the undergraduate environment over which the institution has little control.[31]

Although the original study from which most of these findings were derived looked at the *independent* effects of institutional selectivity and of the independent liberal arts college, it did not look at the combined effect of these two variables; that is to say, it did not specifically examine the effect of selective liberal arts colleges. Since the exemplary educational practices (as outlined above) that differentiate the selective liberal arts colleges from their nonselective counterparts (and from most other types of institutions) have, as I have already indicated, been shown to be associated with positive educational outcomes, it seems reasonable to conclude that students who attend selective liberal arts colleges will enjoy unique educational benefits. Such a conclusion would be substantially reinforced, however, if we could obtain more direct evidence of such effects. Accordingly, for this essay I reanalyzed the data from the original study on an exploratory basis to look specifically at the effect of attending a selective private liberal arts college on two outcomes: critical thinking ability and overall satisfaction with the undergraduate experience. A "selective" college was defined as one where the mean SAT composite score of the entering students is at least 1200. As it turns out, these colleges do indeed show statistically significant, positive effects on both outcomes, a result that clearly confirms the expectation that the exemplary educational practices that one tends to find most often in the selective liberal arts college should lead to positive educational outcomes.

IMPLICATIONS FOR AMERICAN HIGHER EDUCATION

Given that the quality of undergraduate education provided by the residential liberal arts college appears to be unmatched by any other type of institution, one might have expected that this particular approach to undergraduate education would provide the principal model for the many new institutions that came into being following the end of World War II. But quite the opposite seems to have happened in the case of the massive expansion of our higher-education system that took place during the 1950s and 1960s. Instead of relying on smallness, we built very large institutions. Instead of requiring residence, we built hundreds of commuter institutions. Instead of insisting that all teaching faculty place a high value on working with undergraduates, we created dozens of research universities where the only hiring and promotion requirement was scientific or scholarly talent. And instead of effecting a balance between scholarly work and working with students, we created hundreds of community colleges where scholarship was given virtually no weight. While this is not the place to attempt to document all the reasons for these paradoxical trends, it seems to me that there are at least two closely related considerations that guided these policies.

First and most obvious are money and prestige. In the case of the research universities, the massive federal investment in research was just too tempting to resist. Recognizing that outstanding scientists and scholars are the strongest magnets with which to attract federal research dollars, and that having a large stable of such faculty is the key to building institutional prestige, universities initiated an all-out competition for top research talent and instituted unidimensional academic personnel policies that relied almost exclusively on the professor's scholarly performance—"publish or perish." One of the "perks" offered to the top scholars, of course, was a low (or no) "teaching load" (a revealing phrase, to say the least).

The second consideration was more subtle than money and prestige, but no less powerful. In brief, it was the belief that an "undergraduate liberal arts education" could be defined simply in terms of course credits; take such and such an array of courses in these fields, pass them, and ipso facto you've been "liberally educated." Under this view of undergraduate education, it did not much matter how one acquires the requisite degrees or credits: in one institution or in five, in four years or in fifteen years, as a resident or a commuter, through part-time attendance or full-time attendance, in classes of twenty students or classes of five hundred students, with a lot of peer interaction or with no peer interaction at all, with a lot of faculty contact or with no faculty contact, with heavy cocurricular involvement or no such involvement. It did not matter. And if it did not matter, then why inconvenience the student? And why not design the new institutions—research universities as well as community colleges—to operate under-graduate education as cheaply as possible? I might add here that this same kind of thinking, I fear, underlies much of the current interest in "distance education" and the "technology revolution" in higher education.

When I discuss these findings with colleagues in universities and community colleges, I am often told that the residential liberal arts college is "anachronistic" or "not cost-effective," and that what we have learned about its positive effects on students is "irrelevant" to the rest of higher education. A common response is "The modern university is not a liberal arts college." Or "Those findings are not relevant to community colleges, because our average student is thirty-one years old." I must admit that these kinds of responses strike me as non sequiturs, given that all other kinds of institutions *claim* to share one fundamental function in common with the residential liberal arts college: the liberal education of undergraduate students. While it is true that these other institutions perform other functions—graduate education, research, and vocational education, for example—does having multiple functions somewhat entitle an institution to offer baccalaureate education programs that are second-rate? Does engaging in research and graduate education justify shortchanging undergraduate education? Does engaging in vocational education justify offering mediocre transfer education? And while it may be true that the *average* age of community college students may be higher than the average age of students at most liberal arts colleges, we need to remind ourselves that community colleges enroll some five hundred thousand new eighteen- and nineteen-year-old freshmen each fall, most of whom are attending full time in pursuit of bachelor's degrees.[32] This is double the number of new freshmen enrolling at all types of liberal arts colleges!

In trying to understand the larger implications for American higher education of what we have learned about the environments and student outcomes of residential liberal arts colleges, it would be easy to dismiss these findings on the grounds that the key structural feature distinguishing these institutions from most others in our diverse higher-education system—small size—is unattainable for most other types of institutions. Such an argument overlooks the fact that size is confounded with many other characteristics that make it hazardous to generalize from what we know about the effects of the "small college." I use the term "confounded" here to mean that, as the size of institutions increases, *other* qualities begin to appear that substantially alter the capacity of an institution to provide a high quality undergraduate education. These other qualities include public control, a more bureaucratic and impersonal form of administrative structure, a diversification of the clientele served (i.e., increases in older, part-time, commuter, professional, and nondegree-credit students), and larger academic departments. This last quality is especially significant since, as departments grow in size, pressures to emphasize research and graduate education and to seek greater autonomy from the larger institution increase. When this happens, general education—the heart of an undergraduate liberal arts education—tends to become fragmented and marginalized. Indeed, in many of our leading research universities today, regular faculty do little or no advising of freshmen or sophomores and much of the undergraduate instruction is done either by graduate students or by part-time and adjunct instructors.

The key point is that these correlates of large size are just that—correlates—and that *none* of them is a necessary or inevitable consequence of large size. At the same time, being small is no guarantee that these "undesirable" correlates (undesirable, that is, from the perspective of exemplary undergraduate practices) will be absent from the institution (the California Institute of Technology, for example, places an extremely strong emphasis on research and graduate education, even though its enrollment is much smaller than the enrollments of most liberal arts colleges). Moreover, there are structural changes that large institutions can make—for example, the creation of relatively autonomous "colleges" like those at the Santa Cruz and San Diego campuses of the University of California—that can mitigate some of the usual limitations of large size.

Since the issue of comparative costs could be the subject of a separate essay, let me offer just a few observations. First of all, we need to recognize that there is great variation in the expenditures of liberal arts colleges, and that indeed many liberal arts colleges spend less per student than many large public institutions. At the same time, we must acknowledge that the highly selective liberal arts college does indeed spend much more per student than do most other types of institutions. There is no question that costs may well become a significant issue for any institution wishing either to achieve a better balance between teaching and research or to emulate some of the selective liberal arts college's exemplary practices—say, narrative evaluations, essay exams, and generous support of student services. Even so, there is no *necessary* reason why any institution cannot consider more frequent use of some of these practices, with the overall aim of increasing student-student interaction, faculty-student interaction, time devoted to academic work, and other forms of student involvement.

The real danger in pursuing educational reform and educational policy from a purely economic or materialistic view, however, is that we tend to forget the basic values that led us to support the idea of a residential liberal arts education in the first place. The real meaning of such an education goes far beyond merely producing more physicians, teachers, scientists, technicians, lawyers, business executives, and other professionals to fill slots in the labor market. A liberal education in a small residential setting is really about encouraging the student to grapple with some of life's most fundamental questions: What is the meaning of life? What is *my* purpose in life? What do I think and feel about life, death, God, religion, love, art, music, history, literature, and science? What kinds of friends and associates do I want in my life? What kinds of peer groups do I want to associate with?

In many ways the philosophy underlying the notion of a liberal education in a small college setting is a tribute to the power of the peer group. This form of education implicitly assumes that an excellent liberal education is much more than a collection of course credits, and that a little bit of serendipity is a good thing. Allow young people to go away from home and live together in an intimate academic environment for a while, and some good things will happen. Often we really have no idea what these goods things will be, but the students will seldom disappoint us.

ENDNOTES

[1] In its classification of higher-education institutions the Carnegie Foundation for the Advancement of Teaching designates a large number of private liberal arts colleges as "comprehensive colleges and universities" because they had come to award a substantial number of their undergraduate degrees in "professional" rather than "academic" fields (primarily business, education, nursing, and allied health). For the purposes of this essay, these institutions will be considered as "private liberal arts colleges" as long as they claim to offer a "liberal arts education" to undergraduates and as long as their graduate and professional programs are not so extensive that they are considered to be a "university" by the National Center of Educational Statistics. It should also be noted that some private colleges that are self-designated as "universities" (e.g., Wesleyan University) are basically liberal arts colleges and will be considered as such in this essay.

[2] Alexander W. Astin and Calvin B. T. Lee, *The Invisible Colleges* (New York: McGraw-Hill, 1972).

[3] Selectivity is also commonly used as an indicator of academic quality or "excellence," a practice that, in my judgment, does not serve as well. Alexander W. Astin, *Achieving Educational Excellence* (San Francisco: Jossey-Bass, 1985).

[4] Kenneth Feldman and Theodore Newcomb, *The Impact of College on Students* (San Francisco: Jossey-Bass, 1969).

[5] Alexander W. Astin, *Assessment for Excellence: The Philosophy and Practice of Assessment and Evaluation in Higher Education* (Washington, D.C. and Phoenix: American Council on Education and Oryx Press, 1991).

[6] E.g., Burton R. Clark et al., *Students and Colleges: Interaction and Change* (Berkeley: University of California, Center for Research and Development in Higher Education, 1972).

[7] E.g., James W. Trent and Jenette Golds, *Catholics in College: Religious Commitment and the Intellectual Life* (Chicago: University of Chicago Press, 1967).

[8] Ernest T. Pascarella and Patrick T. Terenzini, *How College Affects Students* (San Francisco: Jossey-Bass, 1991).

[9] Astin, *Achieving Educational Excellence*.

[10] J. W. Henson, *Institutional Excellence and Student Achievement: A Study of College Quality and Its Impact on Education and Career Achievement*, unpublished Ph.D. dissertation, University of California, Los Angeles, 1980.

[11] Astin and Lee, *The Invisible Colleges*.

[12] See Henson, *Institutional Excellence and Student Achievement*.

[13] Pascarella and Terenzini, *How College Affects Students*; Alexander W. Astin, *What Matters in College? Four Critical Years Revisited* (San Francisco: Jossey-Bass, 1993).

[14] Astin, *What Matters in College?*

[15] Feldman and Newcomb, *The Impact of College on Students*.

100   *Alexander W. Astin*

[16]Alexander W. Astin, "An Empirical Characterization of Higher Educational Institutions," *Journal of Educational Psychology* 53 (1962): 224–235; Alexander W. Astin, "Differential College Effects on the Motivation of Talented Students to Obtain the Ph.D. Degree," *Journal of Educational Psychology* (1963): 63–71; Alexander W. Astin, "Further Validation of the Environmental Assessment Technique," *Journal of Educational Psychology* 54 (1963): 217–226; and Alexander W. Astin and Robert J. Panos, *The Educational and Vocational Development of College Students* (Washington, D.C.: American Council on Education, 1969).

[17]Astin, *What Matters in College?*

[18]Ibid.

[19]Ibid.

[20]Alexander W. Astin et al., *The American Freshman: Thirty Year Trends* (Los Angeles: Higher Education Research Institute, UCLA, 1997).

[21]Astin, *What Matters in College?*

[22]Ibid.; Alexander W. Astin, Lisa Tsui, and Juan Avalos, *Degree Attainment Rates at American Colleges and Universities* (Los Angeles: Higher Education Research Institute, UCLA, 1996).

[23]Given the strong negative correlation between these measures, it is not surprising that ten of the twenty-one institutions that make up the top 10 percent in research orientation are in the bottom 10 percent on student orientation, and that eight of the twenty institutions that make up the top 10 percent on student orientation are in the bottom 10 percent on research orientation. All members of the former group are research universities (including eight public universities), whereas all members of the latter group are nonselective (mostly Protestant) liberal arts colleges, which places them in the Liberal Arts II category of the Carnegie classification. Finally, of the nine institutions that are in the bottom one-third on both measures, six are public four-year colleges.

[24]Alexander W. Astin and Mitchell J. Chang, "Colleges that Emphasize Research and Teaching," *Change* 27 (September/October 1995): 45–49.

[25]Astin, *What Matters in College?*

[26]Arthur W. Chickering and Zelda F. Gamson, "Seven Principles for Good Practice in Undergraduate Education," *The Wingspread Journal* 9 (June 1987 Special Section): 2.

[27]Astin and Chang, "Colleges that Emphasize Research and Teaching"; Astin and Lee, *The Invisible Colleges.*

[28]Astin, *Achieving Educational Excellence.*

[29]Lisa Tsui, *Fostering Critical Thinking in College Students: A Mixed-Methods Study of Influence Inside and Outside of the Classroom,* unpublished Ph.D. dissertation, University of California, Los Angeles, 1998.

[30]Astin, *What Matters in College?*

[31]Ibid.

[32]L. J. Sax et al., *The American Freshman: National Norms for Fall 1997* (Los Angeles: Higher Education Research Institute, UCLA, 1998).

Peter J. Gomes

Affirmation and Adaptation: Values and the Elite Residential College

SHAPING THE SPACE IN WHICH WE LIVE

SINCE SO MANY OF THE AMERICAN elite residential liberal arts colleges have their origins in the religious imaginations of their founders, to observe such a fact is simply to state a commonplace. In most of the institutions founded before 1900, the most prominent architectural feature of the campus is the college chapel, declaiming in wood or stone the central place accorded the public expression of religion in the life of the school. In many such institutions the geography of the principal quadrangle reflects complementary sitings of the chapel and the library, temples to the twin values of faith and reason by which Christian education in the West has for so long been guided. This shaping of space is most vividly demonstrated in the "New Yard" of Harvard University, since 1936 known as the Tercentenary Theatre. On the northern perimeter of this quadrangle stands The Memorial Church on the site of its predecessor, Appleton Chapel, which had been there from 1855; opposite, on the southern side, is the massive Widener Library on the site of its predecessor, Gore Hall, the old college library that had been built in imitation of King's College Chapel at Cambridge University. Libraries that look like chapels were an architectural conceit, with perhaps the most famous being the Sterling Memorial Library of Yale University. It is said that the donor wished to contribute to a splendid Gothic chapel at Yale,

Peter J. Gomes is Plummer Professor of Christian Morals and Pusey Minister in The Memorial Church at Harvard University.

101

while the University wished a splendid new library: the library was built in the best collegiate Gothic style, the by-then quite aged donor was driven by, she pronounced herself pleased with the splendid new chapel, and everybody was happy.

At Bates College, my alma mater, the college chapel, also inspired by King's College Chapel, Cambridge, was built on the main quadrangle opposite the college library, with residential and academic buildings forming the eastern and western perimeters of the space. When James Buchanan Duke handsomely endowed Trinity College in Durham, North Carolina, and presided over the construction in the 1920s of a magnificent new campus in the collegiate Gothic style, he stated his desire that the whole new space be dominated by a towering church. His wish was followed, and Duke Chapel to this day is the most central and conspicuous landmark of that sprawling campus.

If, in the felicitous phrase with which the president of Harvard confers the several degrees in design, architecture helps to "shape the space in which we live," then simply by looking at so many of our older elite residential liberal arts colleges we are able to imagine both what the founders intended to say about their schools and what is now, for so many of them, the "problem" of that legacy. When in 1974, as the new Preacher to the University at Harvard, I called upon the dean of the Faculty of Arts and Sciences, he showed me the view from his desk, an uninterrupted and splendid view of the tower of The Memorial Church. "A beautiful thing," he said; then, only half in jest, he added, "But if we were starting over again, I don't think we'd put it there."

It may seem odd for a discussion on ethics and the liberal arts in the elite residential colleges to begin with an excursus on chapel architecture and siting, but that perceived oddity is simply an example of the problem we face in discussing the nature and destiny of these remarkable and threatened institutions. In the formative days of the institutions it would have been virtually impossible to conceive of ethics apart from the religious dimension of the institution's life, of which, of course, the chapel was the outward and visible sign. Today the chapel is increasingly a symbol not of unity but of division, an all too visible reminder of the parochial and particular sectarian origins of the school, a cultural liability in the school's necessary positioning of itself to gain market share in an increasingly diverse, multicultural, and secular world. Compulsory courses in the Christian Bible, required attendance at daily and/or Sunday services, and the scholar/preacher/president are all part of a distant past except in those institutions with which most elite liberal arts colleges choose not to compare themselves. All that remains of that inheritance from which most of these schools are descended are the artifactual remains of the chapel, both prominent and forlorn in the center of the campus.

A BROKEN CONSENSUS

This is not an argument for turning back the clock to the religious hegemony of an earlier day; indeed, many colleges define their institutional maturity in terms of their movement away from the often destructive influences of just such a hegemony. The purpose of this essay is to acknowledge that the formative consensus of these institutions and the ethical dimension that flowed from it has been broken, and that for some time there has not been anything to take its place. For what it is worth, the modern American research university has very much defined itself on its own terms in the aftermath of the post–World War II scientific and cultural revolutions, and its culture and the ethical issues associated with it are the subject of studies elsewhere. The elite residential liberal arts colleges have responded to rapid social changes by distancing themselves from their more particular pasts, most noticeably in the role that religion is seen to play in the total mission of the institution, and by fashioning themselves as best they can in the image of the larger secular research institutions. Usually in the name of "raising standards" and "broadening the base," these colleges have largely succeeded in adapting to their own purposes the methods and styles of the larger institutions. A casualty of this wholesale adaptation is often the loss of an institutional character or personality that would justify its existence in comparison with the very places it imitates, and with which it competes.

Increasingly, the elite residentials find distasteful the old, and admittedly woolly, distinction between teaching and research. With some notable exceptions, it was widely accepted a generation ago that colleges taught and universities did research. This distinction of function, alas, implied a distinction in quality. The old bromide "Those who can, do; and those who cannot, teach" increasingly became "Those who cannot do research, teach." Since the flagships of the educational enterprise were the great research universities, colleges where mere teaching was done saw themselves at a disadvantage. "Faculty building" therefore meant supplanting the teaching teachers, products of an earlier and less competitive era, with the best products of the Ph.D. marketplace. Faculty credentials and publication rates increased markedly but at a cost, for the teaching posts were often filled with freshly minted Ph.D.'s who, though exposed to teaching during their graduate student days, were nevertheless the products of a research model of scholarship, and were trained or inclined to do very little else. Many were courted by ambitious liberal arts colleges to fatten up their ranks; many would have preferred to make their careers in the institutions that had trained them, or in institutions very similar to them. Few saw the liberal arts college as a distinct alternative to what they had experienced and endured, and often with the connivance of their new employers they were encouraged to reshape their new college experience in light of their graduate models and ambitions.

Thus, despite the claims of the research-college model so fashionable in the 1970s, many of our liberal arts colleges became small versions of graduate departments often inhabited by people who would rather be in the research university, who saw it as their mission to replicate that environment as closely as possible. The argument was that "good research makes good teaching," and the teacher who is in the forefront of the field, as demonstrated by grants, frequent publication, and professional awards, would in fact be the best teaching model for undergraduates. The trouble was that in order to adapt the residential college to these new expectations certain changes in the culture were sustained. Some, such as the gradual removal of academic deadwood and the stiffening of intellectual standards, were a clear gain. Others, however, such as the transference of professorial loyalty from the college to the guild, meant that college culture was more frequently defined and maintained by professional administrators hired for the purpose and often at a remove from the central academic mission of the school. Residential colleges as self-defining and self-perpetuating communities of shared but differentiated endeavor became more and more compartmentalized, thus in effect replicating the worst aspects of the research university model. Among the casualties of this process were the leisure and will necessary to contemplate the social, moral, and spiritual values that would help to shape a shared life.

This transition in the composition and ideology of the elite college professoriate occurred at the very same time that American culture began to recognize profound shifts in its systems of values. By the 1970s, the secularization process of the culture, which had been so vividly documented in the early 1960s by Harvey Cox, was well under way, and few institutions of higher education were immune to those forces. The "culture wars" of the period allowed little time for dispassionate reflection, and most institutions lurched to and fro as they improvised reactions to the latest internal or external crisis. The small residential colleges, which depended for their successful operation upon a genteel consensus and the faithful transmission of tradition from one generation to another, were especially vulnerable to the breakdown of the institutional and individual trust that was characteristic of the period from 1963 to 1973. Notions of civility, deference, and a treasured sense of continuity fell victim to cries for relevance, engagement, and transformation. The natural intensities of closed communities, such as small residential colleges, turned in upon themselves. Old standards of conduct were suspect, and it was difficult in the state of constant crisis for new ones to achieve the necessary consensus to evolve to take their place.

These college troubles all took place within a national and international climate of cultural anxiety, and institutional self-assessment became the order of the day, with significant examination of constituencies, priorities, and identities. It was within this context that educationalists began to ask how both institutions and individuals might learn to be good. Such virtuous questions had been at the heart of the residential college of an earlier day, but they had been anchored in the moral culture that those institutions had derived from their religious identities. Ironically, as those identities became less and less clear, the questions they once were designed to address became more and more urgent.

THOSE WISE RESTRAINTS

I remember vividly the telephone call from Derek Bok. It came on the Monday morning following the "Saturday Night Massacre" in which President Nixon had fired Special Prosecutor Archibald Cox, and Attorney General Elliott Richardson had resigned in protest. The country was on the brink of a constitutional crisis, and the president telephoned me to ask if he might speak to this matter from the pulpit of Appleton Chapel at our daily service of Morning Prayers. He wanted to say a few words about the civic example of his old teacher and colleague, Professor Cox, and he wished to do so in a setting where the moral import of his concern would have resonance; hence, he wished to speak in chapel rather than issue a statement or give a press conference. The arrangements were quickly made, and the president delivered himself of an excellent and edifying moral discourse, which was all the more remarkable in that it was decidedly not the custom of the president to do so in this context. When later I told him that he had acted in the best traditions of his preacher/president predecessors, he was mildly embarrassed.

His concerns, however, did not end with that one performance. He continued to reflect often upon the quality of moral education in American colleges and universities, whereby those whom David Halberstam once called "the brightest and the best" seemed increasingly devoid of a moral or ethical center. If in our secular age religion could no longer be relied upon to perform that function automatically, providing "those wise restraints that set men free," which many now saw as the function of the law, how could we provide systematic instruction for the young to take up reasoned moral responsibility?

When it came time to review Harvard's creaky "General Education" requirements, President Bok and Henry Rosovsky were determined to address what they regarded as a profound gap in the undergraduate educational experience: instruction in moral education. Certainly there were ethics courses available in the faculties of divinity and philosophy, and religion courses aplenty, widening as the new honors concentration in the comparative study of religion won faculty approval; but there had not been a requirement in ethics or in moral philosophy since before the days of President Charles William Eliot (1869–1909), when such a course was taught over a four-year period by the president himself. It was thus no small thing to propose that what eventually came to be called "Moral Reasoning" be required of all Harvard undergraduates in their first two years of residence.

MORAL REASONING

The case for moral reasoning in college coincided with the development of theories of moral development advocated by such thinkers as Harvard's Lawrence Kohlberg and James Fowler, and by educational practitioners such as Theodore Sizer, formerly of Harvard and by the early 1970s headmaster of Phillips Andover Academy. The context of those theories and initiatives was as much shaped by the decline of religious values in the educational experience both of high schools and colleges as it was by the perceived sense of moral ambiguity in the Watergate crisis. Within the environment of an avowed and aggressive secular culture in schools and colleges, particularly in those elite institutions that had moved markedly away from their religious origins, how was it now possible to teach people to be good? The secular values of civility, tolerance, and rationality, long the hallmark of liberal education, seemed on their own incapable of addressing the question of values and the acceleration of the coarsening of both public and academic culture.

Furthermore, a paradox might be observed in the elite colleges' response to this sense of moral disarray. The cultural revolutions of the 1960s and early 1970s, it is said, precipitated the end of the old residential college principle of *in loco parentis*, the quaint doctrine in which colleges acted in the place of parents with regard to the care and discipline of students. Both parental and institutional authority in this period were subject to ever-increasing assaults, and few residential colleges by the early 1970s would maintain that they had a parental relationship to their students. As the consumer/client model became the controlling metaphor, even the notion of mutual citizenship— also a once-favored model for the relationship between students and their colleges—was eclipsed. Colleges saw themselves as dispensing a product, a liberal education and a marketable degree, and students were no longer older children but young adults, with the assumption that treating them as such meant leaving them alone, imposing upon them minimal institutional restraints, and hoping that by the rigor of the intellectual experience and the tolerance of the social experience they would grow up into reasonable facsimiles not of their parents but of their teachers.

In this context religion ceased to be a public or institutional value and became more a part of the private service industry to which the colleges committed themselves. Thus, chaplains no longer represented the professed values of the institution but became providers of services and counseling on an as-needed basis to students; often, they no longer served at the center of the administration as the president's vicar or alter ego but as one of many professional helpers on the staff of the dean of students. This therapeutic model addressed well the individual and group needs of students in the schools and colleges, but, rather than affirming any institutional commitment to values that transcended the plethora of particularism and individualism, the model served in many ways to emphasize in the name of a much-valued pluralism the cultural divisions that seemed to make impossible, even if desirable, any sense of shared mission and purpose. So, while many institutions could boast of a marked increase in religious activity on their campuses, the institutions themselves would be perceived as having lost their own moral voice and sense of mission, thus making the transition from mission to market, as Richard Hawley of the University School in Cleveland puts it, complete.

The paradox, however, is this: in this very period it was the students who called for their schools to take the moral lead and to provide exemplary institutional leadership for the moral life. Instances of this occurred in the mid-1960s, when students in privileged institutions asked for a public commitment to the civil rights movement, for example, insisting upon student and faculty exchanges with black colleges and arguing for increased minority enrollments in predominantly white schools. The initiative in nearly all of these instances came from the students, who invariably provoked their institutions to action. The cause of civil rights was supplanted by the antiwar movement, in which students defined as the moral issue of the day the case of the war in southeast Asia, stimulated no doubt by their own combined sense of moral outrage, social guilt, and personal anxiety. The colleges—and particularly the elite residential colleges, with their liberal values, their sense of rational and open discourse, and their humanistic hospitality to ambiguity— became the social laboratories for a form of public moral discourse that in many ways they were ill-suited to manage. As institutions withdrew from the preaching of values, students seemed to demand that very thing from them.

GREAT EXPECTATIONS

In more recent times we have witnessed student demands for institutions to take more forthright positions on such things as campus drinking, smoking, and sexual conduct, provoking many a seasoned administrator to wonder if this represents a move to reinstate some of the once-discredited social legislation by colleges that was jettisoned a generation ago in favor of what was thought to be institutional and individual social liberty. More and more, presidents, deans, and governing boards are being asked not only to define the moral mission of the institution but to define and manage the moral climate of the campus. Students appear to want to retain all of their hard-won autonomy, while at the same time insisting that institutions assume a moral responsibility for protecting them from the consequences of that autonomy. In this respect, perhaps, the institutional crisis in the relationship between private rights and public responsibilities may well reflect that of the larger culture.

Part of the difficulty is, of course, the climate of expectation created by the elite residential liberal arts colleges. In order to differentiate themselves from the larger and more anonymous research institutions, such colleges have cultivated their idyllic images as small and intensely caring communities where individuals both count and flourish, and where all of the institutional resources are brought to bear for the benefit of the individual student. In expensive imitation of the old fast-food slogan, such institutions seem to be saying, "We Do It All for You." Parents are promised it, students expect it, and institutions commit themselves to it. Such expectations suggest that the elite residential liberal arts college may create expectations that cannot possibly be met: stress-free, hurt-free, self-actualizing, and affirming communities of achievable ambition that are maximally secure, noninterfering, and nonjudgmental just may not be possible, no matter how efficiently run or handsomely endowed.

It has also become impossible because the elite residential college is "a house divided," as Ernest L. Boyer put it in *College: The Undergraduate Experience in America*;[1] and a house divided against itself, as Jesus pointed out and Lincoln famously quoted in his Cooper Union speech, cannot stand. Archibald MacLeish in 1920 observed, "There can be no educational postulates so long as there are no generally accepted postulates of life itself."[2] Colleges appear to be searching for meaning in a world where diversity, not commonality, is the guiding vision.

DIVERSITY AND PURPOSE

If elite residential colleges have a consensus on anything in addition to the rationale for their own survival, it has been on the values and virtues of diversity as an institutional goal. It would be an interesting study to trace when this concept first emerged as an educational mantra, but by the mid-1970s in those institutions with which I was most familiar it was a goal so frequently and fervently espoused as to take on the nature of a sacred cow, immune to criticism or examination. Those who did risk a challenge to the concept were consigned to the ranks of the sentimental or self-interested old guard, who refused to recognize the new demographics of America and longed for the old boy network of the past. The great conundrum of diversity, however, was not in its variety but in its purpose.

For what end was this new and diverse student population created? What purpose, other than statistical, was to be achieved by the new diversity? Would the new diversity render any such shared purpose impossible? Another of our educational paradoxes was that diversity became the ambitious goal of the residential elites at the very point where those institutions seemed less and less secure about their meaning and destiny. Thus, communities of diversity came either to confront or replace any sense of shared communal purpose that was defined not by those admitted but by that into which they were admitted. This dilemma perhaps accounts for the fact that the two most typical institutional self-defining statements, the matriculation address and the baccalaureate sermon, have become such bland parodies of their former selves. The typical welcome address to new students can be summarized in the pious hope of Rodney King that "we all just get along"; and the baccalaureate sermon, when given by an insider rather than by an outsider to the institution, wishes the candidates luck despite their college experience. In most schools these are the only two occasions in which the class is assembled in some semblance of academic convocation, the first occurring when the students are too inexperienced to know what they are getting into, and the second when it is manifestly too late to do anything about it. No wonder presidents and deans are at a loss as to what to say or to do on those occasions.

This was not always the case, as any old collection of "College Talks," "University Sermons," or "Presidential Addresses" will testify. It would be no waste of time to consult some of these, now consigned to the archives and libraries of teachers' colleges and education schools, to see how visions and tasks were once articulated; and it would not be so much an exercise in institutional nostalgia as it may seem, for by such a project one might begin to ask how we would articulate our goals and ambitions under these modern and difficult circumstances in the way our predecessors addressed their moments and opportunities. To do so with a particular attention to the relationship between private opportunity, public responsibility, and liberal values in a material and secular world might prove an instructive lesson.

As early as in 1910, William Jewett Tucker, president of Dartmouth College, recognized the gathering burden upon the residential liberal arts college to "assume the responsibility for the very considerable amount of intelligent but unquickened life in a prosperous democracy," if schools were only concerned with the pure stuff of scholarship. According to Tucker, though, the age demanded a larger duty, a "social duty," as he called it. "The method of discharging this social obligation, of quickening, that is, the sense of personal power in the average college student, is," he noted, "one of the most perplexing questions of college administration."

> Difficult as it is to provide the means and facilities for instruction, it is still more difficult to insure the moral supports of instruction. The intellectual impulse is seldom sufficient for the proper demands of the intellectual life. The rightly adjusted will, and the motive, are essential elements in the intellectual growth of the college man. Furthermore, it must be considered that the process of moral education in our colleges is very largely that of the education of the individual through the mass, a slow, hard, and often unsatisfying process, but one for which this is no equivalent, for which there can be no substitute. The average student will not be made better except by the use of such motives and influences as are able to lift the whole body of which he is a part.[3]

Having defined the problem, Tucker notes, "The Sunday Vesper service in Rollins Chapel at Dartmouth gave me while president of the college the unusual opportunity of attempting to supply to some degree what I have called the moral supports of instruction." Mere sermons, the secular age responds; and what modern college president in the age of the shrinking college presidency has either the time or the inclination to submit himself and his thoughts to a weekly or even quarterly hearing of the community? These concerns notwithstanding, perhaps the luxuries of an earlier age might provide some stimulation for the necessities of the present. Tucker took on a four-year series, addressing a different topic to each entering class, "designed to emphasize the distinctive objects of college training." In his first talk he spoke of the obligation of the college to "train men to become gentlemen." In the second year he asked, "Are the colleges of today sufficiently honoring the claims of pure scholarship?" In the third year he spoke of "the relation of the American college to citizenship"; and in the final year he proposed to consider the question "Are our colleges now producing under other forms the equivalent of that altruism which, at the origin of the older colleges, found its immediate and most vivid expression in religious consecration?"[4]

It is instructive to note that Tucker made these addresses at the beginning of each college year rather than at the end; and while their conclusions did not substitute for institutional policy, they did communicate the institution's public musings and consideration of its work in the face of those young and formative students who had come to share life as temporary members of an ancient community.

MORAL EDUCATION AND WISHFUL THINKING

Forty years ago, in his baccalaureate sermon to the class of 1959, Harvard's president, Nathan Marsh Pusey, preached on the subject of "College Education and Moral Character." A historian of his own college and of his predecessors in office, Pusey spoke of the early goals of Harvard and its sister institutions, which included the advancement of religion, the training of the mind, and the development of moral character. This emphasis on moral training and the cultivation of character, while central to the earlier enterprise, would by 1959 seem strange and unfamiliar. Pusey observed, "We tend almost instinctively to shy away from the subject, or at least to pass by it in silence."[5] Pusey, it should be remembered, was speaking not simply from his experience as president of a university that since 1886 had been known as "godless Harvard," but out of an earlier and distinguished tenure as president of Lawrence College in Appleton, Wisconsin, a small elite residential liberal arts college. In his sermon Pusey gave a brief account of the history of instruction in moral philosophy, a task that usually fell to the president, and he noted the work of Francis Wayland of Brown University, who "devoted three weeks of his course to the subject of slavery, speaking sharply in favor of emancipation in 1849, at a time when a fourth of his class were southerners." Pusey then put the question:

> For several generations this course was taught in many colleges by men of conviction whose conviction was itself contagious. The question I would set before you today is this: "Where in our college has this course gone?" Clearly the president does not teach it— certainly not in a baccalaureate! Nor does anyone else, by himself.[6]

Somewhat wistfully Pusey answered his own question, at least in part, by suggesting that "... students, teachers, all of us, with those who have been here before us—together perhaps do. From the beginning this course set for itself aims which cannot be taught, but they can be learned, and it is my belief that, as in an earlier day, so they continue to be learned here now."

Was the collective "we," however, even at Harvard, capable of the ambitious goals of the old course in moral philosophy, which was intended to "instill into the minds of youth ... the principles of morality and rectitude which will give them a true and happy direction in the pursuit of all public and private virtues, and by the exercise of which they may become useful to themselves, good members of society, and ornaments to their country"?[7] It was Pusey's hope that this was the case. In his baccalaureate sermon to the class of 1962, entitled "The Quality of Life," he would return to this theme in an expression of the college's expectations of its graduates:

> What Harvard wants more than anything now to give to our country and the world is educated men and women of character. It is her hope that there will develop here generation after generation, now as in the past, thoughtful men who through their beliefs and actions will go on to renew and strengthen true quality in the world's life; men and women of knowledge and faith who, ready to learn from others, will make an effort at honest appraisal of their culture, will recognize both its strength and its weakness, will try to see these aspects separately and fairly, and who then, not complaining, or criticizing unreasonably, or turning away in su-

percilious indifference, will steadfastly set about working where they can—first of all perhaps with themselves—to improve that culture and to make not its shabbiness but its goodness available to others.[8]

The sentiment is noble and honorable, splendidly put, but doomed. First, such instruction and inspiration, difficult to sustain under the best of circumstances, is almost impossible to sustain by self-generation and osmosis. People do not teach themselves to be good. Secondly, the sentiment seems like a final appeal to a reasonable hope in the face of an impending apocalypse, "a little cloud like a man's hand rising out of the sea."[9] Within a very few years the notion that colleges had a common set of values beyond teaching, research, and survival, and an institutional moral responsibility to shape the character of their students, would be regarded as antique.

MORAL EDUCATION AND A NEW OPPORTUNITY

It would be reassuring to believe that what was less and less possible in such great research institutions as Harvard and the state universities was still a viable and cherished ideal in the small elite liberal arts colleges. As we have seen throughout the course of the last century, however, such colleges have often chosen to define themselves in imitation of the research model, taking their conduct of scholarship, appointments and promotions, and institutional identity from the larger model. The result has been a general blurring of distinctions between the function of these residential elite schools and the larger institutions from which they receive their instructors and to which they would send their best graduates. With regard to the particular role of moral education, of which ethics is a part, while it is both regrettable and understandable that the modern secular research university—with some notable exceptions in graduate and professional education—generally does not pretend to instruct in this area of responsibility and is perhaps not well suited to do so, it is unfortunate and self-defeating for the residential elites not to claim a particular responsibility in this area of education, which often is consistent with both the historic mission of such institutions and a felt need of society. In other words, taking up once again the cause of moral education in the undergraduate experience might be a key strategic move in establishing for the residential elites a unique and marketable identity in contemporary American higher education.

CONCLUSION

From this examination of values and the elite college model, several points emerge as particularly salient. Most importantly, if the residential liberal arts college wishes to see itself as "the conscience of American undergraduate education," it will have to embrace as central to its distinct mission the formation of conscience in all of those committed to its care. It will have to adapt the historic function of moral education to the contemporary needs of the residential liberal arts college. Contrary to certain libertarian views of the college as a value-free arboretum for private individual development, the liberal arts college must be prepared to reassume its responsibility for helping to shape values, recognizing that while moral education has as its objective the development of morally responsible citizens and individuals, moral education is too important an institutional and societal value to be left in its entirety to individual and private cultivation.

Diversity can no longer be seen as an institutional or societal goal in itself, but must be regarded as a means to include a diversified population in shaping shared goals to enhance the quality of our common life both in college and in the wider world. Schools with a distinct religious heritage should not be embarrassed by that heritage or seek to distance themselves from it in a misguided attempt at pluralism. While welcoming a variety of religious experiences to the college, the college's own religious inheritance ought to be affirmed as a way of reclaiming the moral dimension of undergraduate education. The issue of religion as an element in institutional moral discourse should at the very least be discussable.

The promise of "community" as a distinguishing feature of the residential elite colleges must be understood as more than institutional neutrality in the face of self-defined communities. Proximity in itself is not a virtue, and the institution must be prepared to define and defend its own value system while seeking quite explicitly to influence and enhance the value systems of its members. Codes of conduct are less important than the climate of instruction and living. In other words, institutional expectations must be articulated early, regularly, indeed frequently, in ways that promote discussion and reflection across the constituencies of the college. Thus occasions for public assembly should be cultivated apart from the opening assembly for new students and the commencement exercises. These need not be "chapel" in the old compulsory sense of religious exercises, but if community is to be more than a marketing device or a collection of semi-autonomous affinity groups, then the community must be gathered and seen to be gathered on some regular basis. The small residential colleges still can achieve some version of the assembly with a far greater chance of success than the universities. If the colleges are "too busy" to orchestrate such gatherings, or have other priorities, then what the college is spending its time doing should be reevaluated and a new scale of priorities identified. In such areas the president perhaps more than any other single individual must be prepared to give leadership, although the responsibility for setting the climate must not be left to the president alone. Chaplains, deans, and professors, together with professional staff, must share in the shaping and maintenance of a climate in which moral education can take place at many levels. The "quality of life" issues in the residential elite colleges are too important to be left alone to the administration or the professionals, and hence some way must be found to reintegrate a system of faculty citizen-teachers at the core of the life of the institution.

While curricular revision is second only to calendar reform in assuring institutional inertia and illustrating the intractability of conflicting interests in the residential elite liberal arts college, the present market and identity crisis may provoke these schools to consider their unique contributions to higher education. Moral education may be that ingredient that will help give a renewed definition of purpose to such institutions. The intellectual challenge will be to develop a course of instruction that is not exclusively curricular, that addresses the college's commitment to moral education in the new century as the old combination of chapel, presidential discourse, and instruction in moral education served in the last century. Given the complexity of the residential college community in both faculty and student body, the demands of such a task cannot be underestimated; and given the fact that the very existence of the residential liberal arts college is likely to be less and less secure, no effort, including this one, should be regarded as beyond the institution's competence.

Questions of values, virtue, and morality have become of greater importance to the national discourse in the past quarter century. Leadership is required to help shape the conversation on these topics, and a natural place to turn for leadership and guidance in these areas is to the places where the discussions first took place: the elite residential liberal arts colleges. Their institutional heritage, their size, their relative wealth, the humanistic traditions that still guide their teaching and research, and the surprising degree of confidence that the general public still reposes in such institutions make liberal arts colleges an essential ingredient in making better citizens and better lives.

Perhaps after the fashion of much of postmodern architecture, the elite residential liberal arts college may well find that its best move forward requires a step or two backward in an adaptive reuse of certain of its historic assumptions and responsibilities. The inspiration for such institutional renovations will no longer come from the elite research institutions in whose shadow the liberal arts college has for so long lived in pale imitation. The way of the future for such institutions may well come from a reappropriation of aspects of their past. If older models of moral education no longer work as they once did, the problem is not that this shaping is no longer desirable or even possible, for an ear to contemporary culture will demonstrate that it is very much desired indeed. The ambition of the residential elite college, then, ought to be the reaffirmation of this formative aspect of its mission, and its still-considerable resources—intellectual, moral, and capital—should be devoted to a contemporary adaptation of the goal as cited by President

Pusey, to "instill into the minds of youth . . . the principles of morality and rectitude which will give them a true and happy direction in the pursuit of all public and private virtues, and by the exercise of which they may become useful to themselves, good members of society, and ornaments of their country."[10]

ENDNOTES

[1]Ernest L. Boyer, *College: The Undergraduate Experience in America* (New York: Carnegie Foundation for the Advancement of Teaching, 1986).

[2]Ibid., 3 and note 3 on p. 301.

[3]William Jewett Tucker, *Personal Power: Counsels to College Men* (Boston and New York: Houghton Mifflin, 1910), preface, vi, viii.

[4]Ibid., 242.

[5]Nathan Marsh Pusey, *The Age of the Scholar: Observations on Education in a Troubled Decade* (Cambridge, Mass.: Belknap Press of Harvard University Press, 1964), 139.

[6]Ibid., 142.

[7]Ibid., 144.

[8]Ibid., 204.

[9]I Kings 18:44.

[10]Pusey, *The Age of the Scholar*, 144.

There is a rusting irony in the reversed fortunes of art and science, already visible in the mid-nineteenth-century writings of scientists. Alexander von Humboldt sadly reflected in 1844 on the contrast between ephemeral science and enduring literature, saying, "It has often been a discouraging consideration, that while purely literary products of the mind are rooted in the depth of feelings and creative imagination, all that is connected with empiricism and with fathoming of phenomena and physical law takes on a new aspect in a few decades, . . . so that, as one commonly says, outdated scientific writings fall into oblivion as [no longer] readable." By 1917 Max Weber could regard the opposition of transitory science to stable art to be a platitude, one that made it difficult to understand what sense it made to pursue science as a career. Near the end of World War I, addressing an audience of Munich students who desperately wanted him to explain how science illuminated the meaning of life, Weber flatly asserted that science provided no such answers; science could hardly answer the question of what the meaning of a scientific career was. Why should one devote a lifetime of labor to producing a result that "in 10, 20, 50 years is outdated"? Subjective art endured, but objective science evaporated. Weber's own answer crowned this irony with yet one more. The spiritual motivation and reward for a lifetime devoted to science was exactly the same as for a lifetime devoted to art: science for science's sake, art for art's sake, the immolation of the personality in the service of "the pure object alone." Having disavowed the artistic imagination and having lost the permanence of artistic achievement, science nonetheless aspired to the ascetic single-mindedness of art.

—Lorraine Daston
"Fear and Loathing of the
Imagination in Science"

from *Dædalus*, Winter 1998
"Science in Culture"

Geoffrey Canada

The Currents of Democracy:
The Role of Small Liberal Arts Colleges

AS THE ONLY REMAINING SUPERPOWER the United States has the opportunity and burden of demonstrating the advantages of a free democratic society. It is my belief that small liberal arts colleges will play an important role in the coming global debate about the success or failures of American-style democracy. Having an honest conversation about democracy in the United States is difficult because of our country's painful history; Americans are uneasy talking about it outside of our particular comfort zones—ethnic groups, racial groups, religious groups. Our country has limited, by law in most instances and by custom when laws were challenged or seemed too blatantly discriminatory, the participation of some of its citizens in the democratic process. The most obvious examples are those presented by the enslavement of blacks, the subsequent Reign of Terror, Jim Crow laws, and the continuing struggle of blacks for equality. But there are many groups that have struggled to be equal members of our society whose stories may be less obvious, though no less painful: Native Americans, Latinos, Irish and Italian immigrants, women, gays and lesbians, and on and on.

The goal of full democratic participation in our society, while still a long way from being met, is much further along than it was when I started college some twenty-nine years ago. And it is my belief that the process of democracy in our country, a process that often entails streams and currents of different

Geoffrey Canada is President and CEO of the Rheedlen Centers for Children and Families.

121

groups coming into intimate and sustained contact with one another, can be well served by the small liberal arts college.

My belief is not based on research or an exhaustive study of the literature; it is simple, uncomplicated, and formed from personal experience. Twenty-nine years ago, at the age of eighteen, I graduated from my all-black high school and left for Bowdoin College in Brunswick, Maine. It was 1970, and the country was deeply concerned about the nature and future of democracy. Indeed, even my decision to go to Bowdoin was largely influenced by the questionable inequalities in treatment of the citizens of our country. The times were tumultuous: President Kennedy, Robert Kennedy, Martin Luther King, and Malcolm X had been assassinated. The black ghettos of the country had burned summer after summer. And one of the most divisive issues of these times, the war in Vietnam, was being debated with vitriolic voices all over the land.

It was this last issue, the war, that led me to Bowdoin and changed my life forever. I was against the war. Even now that statement sends shivers down my spine, because in 1970 being against the war was tantamount to being against America. There were many blacks who were against the war and against America. The hate-filled rhetoric of a then-angry Malcolm X, the Black Panther party's declaration of armed struggle, H. Rap Brown's pronouncement "Burn, baby, burn!"—these filled the airwaves of my adolescence. During my teens I was not against America, but I was ambivalent about my feelings towards my country. The television screens were constantly filled with images of how much we, blacks, were hated. Pictures of fire hoses knocking over demonstrators, dogs biting and ripping our blackness, churches burning, and the remains of children smoldering, along with the resulting charred hopes of a people, were what made up the six o'clock news. It is hard to love a country that makes it clear that it does not love you. Like most minorities, I wanted to be accepted at least, if not loved. And all of this was going on in the midst of a war.

I became eligible for the draft in 1969, and the lack of fairness in the laws of the land was manifested in who was drafted to fight in Vietnam. If you went to college, you could get a deferment and avoid the draft entirely. Going to college was still a dream for many Americans, both black and white. But for blacks the centuries of racism and prejudice were just beginning to abate; many colleges had started to accept blacks, though often only a few were admitted each year. So if you were black in 1970 and not in college, and most were not, then you knew you were going to war. I considered myself one of the lucky ones because I had a full scholarship to the State University of New York at Stonybrook, which meant I was not going to war. I knew it was unfair that my friends who were not going to college would almost surely be drafted. While I studied and partied, they would be in Vietnam, but like most teenagers I did not lose any sleep over it. I thought that was just the way things were.

You can imagine my surprise in July of that year when I decided to check in with Stonybrook, having not heard anything from them, and was told: "We have no record of your being accepted at this institution. You will not be attending classes this fall." I was dumbfounded. How could that be? I had won a scholarship from the Fraternal Order of Masons and completed all the paperwork. In April I was told by phone that everything was fine. How could they claim to have never heard of me?

I sat on my bed at home, holding my head in my hands, saying over and over again: "I'm going to be drafted and sent to the war. I can't believe it." Suddenly I remembered that I had been accepted to another college—Bowdoin. I had never heard of the school and had no interest in going there, but at the insistence of a school secretary, who had been unrelenting, I had applied. I had thrown the acceptance letter in the bottom drawer of my dresser, a junk drawer into which I tossed every piece of paper that I knew I would never need but thought I had better keep just in case. I now found myself head down in that drawer flinging papers left and right as I tried to find the acceptance letter from Bowdoin.

My relief at finding the letter was short-lived as I read that the date to respond to their acceptance had long passed. I had no choice but to try to talk myself into that fall's freshman class. I called the admissions office and politely informed them that I was calling to find out about my room assignment. I was told that the school had never received a reply to their invitation to attend the school. What followed next was an outright lie, as I accused the school of misplacing my paperwork (which did not work), and then an impassioned plea for mercy since I did not want to end up in the jungles of Vietnam. This at least brought me a "Hold on a minute while I talk to the Admissions Director." I knew my life hung in the balance of the decision that would be made in the next few minutes.

What I did not know was that the spring semester of 1970 had been a troublesome one at Bowdoin, as it had at college campuses all over the nation. Students were striking, demonstrating, taking over college buildings, protesting any number of things: the war, school policies, or, at Bowdoin, admission rates for minorities. Even the relatively rural and isolated Bowdoin could not escape the clamor for rights: civil rights, political rights, the rights of women, and the right to have colleges reflect the demographic diversity of our nation.

The woman at the admissions office got back on the line after a few minutes and said, "Although we did not receive your acceptance letter, I'm sure that if you said you mailed it, you did. We are pleased to admit you to Bowdoin. Freshman orientation begins the first week of September. Congratulations."

I hung up the phone thinking "Boy, am I slick. I sure fooled those people." I never realized that the forces that were pushing and pulling on Bowdoin, just like the forces that were shaping and reshaping our nation, were really responsible for my triumph. At the time, there was a national movement to pressure institutions that had intentionally or unintentionally denied citizens the rights granted them by our democratic way of life to redress those wrongs. The shock troops of this movement—students, professors, religious leaders, and common citizens—were fighting for an America that reflected the principles in which they believed. Some folks in Brunswick, Maine, believed that more poor, minority, inner-city students should attend Bowdoin. Students and professors yelled and demonstrated and had allies in the admissions office who shared their belief, and the school began to seriously recruit minority students. In 1970, however, after sincerely trying to recruit significant numbers of blacks to Bowdoin, they had fallen short of their goal. The admissions office knew there would be more demonstrations, more speeches, more denouncements of a biased, prejudiced, racist recruitment policy—a blemish and maybe even a black eye for this liberal institution. Bowdoin had prided itself on having the third African American to graduate from a United States college, John B. Russworm in 1826, and yet it was being accused of being just as guilty of not doing its part as Ole Miss.

This was the context of the times when I called the admissions office in July 1970. The truth was that I fooled no one with my story of replying to Bowdoin's acceptance letter. I was exactly who the school had been working so hard to recruit. I was black and, just as important, poor and from a poor community. It took less than five minutes to make the decision; I was in, though I would later come to understand that I had no idea what I was in for. I thought I was ready for Bowdoin, but I was wrong.

To understand the culture shock I felt in coming to Bowdoin one has to understand how segregated the two communities were then (and appreciate that they are even more segregated now). I grew up in the South Bronx in New York City. My family consisted of my mother and my three brothers. Our father had deserted us when we were infants; my mother worked when she could and received welfare when she could not find work or child care. As the neighborhoods we could afford to live in became more dangerous because of the heroin epidemic in the late 1950s and early 1960s, families that could afford to move away did. The civil-rights struggle provided more opportunities for middle-class blacks to move to "better" neighborhoods. Those of us who could not leave found that our neighborhoods were increasingly made up of other poor families. The first sign that things were changing was when the few whites that lived in the neighborhood moved away, followed by the blacks who had decent jobs. Those of us who remained were left with little contact with whites and black middle-class families outside of businesses and schools. We were growing up poor, segregated from other races, ethnic groups, and economic classes. This was the way I spent my entire elementary-, middle-, and high-school years.

The fact that Bowdoin's student body was 90 percent white and largely middle and upper middle class was a shock for me from the minute I first set foot on the campus. But it was not the only shock. One of the reasons I had wanted to go to Stonybrook was that it was considered a really good party school. At eighteen I felt that going to great parties would be an important part of my college experience. As I stood in the admissions office at Bowdoin, I saw only young men coming and going. As I looked out the window at the beautiful campus, I saw only young men strolling along, playing frisbee, sitting under trees talking.

"Excuse me, is this college divided into a boys campus and a girls campus?" I inquired. The young woman who was helping me find my dorm room smiled and looked up at me so she would not miss the look on my face as she said, "Bowdoin is an all-boys college." I looked at her as her words slowly registered. Years of tough training on the mean streets of New York City had taught me how to mask my feelings, and I called on all that experience and asked, "All boys?" She nodded her head yes even before I got the question out. I saw a look of sympathy in her eyes as I realized that the shock of what she said must have registered on my face.

I tried to pull myself together. That someone could think it was a good idea at eighteen years old to go to a single-sex school did not make any sense to me. What was the sense of getting away from your parents and living on your own if there were no girls around? I mean, sure, I wanted an education, but if you ranked sex, a good education, and playing your stereo loud, a good education would come in second (and after six o'clock in the evening, third) every time. I began to panic and looked out the window again. All the boys seemed quite content. Why, I wondered? They obviously knew that this school was all boys, so why had they come? Maybe they knew something I did not, like where the great parties were in the city of Brunswick. Of course. That had to be it.

"Excuse me again. But could you tell me where the blacks live in Brunswick?" I asked the young woman who had continued to watch me out of the corner of her eye. Wherever the blacks lived would be the first place I would head once I dropped my bags off at my dorm room. No matter what kind of tough inner-city Brunswick had, I would feel quite comfortable there. It could not be any worse than the South Bronx. I would hang out, make a few friends, maybe even meet a girl.

"Well, I don't quite know how to tell you this," the young woman began. My heart began to sink. "But Brunswick is a very small city, and I'm afraid it's nothing like New York. I think there is a black family that lives here, but I really don't know." She decided that she would give me the whole dose of medicine quickly to spare me a slow torture. "With your entering class we have a total of about sixty-seven blacks on campus. This is the most concentrated group of blacks in the state of Maine." I stumbled over to a chair, forgetting the young woman was still watching me. I thought to myself, no girls, no blacks, what black teenager would voluntarily come to a place like this? Right then and there I knew this was not my kind of place.

But Bowdoin was my kind of place. I spent four years there and would not trade those four years for any other college experience in the world. There are many reasons I grew so fond of the college, not the least of which was its academic excellence. I came to Bowdoin thinking I was a good student. I had always excelled in my classes in high school. The harsh reality of how far behind I really was hit me during the first week of classes. I did not know if I would make it through the first semester. It all seemed like too much. Bowdoin had a pass/fail system where a pass was really considered a C by the students who cared about grades (which was almost the entire student body, no matter how much they claimed otherwise), an H or honors was considered a B, and an HH or high honors, an A.

I spent my first year at Bowdoin just trying to keep my head above water. I was not alone. There were many students, black and white, who found the academic rigors of Bowdoin a real challenge. The thing that saved me was the same thing that saved most of the students who found themselves in my predicament—other students and the faculty. There is something about the smallness of Bowdoin that brought about an intimacy that I will never forget. People cared about one another. Students would go out of their way to help you if you needed it. A student who left school because of poor academic performance, although a rare occurrence, was felt to be a real loss by the student body because we all knew one another. The longer we were at the school, the more we felt responsible for those who followed us.

The faculty seemed to feel the same way. Our classes were small, so you could not help but develop a relationship with the faculty. And what a faculty they were. We were in awe of them. They cared passionately about the subject matter they taught. They were fiercely independent, often at odds with the administration and, just as likely, with the student body. Even acknowledging the tendency to romanticize one's youth, I still feel that this was a time of great change in our nation. The debate was never more intense, never more encompassing, and schools like Bowdoin were right in the middle of it. The issues were racism, sexism, multinational corporations, socialism, communism, sex, drugs, the war; the debates were passionate. We were concerned with "selling out" and whether places like Bowdoin were part of the solution or part of the problem. These debates raged in our classes, in our dorms, in our lives.

I majored in two areas, psychology and sociology. Bowdoin did not have a major in education, but I took all of the education classes that were offered. I was convinced that I could begin to find the answers I sought in these three disciplines as I prepared to go back to poor communities and try to help even the playing field for children. I knew that the problems poor families faced were complex and intricately interwoven with larger societal issues, such as poverty, failing schools, and the breakdown of community. By the time my senior year rolled around, the pieces of the puzzle had started to fall into place. I began to have an inkling of what the issues were and what some of the solutions might be. I took courses in physiology and pharmacology that year as I tried to understand why drug abuse was such a problem in poor communities. I began to feel that I was getting close, but time was running out. My years at Bowdoin were coming to an end.

I will always think fondly of my senior year at Bowdoin. It was then that I discovered one of the secrets of a small college: you can talk to the professors. The more I learned, the more I wanted to know, and yet so much of what I wanted to know could not be taught in the classroom. I had questions that had no definitive answers, only strong theoretical possibilities. I spent countless hours talking to professors about what might be possible. We talked over dinner, over lunch, and while walking in the magnificent Maine countryside. I learned as much from these conversations as I did from all of my course work.

It is the bringing together of the rich diversity of our nation in an intimate setting that makes colleges like Bowdoin so necessary to the continued struggle for full democracy in our country. My years at Bowdoin were spent during times that signaled the end of the civil-rights era in America. Many of us thought that by the time we reached middle age our country would be further along in the areas that we debated with so much youthful enthusiasm. To be honest, the country has moved steadily in the right direction. We may not have moved as quickly as many would have hoped, but we have moved forward.

I came to Bowdoin wanting to do several things: having a great social life was one, learning how to help poor children was another. The reason I stayed at Bowdoin for four years had nothing to do with my social life, although I must admit it improved dramatically when women were admitted to the school my sophomore year. It had to do with the training and preparation I received. I knew that the only way to help poor children in this country was to improve their educational opportunities, and my dream was to learn everything I could to create a world where this could happen. Bowdoin offered me support for that dream. No one laughed at my dream and no one said it was not possible. Rather, people said, "If that is what you want, this is what you need. It will be hard, but I'll help." It was said by students, by faculty, and, seemingly, by the college itself.

The college was serious about its mission of educating the future of America. I like to think I did not waste the college's time. I took advantage of the opportunities to learn from people of different races, economic classes, and regions of the country and the world. When I graduated from Bowdoin, I was a different person than when I entered. I knew my vocation would be to work in the poorest communities this country had to offer—it was my calling when I came, it was my calling when I left. But being at Bowdoin was like being plunged into a brave new world. The people had changed me. I had grown in breadth as well as depth, which can only happen if we intentionally encourage diversity in our nation and on our college campuses. Small liberal arts colleges force the members of their communities to live with and therefore know other kinds of people; for those who come having had limited experience with this, it is an opportunity to grow and learn. I left Bowdoin better prepared to tackle the job I wanted to do. By my senior year I had mastered how to learn. I went from being a mediocre student to one who received straight High Honors my senior year. My success was less a testament to my brilliance than a tribute to the hard work of professors and students who believed in me, challenged me, molded me, and finally sent me out into the world to do what I had to do.

Changing the conditions for the poor children of this nation is a tall order and much too ambitious for any one individual, so I have focused my work on a small piece of this nation: the children of Harlem. Twenty-four years after leaving Bowdoin I am where I want to be, doing what I always wanted to do. The not-for-profit agency of which I am president works with over four thousand poor children from Harlem. In each one of our children I see myself. I know what it feels like to be poor and a minority, and to think that you are all alone. My challenge each day is to demonstrate to my children the trust, faith, and belief that the faculty and students had in me many years ago when I was at Bowdoin.

The Rheedlen Centers for Children and Families provides a range of educational, social service, cultural, and recreational supports for our children. Each new American crisis—AIDS, violence, crack cocaine, fatherlessness—hits our children the hardest and adds another burden to families that have no financial, educational, or emotional reserves. Two years ago we decided to try a bold new experiment. Instead of working with individual families in need, we would work with an entire community. The challenge would be to rebuild the fabric of a community while strengthening essential community institutions. We created a new program called the Harlem Children's

Zone (HCZ). The HCZ is a geographically targeted, comprehensive, community-building initiative that focuses on a twenty-four-block area of central Harlem. The concept is to support every child and family in the Zone (currently there are approximately twelve thousand residents in the Zone). We are also working with the three elementary schools to increase academic achievement, with the churches to do more for children, and with other community-based organizations. We have organizers forming block associations, and we will be opening a counseling center and an employment center. With residents, we are planning how to increase the availability and use of technology, increase resident leadership, and improve the housing.

The Harlem Children's Zone is a large and complex initiative, and Rheedlen could not do it alone; in my small corner of the world, I am not alone. On these same streets of Harlem where I have seen so many of my children struggle to make it—where making it sometimes means you go to college and sometimes means you stay alive—others have come. They are from Bowdoin, and their lives are very different than the one I have chosen to live. They come to see me, to walk these streets with me, to share for a moment the danger, the hope, the promise that the children of Harlem represent. They come to help.

When we look at our country today, it is more segregated than ever, not just by race, but by class. The difference between the rich and the poor has increased. Most people do not have friends outside of their own racial or economic class. I find it significant that many of my closest friends are people who went to Bowdoin, and they are rich and poor, black and white. They come to help me because we all went through something together that made us aware of the real promise of America: a democracy that works, equal opportunity for all, a system of government where your station in life is based not on your color, race, religion, or sex, but on your achievement. And we still believe in those things.

So my friends from Bowdoin come to Harlem to whisper encouragement in my ear, to bring their resources both professional and personal, but more importantly to hug a friend, to see his vision of our nation and to accept it as their own. If my children from Harlem can make it, so can America, so can our democracy. When you see that vision you recognize how awesome it is, how awesome the promise of America is, and why liberal arts colleges like Bowdoin, where that vision was nurtured and continues to be supported, are critical to making that vision a reality for all the country and indeed the world.

Eugene M. Lang

Distinctively American:
The Liberal Arts College

P ATENTS ON THE TRADITIONAL MISSION of liberal arts education
have expired. Generic versions of that mission are now
regularly included in even the most specialized undergraduate curricula. In the marketplace, meanwhile, the undiluted liberal arts experience is battling the pressures of escalating costs, rising tuitions, and increasing demands for career
training as a primary component of undergraduate study. These
pressures alone weigh heavily on the future of independent
residential liberal arts colleges. However, their impact is compounded by the contemporary environment of social change
and societal demands. As a result, the educational estate of
these colleges is being fundamentally challenged and their continuing viability seriously threatened.

This essay will address the following questions: In view of
their acknowledged problems, have liberal arts colleges lost
their relevance and do they, *in terms of their traditional mission
as liberal arts colleges,* face extinction? If so, and the "natural
selection" process is allowed to proceed, does it matter? If it
matters, why? What are the options for survival? And would
"responsible citizenship," as an active ingredient, contribute
significantly as a force for breathing new life and viability into
the liberal arts mission?

There are some thirty-five hundred colleges and universities
in the United States. Under sufficiently elastic criteria, about

*Eugene M. Lang is chairman emeritus of the Board of Trustees of Swarthmore
College, founder and chairman emeritus of the "I Have a Dream" Foundation,
founder and chairman emeritus of the Conference of Board Chairmen of Independent Liberal Arts Colleges (CBC), and trustee of the New School University.*

eight hundred of these might claim a liberal arts identity and at the same time qualify as "independent" and "residential." However, the latest Carnegie classification lists only 125 colleges as baccalaureate (Liberal Arts I) institutions, that is, "primarily undergraduate colleges with a major emphasis on baccalaureate (*liberal arts*) degree programs."[1] The list does not include doctoral universities that offer baccalaureate programs or colleges with baccalaureate programs where fewer than 40 percent of graduates receive liberal arts degrees. While this essay is focused on the baccalaureate (Liberal Arts I) group, in obvious respects its comments apply to higher education more broadly.

While sharing the Carnegie liberal arts classification, these 125 colleges differ greatly in their characteristics of smallness, independence, academic and nonacademic programs, resources, and facilities. It is also noteworthy that only one college in this group was founded after 1950—while, over the same period, the total college population of the United States almost quintupled. Further to the point, since 1950 many liberal arts colleges have closed their doors or sought survival by merging or abandoning their liberal arts identity, while the number of four-year colleges offering the bachelor's or first professional degree as their highest degree declined by more than 12 percent.

THE HISTORIC LIBERAL ARTS MISSION

Liberal arts colleges—like many other colleges and universities—have their philosophical roots in a tradition that began in New England over three hundred years ago with the establishment of the first enclaves for educating privileged white males. Their select young students were groomed in a tightly disciplined Anglo-Saxon educational tradition that was presumed to instill qualifications for leadership of a theocratic community. While imparting knowledge, their academic regimen was also intended to develop personal character and intellect—to turn out what continues to be confusingly styled "the whole person," prepared to function knowledgeably within a framework of civic responsibility. Woodrow Wilson, as president of Princeton, referred to this tradition when he spoke of "the generous union then established in the college between the life of philosophy and the life of the state" in the early years of this country.[2]

Today, unlike their forebears, liberal arts colleges do not as a general rule feel impelled to exercise a proactive role in preparing students for service in their communities. Contemporary liberal arts curricula are seldom designed to implement that civic dimension of their missions by reaching beyond the campus environment. Rather, conscious of their established prestige and historic role in higher education, they are substantially consumed by internal academic agendas.

This change came about over the past 150 years as America's steadily expanding population and evolving agricultural-industrial-service economy generated new educational demands. Institutions of higher education that were established to satisfy these demands included land-grant colleges, vocational schools with science and engineering disciplines, research universities, and graduate and professional schools. While higher education was thus becoming more integral to American life, liberal arts colleges continued to focus steadfastly on their traditional curricula and became more and more detached from the community. They came to be virtual academic islands that regarded applied learning as somewhat déclassé.

Reformers of liberal arts education have considered the need for adapting attitudes and curricula to encourage more significant relationships with community problems and social change. Indeed, college years now abound with serious discussions and random initiatives of voluntarism that evidence social concern. Issues of diversity, multiculturalism, poverty, freedom of speech, empowerment, environment, demographic and economic changes, affirmative action, gender, and equal opportunity permeate the curricula of the humanities and social sciences. Qualities of responsible citizenship as demonstrated by student engagements with social issues are applauded; but rarely do colleges engage these issues in ways that meaningfully prepare students for active roles as citizens in recognizing, understanding, and responding to them.

The social philosophy of Plato, with its mandate for responsible citizenship, is recognized as a building block of the liberal arts canon. The stated mission of virtually every liberal arts college attests to this. However, while professing allegiance to the canon, liberal arts curricula are not explicitly designed to inculcate qualities of civic responsibility, that is, to impart the knowledge, understanding, and ability to make thoughtful and ethical judgments of social issues—to feel the motivation and moral responsibility that encourage constructive participation in a democratic society. Liberal arts colleges seem content to presume, with some justification, that the traditional liberal arts education in itself infuses special qualities of citizenship into student psyches that eventually emerge in various ways as postgraduate dividends to society.

The limited civic responsiveness of liberal arts colleges may in part reflect a muddled understanding among their constituencies—administration, faculty, students, trustees, alumni—of the social issues and the "buzzwords" by which they are identified. It may reflect ethical uncertainties and substantive disagreements in assessing the relevance of the issues to liberal arts education—or, in any case, the priority of their claims to attention. It may reflect fears of getting trapped in positions where responsive actions might open a Pandora's box of more serious problems and controversial reactions. As Gregory S. Prince, Jr., wrote, "Educating for civic responsibility is educating for changes, and that task creates tension, resistance and even anger."[3] Finally, colleges may fall back on the minimalist concept that "learning for its own sake" needs no extracurricular rationale.

Whatever the explanation or excuse, the disengagement of colleges does not reflect the readiness of most of their students to initiate or become involved in social causes that touch their idealism, emotions, or sense of justice. Arthur Levine has pointed out that 64 percent of all college students are currently involved in some form of community-service activity.[4] However, lacking an institutional imperative, these activities are mostly random off-campus extracurricular ventures that are peripheral to academic programs, undertaken with insufficient understanding of the problems they address and the qualifications needed for dealing with them. Their goals often lack definition, criteria for evaluation, mechanisms for continuity, and responsibility for accomplishment.

Issues of citizenship and social responsibility impact all colleges and universities—their governance, budgets, staffing, internal relationships, and academic life. They provoke the collision of diverse perspectives and perceived interests of faculty, administrators, students, trustees, and alumni. Most of these institutions are in some measure shielded from the impact by their institutional characteristics, their curricular orientations, and their positions in the marketplace. Academic programs that are heavy in the sciences, research, or professional and vocational training can dull the cutting edge of social concern and temper motivation for activist diversions.

Independent residential liberal arts colleges, by contrast, are by their nature uniquely vulnerable to these collisions. Smallness and limited resources compound the difficulties of maintaining a liberal arts character as they try to contain or accommodate the insistent demands of diversity, financial aid, alternative lifestyles, new technology, community relations, and requests for student services. For these live issues and others that touch directly upon questions of citizenship and social responsibility, procrustean responses accomplish little and may even exacerbate the problems.

Beyond issues associated with socially responsible citizenship, liberal arts colleges also have the problem of sustaining their traditional academic character in a competitive environment in which, on the one hand, they have lost the exclusivity of their liberal arts franchise and, on the other, more and more of their prospective students insist on undergraduate education that also offers attractive vocational substance. This is not to suggest that the value placed on the liberal arts has diminished. On the contrary, and perhaps for the very reasons that threaten its future, the educational preeminence of the liberal arts canon could be more important than ever as an attribute of democratic culture and a qualification for leadership. Indeed, as professional and service activities have become major growth sectors of the American economy, a liberal arts degree has come to be regarded as a valuable and often essential employment qualification for future managers.

CHANGE: A LIBERAL ARTS CONSTANT

Like most systems that relate to intellectual or spiritual life, liberal arts education must periodically refresh the substance of its mission—most immediately by adapting its content and structure to address the needs and objectives of a democratic society that has undergone and continues to undergo major transformation. There is nothing new about this. Pressures for change have been a historic constant in the lives of liberal arts colleges. Among many influences, the innovations of prominent educators—such as Charles Eliot, John Dewey, Frank Aydelotte, Alexander Meiklejohn, and Arthur Morgan—plus the perennial need to recruit the next class of qualified students have stimulated colleges to respond in various ways.

Claims to elitism have become more restrained. Discriminatory practices are much less apparent. Visible evidence on campus of racial diversity is a must. Rights and considerations of gender are generally respected and substantially accommodated. A cornucopia of curricular concepts have entered the liberal arts lexicon—"free electives," "distribution requirements," "cores," "majors" and "double majors," "minors," "concentrations," "internships," "honors," and "interdisciplinary" activities of all types. Curricula have been modified to dilute the European tradition of Platonic idealism with the American tradition of philosophical pragmatism. Thus, they now offer more languages (often without Latin and Greek), somewhat greater cultural diversity, updated and revisionist reading lists, and larger doses of both the sciences and professional studies. On the negative side, as rising operating costs have compounded the urgency of recruiting an adequate student body in an increasingly competitive market, many colleges—especially those with severely limited financial-aid budgets—must contend with the questions of economizing on instruction and lowering standards of admission and academic performance.

Like all colleges and universities, liberal arts colleges in recent decades have also been obliged to cope with burgeoning external forces—new and challenging frontiers of knowledge and communications, dramatic new learning tools, maintenance and obsolescence, global considerations, increasingly diverse constituencies and their growing service demands. Thoughtful responses to these forces have rarely come easily or uncontested. Responses are tempered by the need to surmount barriers of academic process and prerogative, sensitivity to relationships with peer colleges, costs and financing, internal conflicts over the allocation of resources, strong individual biases, and the viscosities of tradition.

There are also strong internal forces, with none more powerful and insistent than the faculty. Adam Yarmolinsky rightly depicted faculty as the legislative body of any college.[5] Without their consent, no program of instruction can be offered, no student can graduate, no faculty member can be hired. Their prerogatives and the advocacy of their disciplines, matters of tenure, maintenance of quality, and intramural competition for resources are influential ingredients of just about every curricular and institutional policy decision.

Liberal arts colleges boast faculties that are distinguished by sustained dedication to undergraduate teaching and the values of a traditional liberal arts environment. As Vartan Gregorian put it, "At the heart of liberal education is the act of teaching."[6] However, many good teachers have been gravitating toward the scholarly and monetary rewards of specialization—committing themselves to increasingly narrow segments of their disciplines, giving their research priority while offering only part-time instruction to students. Absorbed in their disciplines, more and more teachers confine their responsibilities to the classroom and laboratory, competing for student majors who can be trained according to research needs with slight regard for the content or direction of their nonacademic lives. Frank Wong observed that such specialization geared to "careerism and credentials" is a very serious concern when, narrow and dominating, it becomes disconnected from human values, social needs, and the personal development of students.[7]

No less than faculties, administrators and trustees of liberal arts colleges also find themselves turned inward. Except when associated with campus crises, concerns over issues of citizenship and social responsibility are understandably displaced by operating and budgetary priorities. Published mission statements and annual reports almost invariably include references to these civic issues. However, such language usually represents a ritual of righteous rhetoric rather than functional liberal arts credentials. The rhetoric suggests de facto decisions that, beyond organizing the intellectual life of students, colleges do not accept a responsibility for cultivating responsible citizenship.

REVITALIZING THE FUTURE OF LIBERAL ARTS COLLEGES

Leon Botstein asserts that the organization of knowledge and the modes of transmission are inherently part of a fabric of social ideas and action.[8] Drawing on management guru Peter Drucker's statement that the purpose of any organization can be found outside of the organization, James Mingle maintains that while the tradition of an institution gives it strength, external engagement governs its future.[9] The operating agendas of liberal arts colleges are not consistent with these precepts. If liberal arts colleges *as such* are to retain a significant role in higher education, they will have to redefine their missions in contemporary terms. Beyond rhetorical therapy, redefinition will have to invoke a philosophy of enlightened self-interest that clearly makes "social ideas and action" and "external engagement" the subjects of aggressive attention. It must effectively associate both institutional and student objectives with those of the community and responsible citizenship. To achieve the development of students as the "whole persons" that liberal arts curricula are said to intend, classroom and campus boundaries must not limit institutional responsibility for intellectual growth and academic experience.

The philosophy of liberal arts is the philosophy of a democratic society in which citizenship, social responsibility, and community are inseparable. An educated citizenry is the essential instrument for promoting responsible social action and community well-being. It is characterized by an ongoing effort to develop informed, humane, and thoughtful judgments of social issues and to act appropriately on these judgments. Such issues may be identified by their impact on the rights and well-being of human beings, their relationships to the community, the environments in which they exist, the rules by which they are governed, and the equity with which they apply.

Some 150 years ago, Alexis de Tocqueville, commenting on the qualities of citizenship, observed that, unlike peoples of other countries, Americans as individuals took a particularly active responsibility for the well-being of their neighbors and their community. Since then, the massive demographic, cultural, and economic changes of this country's expanding and increasingly diverse population, together with the forces of new technology and globalization, have eroded this characteristic. Most people now tend to ignore or reject more than casual involvement with social issues that they do not perceive as affecting them very directly. Respect for the rules, processes, and institutions of our democratic society has been largely displaced by suspicion and cynicism. Popular sentiment has become increasingly disenchanted with politics, political decision making, and the quality of political leadership. So pervasive is political apathy that it is unusual when even half the citizens who enjoy the right to vote do so in an election. The bonding sense of pluralism associated with America's melting-pot tradition has been abraded by multicultural separatism that is often blind to shared values. The causes that inspire strong civic reaction today are often thoughtless and narrowly orchestrated "us versus them" expressions, most notable for their qualities of cultural bias, ignorance, or lack of understanding among community groups.

These conditions also point to major deficiencies in the responses of American education to the needs of a vastly changed society. By almost any statistical measure, the public education system—indispensable to the existence of a free democratic society—has deteriorated. Especially at primary and secondary levels, it fails to meet the educational needs of youth who must learn to live their lives in a society very different from that in which their parents came to maturity. Almost half the children who started school this year have no credible expectation of a college education—and this in an era when 80 percent of all new jobs require entry-level skills equivalent to at least two years of college. Among other negative consequences, these deficiencies have greatly restricted the number of students who qualify for higher education—a consequence of particular severity for liberal arts colleges.

Higher education, generally, and liberal arts colleges, specifically, have done little to help rebuild the condition of the nation's educational system. From their prestigious position at the top of the educational ladder, colleges and universities generally have shown little disposition to reach down with sustained commitment to help make the total process of education work effectively for everybody. There has been no long-range cooperative outreach geared to the assumption that "a rising tide raises all ships." Rather, the recruiting efforts of institutions strive to compete more intensively within the limited pool of qualified students who are able to climb the educational ladder with minimal supportive intervention.

The undergraduate years are the most fruitful—and, for most students, the last—period for nourishing their ideals and expanding their social perspectives and intellectual horizons in preparing for their eventual places in society. Whatever the nature of the institution or its curriculum, the processes of undergraduate education both in and out of the classroom should be designed to enrich the experience of students by inculcating democratic values, respect for the institutions of democracy, ethical perspectives, civic duty, and social responsibility. As a distinguishing element of their mission, liberal arts colleges can take the leadership in making this happen.

AN OPEN-ENDED CHALLENGE TO LIBERAL ARTS COLLEGES

The development of curricula and delivery systems for providing such enrichment is a general and open-ended challenge to higher education. Although higher education institutionally would surely applaud such objectives in principle, most colleges and universities are likely to find the challenge intimidating, impractical to implement, unaffordable, or beyond their educational charter. Few would willingly recast their educational programs to satisfy intangible and perhaps controversial social objectives that may seem remote from current academic agendas. Some might insist that their existing agendas already deal adequately with civic concerns.

Liberal arts colleges cannot so readily dismiss this challenge. For one thing, to do so could properly be regarded as disavowing a moral responsibility and repudiating their traditional role in higher education. For another, there is the serendipitous fact that major social issues bound up in the challenge include some that liberal arts colleges must in any event confront—if they are not already trying to do so. But especially important, it would squander their special qualifications for meeting this challenge.

Liberal arts colleges are natural laboratories for undertaking long-term institutional commitments to serve social objectives. They are relatively homogeneous bodies and free from cross-currents of interests and territorial imperatives that character-ize the operations and politics of large university complexes. As small communities in their own right, these colleges provide favorable environments in which to develop and test elements of curriculum and related programs for making responsible citizenship a meaningful part of undergraduate experience. When undiluted by vocational priorities, their academic do-main and campus attributes provide opportunities to encourage thoughtful and creative initiatives. Their liberal arts disposition tends to be responsive to projects that associate intellectual commitment with human concern—an association that propels social action. They are practiced in consulting and cooperating with their internal and external constituencies when consider-ing and carrying out major policy decisions and commitments. As Michael Sandel has noted in substance, liberal arts colleges are positioned to develop "the capacity of individuals to bal-ance individual and community responsibilities, civic responsi-bility against individual freedom, and procedural aspects of institutions with the content of their mission and program."[10]

Taking their problematic future into account, liberal arts colleges may well regard the challenge of enriching American education as a special opportunity to reconstitute the viability of their historic role in higher education and their distinction in the marketplace. Instead of seeking survival by compromising their mission and adapting their character to more merchant-able denominators, liberal arts colleges can find new vitality and appeal by adding responsible citizenship as a discrete un-dergraduate dimension. Obviously, the dimension will not, like Athena from the head of Zeus, emerge on any campus as a fully fashioned creation. Rather, over time it will develop incrementally in substance and effectiveness from the initial projects and programs and the related collaborations among college and community constituencies.

Moreover, packaged with the experience of organizing and administering them, programs and related projects could, as tested models, become available to all colleges and universities for adaptation and replication.[11] With the galvanic influence of success, these models of liberal arts experience could do much to encourage other institutions to bridge the critical gap between approval of program objectives in principle and positive engagement to achieve them. In effect, the challenge may be said to offer liberal arts colleges the ultimate opportunity for institutional revitalization by serving what has become this country's highest priority: to assure a genuine opportunity for a quality education to every child. It is important to realize that every major problem America faces—political, economic, social—is at least in part rooted in the disarray of American education. According to a U.S. Department of Education survey published in 1993, over one-third of this country's adult population is functionally illiterate—a condition that must surely be reflected in the nation's productivity, economic growth, racial disharmony, poverty, crime, competitive position in world markets, and, ultimately, its viability as a free democratic society.

AN AGENDA FOR ACTION

There are many paths to responsible citizenship, just as there are many ways—instructional and experiential—to cultivate its qualities. As a starting point for making responsible citizenship a substantive element of undergraduate experience, political scientist Benjamin Barber provides a broad blueprint of the qualities desired: "The willingness to engage in public issues (which grows out of self-esteem); empathy and respect for differences; commitment to nonviolence and conflict resolution; and the ability to analyze information, evidence, and argument."[12]

I do not profess expertise or presume upon professional prerogative by prescribing details and process for teaching and cultivating these qualities. However, John Dewey prescribed three essential elements: it should engage students in the surrounding community; it should be focused on problems to be solved rather than academic discipline; and it should collaboratively involve students and faculty.[13] Within this prescription, programs can be planned to provide opportunities for constructively expressing the idealism and socially driven energies of students, joined with the experienced guidance of faculty. Such programs could foster socially oriented collaboration and volunteerism within the institution and community. As Alfred H. Bloom wrote, such programs should "educate students for the kind of ethical intelligence that is required for our time, to transform values to strategies for social change, [and] to provide exposure to [social] problems so vivid that it will develop in them a lifelong commitment to respond."[14] There is, however, one major caveat: without infringing upon "first amendment" rights, the form, direction, content, and conduct of programs must be consistent with approved institutional policies.

Thus envisioned, the undergraduate learning experience for responsible citizenship would function in three contexts:

In the classroom. Courses on citizenship can teach its meaning philosophically and practically. They can foster an understanding of the fundamental significance of pluralism in society—to appreciate the common values of diverse cultures and to respect their differences. Students can learn to take pride in their ability to contribute usefully to public affairs, to believe that they can make a difference, and to recognize the importance of experiential learning. Faculty can relate elements of existing courses in their disciplines to civic issues for student consideration. Students can be encouraged to ask penetrating questions and learn to communicate effectively with understanding and respect for the sensitivities of individuals and groups.

On the campus. Aspects of citizenship and social responsibility associated with living together on campus and the problems of institutional life can be subjects for communal discussion and resolution. They can be central considerations in establishing facilities, organizing and extending campus activities, and stimulating student initiatives. They can promote interactions among interest groups. Campus publications, special research, and involvement in conflict resolution can promote thoughtful intramural dialogue on aspects of campus activities and policies relating to concerns such as diversity, multiculturalism, racism, harassment, social conduct, and academic performance.

In the community. Local communities provide colleges with a broad range of options for program-related projects and an opportunity for imaginative initiatives. Projects can be long- or short-term undertakings and associated with classroom studies. Areas of outreach, whether local or distant from campus, can include education, the environment, health care, economic development, cultural enterprise, and social services. Projects can be internships or established community actions that invite college participation. They may network with established public- and private-sector educational and social service programs, or join in establishing new ones. They must have reasonably defined parameters with specified objectives and competent oversight, as well as providers with performance responsibilities who are or can be qualified to fulfill them. Moreover, well-intentioned though they may be, projects must be more than extracurricular "feel good" exercises that confer little benefit, and that may be seen as superficial or patronizing.

AN AGENDA FOR COLLABORATION

For programs to be effective, colleges must from the beginning seek to establish collaborations that relate to each of the three contexts of program operation—classroom, campus, and community. These collaborations are needed to contribute useful experience and judgment in the planning, organization, and oversight of programs and for dealing with related problems and policies. Collaborators must fully understand the program, recognize the significance and credibility of its objectives, know what is expected of them, and demonstrate enthusiasm for being part of it. They can have an appropriate role in program governance.

Upfront collaboration that represents participation of the entire college community is fundamental. Each in their own way, administrators, faculty, students, trustees, and alumni—as individuals or representing a constituency—can contribute constructively to some aspect of the program and its related projects. In so doing, not only is the campus spirit of community enhanced but, particularly important, institutional commitment to the program as a contemporary element of mission is affirmed.

Off-campus ingredients of the program require that collaborations involve members of the local community—corporations, public and private social-service agencies, church and civic groups, schools and community colleges, and individual volunteers. These collaborations may deal with projects that respond to specific community concerns in education, environment, health, economic development, and poverty. Collaborators as a group should reflect the diversity of the community, and take care that interactions among themselves and with the community are considerate of the rights, experience or inexperience, sensitivities, and interests of those affected. In addition to personal fulfillment, the services of collaborators can provide inspirational models of college leadership, responsible citizenship, and town-gown relationships.

Institutional collaborations among liberal arts colleges, perhaps under the auspices of existing associations, can be of greatest importance for program development and significant accomplishment. The structure and details of individual college programs must obviously be shaped by local circumstances—and programs may differ accordingly. However, their common thrust will generate experiences and information that can be usefully exchanged, and raise problems and policy questions that can usefully be discussed. Over time, a basic agenda for promoting responsible citizenship, adaptable but with conceptual integrity, would be collectively developed as a kinetic dimension of liberal arts curricula.

Liberal arts colleges share some critically important objectives that, by their nature, can be best served by collaborative attention—and without antitrust concerns. Thus, probably all of them and their student bodies are now engaged in various socially motivated projects on their campuses and in their communities. Without intruding on their individual integrity, many of these projects could be advantageously associated with the program's broad agenda of preparing students for responsible citizenship.

Most urgent among the common concerns of liberal arts colleges is the tremendous need for enlarging the pool of students who want a college education and can meet admission requirements. This need—a bottom-line aspect of America's currently paramount concern with education—bears on other college problems such as recruiting, academic standards, diversity, and financial aid. As a primary building block of a program for responsible citizenship, liberal arts colleges—perhaps using projects of the nationwide "I Have a Dream" program as models—can most appropriately work together to address the urgency of assuring every child a genuine opportunity for a fulfilling education.

To that end, liberal arts colleges should reach out insistently into their communities, where, by their nature, they are important members—commanding respect and contributing intellectual and economic value. Understandably, except when interests unavoidably collide, colleges usually prefer to avoid initiatives or gratuitous involvements in community concerns that might invite controversy. However, it is reasonable to believe that, as an acknowledged means of promoting responsible citizenship, projects associated with community needs provide common and inviting grounds for college-community engagement.

Through the combined efforts of administrators, faculty, and students, colleges can mobilize local businesses, public and private agencies, churches, and civic groups to join in planning and carrying out projects that address specific community needs— in particular, helping their children climb the educational ladder. Where possible, these projects would cooperate as auxiliary support facilities to complement the regular public services of the community. Special attention might be directed to developing the important resource found in community colleges, as a reservoir of disadvantaged students who are at least preliminarily committed to pursue higher education.

This essay recognizes the fact that no educational program involving change is without cost—and that the cost of undertaking to establish a comprehensive program to make responsible citizenship an active part of the liberal arts mission could, over time, be quite considerable. However, it seems premature to be put off by the question of cost and related funding until the liberal arts community or its leaders can assess the value of its benefits and establish a clear sense of direction by answering the questions with which this essay began—and deciding whether responsible citizenship is to be reestablished as an active ingredient of a liberal arts education. That decision speaks to the future of liberal arts colleges—to the revitalization of their tradition as a distinctively positive force in American education. It also speaks to the direction of higher education generally in fulfilling its responsibilities to the national community.

ENDNOTES

[1]Carnegie classification as published in the *Chronicle of Higher Education*, 23 October 1998.

[2]Woodrow Wilson, "Princeton in the Nation's Service," *Forum* XXII (December 1896).

[3]Gregory S. Prince, Jr., "Are We Graduating Good Citizens?" *Educational Record* (Summer/Fall 1997).

[4]Arthur Levine and Jana Nidiffer, *Beating the Odds: How the Poor Get to College* (San Francisco: Jossey-Bass Publishers, 1996).

[5]Adam Yarmolinsky, "Constraints and Opportunities," in *Rethinking Liberal Education*, ed. Nicholas H. Farnham and Adam Yarmolinsky (New York: Oxford University Press, 1996).

[6]Vartan Gregorian, inaugural address at Brown University, Providence, Rhode Island, 1989.

[7]Frank Wong, "The Search for American Liberal Education," in Farnham and Yarmolinsky, eds., *Rethinking Liberal Education*.

[8]Leon Botstein, *Jefferson's Children: Education and the Promise of American Culture* (New York: Doubleday, 1997).

[9]James R. Mingle, "Responding to the New Market for Higher Education," *AGB Priorities* (11) (Summer 1998).

[10]Michael J. Sandel, *Democracy's Discontent: America in Search of a Public Philosophy* (Cambridge, Mass.: Belknap Press of Harvard University Press, 1996).

[11]Unless obviously used in another context, the word "program" in this essay refers to a comprehensive program for preparing college students for socially

responsible citizenship. The word "project" in this essay refers to any activity or undertaking that is part of a program and its implementation.

[12]Benjamin R. Barber and Richard Battistoni, *Education for Democracy: A Sourcebook* (Dubuque, Iowa: Kendall-Hunt Publishers, 1998).

[13]John Dewey, *Democracy and Education* (New York: Macmillan, 1916).

[14]Alfred H. Bloom in *Swarthmore Papers*, ed. Barry Schwartz (n.p., January 1993).

Eva T. H. Brann

The American College as *the* Place for Liberal Learning

NOT BY THE PERCENTAGES

I N EDUCATION, as in most facets of present-day life, it is the best of times and the worst of times. We may infer that it is the worst of times from the multitude of jeremiads on the topic as well as from our common experience as teachers. Among students there is a perceptible decline of the privately nourished passion for deep and difficult reading; among parents, an anxious preference for career preparation over liberal learning; among officials, an unexamined rage for quantifiable results; among executives, an appetite for bending education toward the training of a workforce.

Moreover, the case for liberal learning and for the American college as the place where it is most naturally situated is not usually defended with anything like the vivid aggression that dominates the propaganda for job-related training. The latter appeals to American productivity and the global future and other such compelling articles of secular faith. But open a representative catalog of a liberal arts college and you will find commonplaces and compromises, embellished by arcadian pictures and references to the distinguishing local amenities.

It is not so much that "the best lack all conviction, while the worst are full of passionate intensity." It is rather that the best lack *well-grounded* conviction and the others abound in clueless good intentions. Thus the American liberal arts college, that

---

Eva T. H. Brann is tutor and former dean at St. John's College, Annapolis, Maryland.

151

endangered species, has allowed itself to be driven into an alien terrain for its defense: graduation rates and completion times, advanced degrees and career choices, employment records and magazine ratings. Rarely does a college say to its public, especially its prospective parents: "Listen to us. These ways of gauging the value of an education are all wrong. Efficiency in learning is ineffective, and training for the future is, in the words of Octavio Paz, 'preparing a prison for the present.' We offer an education that is, to be sure, extended, expensive, nonutilitarian, uncertain (and certainly unquantifiable) in outcome, and possibly destabilizing. But here we love learning and are ready to help your children love it, and we are, moreover, prepared to tell you in detail why we do what we do: what the good of it is, and why we think that these four years are the proper completion to the upbringing you gave your children and the best insurance for a good life."

This rhetoric of conviction is failing in education as it is in many departments of American life. We live in a time when openness is understood as indeterminacy and accommodation is a last civic duty. The reason that the rhetoric of higher education is flaccid is that its defenders think it their duty not to know how to become specific, concrete, and—Heaven forfend—prescriptive. But it seems to me that it is the business of college teachers and the officials that speak for their colleges to have determinate opinions about the right shape of a liberal education—and not just about the prerogatives of their own departments, either. So from the point of view of both outside pressure and inside vulnerability, it is indeed a bad time for liberal education.

But from a different perspective, it is the best of times in the world of learning. Forget the dangerous decline in the number of students taking humanities courses; forget that the American liberal arts colleges, though still a few thousand strong in number, capture a declining share of students. Forget even that the conversion of liberal reading into theory and critique increasingly trickles down from the universities. Take instead as a criterion the least regarded of contemporary accomplishments—learning Greek. By the percentages it is a vanishing study, but in absolute numbers, those enthusiastic late learners of Greek, Thomas More and Erasmus, would think themselves in a humanist heaven, with thousands of fellow students and a profusion of well-edited texts, ingenious textbooks, and convenient commentaries. The same goes for modern studies. Judge Woolsey decreed in 1933 that though *Ulysses* "undoubtedly is somewhat emetic, nowhere does it tend to be an aphrodisiac . . . [and] may, therefore, be admitted to the United States," yet I remember that even in the fifties I had to scare up a copy in Europe, while now we have editions and commentaries galore, and the aphrodisiacs to boot. And though the best books shamefully go out of print, they eventually come profitably back in. Therefore, from the perspective of the availability of the tools of learning, this is the best of times. And it is not just the profusion of books and scores and visual aids that makes this a high time. Some fields are in their fullest glory: mathematics, for example, and the writing of novels, particularly of the kind pronounced dead by critics, the realistic genre, both magical and sober. But if the decline of liberal learning is not due to a dearth of fine means and great matter, what other reasons—at least institutional reasons—might be found?

It is one aspect of majoritarian democracy to rule life by percentages, and a complementary grace to care about individuals. The American college has no present chance of dominating by numbers, but it is good for—one might say it is our last best chance at—shaping well-formed human beings. The nonsectarian, independent colleges are sometimes attacked with that most thoughtless of charges, elitism. If elitism is willful exclusionism, no institution is less elitist or more anxiously diverse. We are, most unfortunately and not entirely by our own fault, prohibitively expensive, but even the so-called elite colleges make near-heroic compensatory efforts to be demographically inclusive. In fact, they might do better to recall that if it is the pedagogic benefit of diversity they are after, no two human souls are more diverse than siblings brought up in the same household, if diversity is taken in a humanly ultimate sense. For who presents the most impenetrable mystery but one's nearest and dearest? It is an accompanying thought that these small institutions are not the right venue for effecting social change. Education is inevitably a social program in respect to the public schools and that part of the great public universities that is not dedicated to pure research. Though their aims are not invariably in tune with those of the American public, at least they have the capability to work social change. The small independent colleges, however, ought not to have these aims and cannot have the power. Their immediate business is much closer to the salvation of the soul than to the rectification of the world. The Laputan large-think and the quantifying administrative language that goes with it—schools as delivery systems, students as clients, their education (or they themselves) as products—are particularly alien to these little places, and they compromise themselves in acceding to these terms.

One more reason that so much that issues from the colleges on liberal education is weak is that it has no real author. Blessedly, there is no system of higher education in this country. There are, to be sure, regional and national administrative organizations like the accrediting agencies and the governmental departments of education. There is also that marvelous exemplar of the Tocquevillian conformity that is so often the unintended consequence of freedom of choice in America—the almost total uniformity of administrative and intellectual organization of our schools of higher education: governance by citizen boards and presidents, departmental divisions following near-identical organizations of knowledge, specialized courses elected by students, and some unstable vestiges of cores, distribution requirements, or freshman seminars. The governance arrangements seem to me to be a spectacularly successful example of American civic life, the curricular plans somewhat less so, stymied as they are between the intellectual revisionism that trickles down from the universities and the conservatism of a professoriate whose members received their credentials by meeting graduate-school requirements as grueling as they are deforming to the liberal spirit of learning and teaching.

Consequently, colleges distinguish themselves by small differences—campus layout, local traditions and rituals, types of sociability. They show the same down-to-earth pluralism as does the American small town, a pluralism based on the stable particularities of place and the ever-fresh differences among the human participants. These places attract lasting affection; in Daniel Webster's rousing peroration to the legal decision that made America safe for colleges, the Dartmouth College case of 1818, he states, "It is, sir, as I have said, a small college, and yet there are those that love it." The colleges really cannot speak with a common voice: on the curricular front there is not much news, while their human setting is rightly localized.

For the same reasons, they are not really a unitary addressee. The multitude of panel reports and position papers on the reform of higher education address no one and nothing. In any case, they are mostly flexings of the iron fist of economic exigency and government interference in the velvet glove of educationese. In fact, these productions often have no real author; they are produced by staffers collating the "input" of panel members who appear to be mostly untouched by the passion of learning.

It follows that an attractive exposition and a persuasive defense of liberal education is not very likely to come from the colleges speaking as a species and is near-certain not to come from concerned outsiders. Here is what is wanting and what is called for against all odds: reaffirmations of liberal education by the individual working communities where it is located, and a thoroughgoing, even radical review with specific reformulations of the elements of liberal education as practiced at each college. I do not mean vaporous mission statements or curricular tinkering, but rather localized and vivid expressions of such fundamentals as faculties can see their way to agreeing on with conviction. It is true in matters of education as in matters of faith that "because thou art lukewarm and neither cold nor hot, I will spue thee out of my mouth."[1] Being both determinate and determined does not necessarily mean being closed-minded, but I think educational pluralism, that peculiarly American blessing, requires a certain sane schizophrenia: believing wholeheartedly in one way while entertaining an appreciative interest in alternatives.

LIBERAL EDUCATION, UNABASHED

An example is called for to explain what I mean both by the affirmation and the specification of liberal education. Liberal education is in need of reaffirmation not only because of the aforementioned unjust charge of elitism but also because of the vague imputation of "irrelevance"—usually without the benefit of the completing prepositional phrase required for definite sense.

From its very first extant description, the essence of liberal education was indeed to be irrelevant to something, namely, narrow vocationalism. Aristotle says in his *Politics*:

> But that [the young] must not be taught all of the useful arts is evident, once free pursuits have been distinguished from those that are unfree—and also that they must take part only in those useful pursuits that will not make the participant [merely] mechanical.[2]

The negative distinguishing mark of "free," that is, liberal, education seems to me still that it is not aimed at making a living or a career or even at preparing for a profession. It should not be defended to the general public or to paying parents on grounds of utility, not even of the nobler sort. To be sure, the facts skew even the purest intentions of those representing such an education. It is simply the case that our students almost universally declare their education to have been of the greatest use to them: in keeping them from being merely "mechanical," it has made them both brave and versatile in facing practical problems. The kind of education I am about to delineate perhaps could not survive if not for the fact that learning undertaken for its own sake—not as a means but as its own end—turns out to be a means to moderate worldly success as well. This circumstance may not be a gratuitous accident but may instead speak to the logic of a world that is after all hospitable to liberal learning. However tempting favorable Graduate Record Examination scores, career statistics, and alumni tracking may be, they are not the right and finally not even the most persuasive defense of an education to which they are merely, if happily, incidental. And though I have great faith in the close relation of thoughtfulness to goodness, even the development of useful citizens should not, I think, be cited among the *direct* aims of liberal learning; it is an obliquely achieved though ardently desired by-product.

In *The Use and Abuse of History*, Nietzsche recommends to the latecomers of a great tradition that they exchange their "painful ironic modesty for a certain shamelessness."[3] Such uninhibitedness about our offerings seems to be indicated. Our students may become economically productive, civically responsible, personally fulfilled, and all the other good things the catalogs suggest, but the first and last unabashed answer to the question "Why engage in liberal learning?" is "To learn something worth knowing for its own sake." It is said that someone who was beginning to study geometry with Euclid asked, "But what shall I get by learning this stuff?" and that Euclid told his servant to give the person three pennies, since he needed to get a profit from his learning. There are softer ways to send the message, but we should not fudge it. As I said, I am unsure of the ultimate defensibility of nonutilitarian learning if our natures and the world were not made so that such learning is also morally and practically effective. But as it is, we should unabashedly ask our students to study for the love of it. The implications for the form and content of such study are momentous.

Aristotle clearly saw liberal studies as easily distinguishable from those that are "mechanical" and useful. But I think that liberality can turn up in human activity in two ways. From one point of view, the one that should be taken by institutions of liberal learning, subject matter is of the essence. But for life in general, I would say that any pursuit can be carried on in a liberal spirit, from accountancy to ontology. I have seen a new initiate into double-entry bookkeeping as fascinated with it as I was when I first saw the Pythagorean Table of Opposites: here was a whole accounted for by a dual list of equally weighted correlatives. From this wide perspective the mark of liberality is simply disinterested delight-taking.

ILLIBERAL NOTIONS

The four college years are spent surrounded by learning that may be liberal in spirit but not in intention. There is a well-known distinction between education and training, the latter being a sort of mechanical habituation for practical purposes. The upbringing of children is largely training, as is the instruction of professionals. These are nonliberal but not illiberal modes; they are necessary, and though graduate training, at least, often results in a permanent professional deformation of the intellect, this is not a direct or unavoidable result. I believe that recent efforts to smooth out the transitions of schooling, to erase the boundaries between high school and college as well as college and graduate or professional school, are more harmful than helpful. These four years of earliest maturity, when most have had some experience of erotic love—the indispensable psychosomatic prelude to higher learning (though also a chief distractor)—and when they are between their parents' control and the world's demands, should be distinct from the other periods of life: free for the alternation of study and reflection, the ups and downs of illumination and confusion, the oscillations of wasted weeks and midnight intensities. I do not mean that the college years should be a unique epoch in people's lives; on the contrary, it is a paradigmatic time, to long for and recapture throughout life. Thus alumni are indeed, as we so often claim, the perpetuating progeny of their college—if, wherever they are, there crystallizes about them a colony of free learning. But those four years are the determinative initiation into liberal learning, and they should be as unlike high school and graduate school as possible. (Once again, a happy coincidence beclouds the purity of intention. According to a well-informed consultant, certain kinds of applicants to liberal arts colleges look exactly for that break with high school.[4]) The intellectual counterpart of what is referred to in anthropology as culture shock is a good beginning in liberal education, and this opinion has real consequences for the subject matter chosen to study, as I will argue below.

There are also genuinely *illiberal* tenets of education. Many of them are currently espoused as educationist wisdom and recommended as guides to curriculum making. Since the *via negativa* is often a good way to reach the specifiable essence, let me list five curricular opinions that seem to me deleterious, however humanely intended.

First, there is the opinion that we must meet students where they are "at," that the teachers must find the students' level, and that the subject matter must be relevant, presumably to their present condition. As I intimated above, I think the cause of the soul's freedom is served in just the opposite way. Students should be given the opportunity to undergo what in adventist religions is called a "rapture," a seizing-away into a new and possibly higher realm. The books they read, the theorems they prove, or the music they analyze that can send them into these realms will not be of their world or on their level at all but above it—as they remain, if truth be told, above their teachers'. But their teachers' calm assumption for them will be that if they face these works together, almost all will be carried beyond their presumed level by the masterful authors' communicative intention.

Nor do I think that students' interest is best raised by burning topicality. There is, after all, a difference between excitation and interest—the former being a sort of prurience of the reason aroused by framing human extremities in an academic setting, the latter being the long-term engagement of the intellect with the human condition viewed from some distance. Interest is harder to arouse but easier to sustain, first because there is the deep pleasure of finding human affinities over great spans of time and increasing levels of abstraction, and second because these longer perspectives eventually help students to see more significance in their world and to frame more coherent opinions.

But students do not easily pluck themselves from the roiling life that surrounds them; the community of teachers has to do that for them. It is a sort of unwitting self-indictment when faculties turn the choice of studies over to the election of their students. If students already know what it is good for them to learn, what are the professors but providers of expertise? That is a respectable but not very liberal view of teaching. I think that a certain amount of prescription is necessary. And the response to the ever-ready challenge of "Who are you to tell me what to study?" is to tell who you are, and why you are assuming responsibility.

A second illiberal tenet follows immediately: that good teachers are people who know things and tell them, literally "professors." It is a strange fact that the same youths who "question authority" in real life are so willing to sit in rows before a professing authority. But perhaps it is not so strange after all. Attendance at lectures is to them a sort of time investment, present life given up for later redemption in good grades.

Teachers should practice the Quaker art of silence until students are moved to *be there.* And just as they should not quell the students' intellectual motions by talking at them, so should they not keep students from confronting the works to be studied by interposing introductions, backgrounds, interpretations, and other intermediating paraphernalia. But more of the liberal mode of teaching below.

It also follows, third, that it cannot be a direct aim of liberal education to change the world, even for the better. The tenet I am criticizing here as illiberal is not so much the inadmissibility of engaging an institution of liberal learning in political causes as the notion that life and learning, practice and theory, are to be intermingled or concurrent, that society becomes an adjunct laboratory for the school or the school a proving ground for social experiments. Study and reflection, and theory and conversation about theory, are *really* different from practical intervention in the world. It is not so much that, in general, thinking should come before doing, and even less that students in action (on either end of the political spectrum, where they tend to be) are not at their most profitable station. What is at stake is the leisurely, long-term, deeply excited but not agitated development of thought that can eventually be brought to bear on issues. School, as is often pointed out, is an adaptation of the Greek word for leisure; school is time out, free from practical pressures and open to looking at foundations, a time for contemplation, for theory in the original sense, for pure viewing. I think every human being wants a time for this sort of contemplative delving, though not everyone wants it in youth. It seems a possible and glorious thing if in the next decades liberal arts colleges received more and more applications from older, even quite senior, would-be students, intending to begin life again.

It follows that "problems and issues" courses have an illiberal taint on them, from my point of view, for who but a sadomasochist of the intellect would study the current ills of society for their own sake? Such courses, even the most scrupulously nonideological, *have* to be conceived as means for amelioration, as seedbeds of prompt action. On the other hand, deep, disinterested theoretical thought seems to be the better prelude to worldly engagement.

Fourth, the very distinction between learning free of interested motive and training for practical ends implies a recognition of high and low, a hierarchy of worth in matters intellectual. I do believe that to an educated person all things, grand or pitiful, and all studies, pure and applied, are eventually interesting. But I also think that the young especially ought to learn how to live with the array of conditions associated with excellence: that what is finest often denies itself to easy access; that to live admiringly with things above oneself is a source of dignity; that genuine hierarchies confer respect on all their members; that even what is greatest, or especially what is greatest, offers itself for critical judgment. The familiarity with greatness I have in mind is only remotely connected to Arnoldian "culture," familiarity with "the best that has been thought and known in the world"; it is a much more concentrated, particular, and laborious immersion. Its real point is not even to induce disciplined self-respect in the way just laid out but to stock the mind with exemplars of the highest quality, based on the hypothesis that in order to battle the bad you have to know some good. But even that aim is too purposeful. The real point is just that if learning is to be liberal, that is, for its own sake, its objects have to be ipso facto authentically attractive. The unfashionable assumption here is that differential greatness exists and is discernible, and that the teachers should in common acquire the experience to discern it.

There is a consequence for teaching technique associated with the choice of works of high art over documents that are valued not for their intrinsic quality but as testimony to a targeted human condition. Works of high art—from mathematics to music, philosophy to literature—appeal to the passions via the judging functions, and liberal learning addresses itself in the first instance to the intellectual rather than the pathological nature of the student. Therefore the devices used to rouse passions and empathy, such as consciousness-raising and role-playing, really do not fit into a liberal pedagogy. Teachers may be themselves exemplars of intellectual passion but must never be the deliberate instigators of emotions in others.

The fifth, and my final, tenet of illiberality is most powerful and most pervasive in our universities and even colleges. It is the exclusion of truth from learning—the *search* for truth. In some sectarian colleges a "truth" is actually taught, and with perfect right since the students have chosen the school in order to learn dogmatically. In such colleges liberal education goes on to a point, after which it becomes theological. But I am thinking of a secular curriculum, in which truths are agreed to be the ultimate objects of a possibly unfulfillable desire. In most classrooms today the question concerning truth is proscribed. Factuality, validity, relevance, interpretability, influence, motivation—all these may be examined, but the question "Is it true, what this book says?" is not admitted. It makes teachers squirm and students snicker. The roots of this embarrassment, which is far more acute than that raised by the mention of more intimately private matters, are as deep as the roots of secular modernity. But the exclusion of the truth question from students' classroom experience, and consequently from their studies, has a devastating effect: It turns all their studies into a high-class game, which they can take or leave.

It is part of liberal education not only to admit that question but even to put it at the center of the enterprise. The first questions will usually be: What is this book saying? What is the gist of this theorem? How is this formula capturing the physical phenomenon? How is this musical phrase related to its verbal text? Of course, in concrete situations the questions will be intricate and specific. But eventually some students will ask: Do I believe this? And do I believe—or reject—it because *I* want to or because the *matter* compels me. This latter compulsion is the initial experience of truth. A liberal setting will be eagerly receptive to such questioning, even if it holds up the works; leisurely delay is the defining tempo of liberal learning.

LIBERAL TEACHING

The mode of teaching that fits liberal learning, then, is just everything that is opposite to the points listed above. Teachers do not strenuously accommodate students' current preoccupations but instead take responsibility for heaving them out of their present contexts by means of hard but high learning-matter. They are scrupulously nonintrusive with respect to their students' emotional life. At most, they hope by the silent influence and the unembarrassed example of their own feeling to turn the students toward the objects of their common attention. These objects are chosen so as to engage the whole community of learning, teachers and students, above its level of comfort, so that the admission of ignorance becomes a virtue of necessity. This community acknowledges hierarchies in the intellectual world, but its practices in the classroom are deliberately egalitarian. After all, one principle of the education I am describing is that "a cat may look at a king," or that ordinary people may confront great matters directly. Before their magnitude, *sub specie aeternitatis*, the "best and the brightest," and the modestly endowed do not seem so different, not to speak of the fact that the quick, brilliant students are not always as thoughtful as the slow, deep ones. But what really equalizes teachers and students is the genuine questions they share. The teachers' perplexity may be better specified, better informed, but whoever does not possess the Socratic wisdom cannot teach in the mode I mean. That "human wisdom" spoken of in Plato's *Apology* is to know that one knows nothing, and to know it in two ways: as a highly specifiable lack and as an irrepressible longing.[5] Such teachers consequently are not authorities or experts but amateurs in the literal sense, lovers of learning, who start students on their way by good questions and help them over obstacles with spare explanations. Above all, they do not postpone or skew the students' direct confrontation with the objects of learning by long, dull, or opinionated scene setting; they do not damp the life of their intellects by preempting the conversation, for conversation is the supporting fluid of liberal learning.

LIBERAL SUBJECT MATTER

It is not quite true that any material serves for a liberal education, and teachers who say that it hardly matters what students
learn as long as they learn in the right way seem to me to be too
easy in their curricular faith. But I do believe that the world is
full of a variety of fine curricular objects—texts, theories,
practica—and that these can be arranged in a multitude of
ways. The point is to make coherent choices and to live by them
with open-minded conviction.

That said, I also believe that there are objects of study and
curricular arrangements that are essentially connected to the
way of liberal learning. I am a teacher at St. John's College, in
Annapolis and Santa Fe, known somewhat formulaically but
not unjustly as a "great books school." What I am about to
describe briefly is our program, though abstracted from the
accretions of detail and tradition that an actual working curriculum will accumulate over six decades and from the strands
of ever-continuing discussion that anchor the foundations of the
program. It is here offered as one example of a coherent liberal
arts curriculum to which a whole faculty has committed itself.

The main objects—both tools and ends—of learning are the
books: books of texts, symbols, notes, figures. The list changes
incrementally, because each addition and subtraction is made
by the faculty, and at least some of the members make it their
business to read each book in question. The criteria for particular choices are well accepted; the modern public can read about
them in essays by writers from Gertrude Stein to Italo Calvino.
There is also an ancient tradition concerning the formation of
whole canons, complemented by a fierce contemporary critique. For us, the primary inherent qualities of program books
include indefinitely rich interpretability without a loss of definite meaning, artful melding of style and matter, and originality
in the double sense of being at the origins or foundations of
human knowledge and of being originative in bringing forth
something new. The programmatically useful characteristics
are a certain coherence—which might be dialectical, that is,
oppositional—with other books and the likely spawning of a
conversation. This last criterion usually means that the book

must have a good deal of self-sufficiency, so that students and tutors need no background preparation except perhaps the earlier books. But self-sufficiency, independent interpretability, is actually yet another mark of a great book for us. The principal effect of such books is self-knowledge in that expansive sense that includes the world.

The fact that the books stand in a coherent tradition suggests a largely chronological arrangement. The earlier books are the students' sole context for the later ones. The quarrelsomeness of this temporally successive tradition assures a balance of views. But the deepest motive for the chronological order is the hermeneutic null principle: mere dates dictate the sequence, and we need introduce no comparative or interpretative schemes. Of course in this, as in all our arrangements, we make reasonable compromises.

"Tutor" is the name we give to the teacher who tries to teach in this mode. There are no ranks, nor do students choose whose class they attend. What is more, they have to *be* in class because there is no making up a missed conversation: the whole program, with some carefully circumscribed exceptions, is required, and for two reasons. One is that we endeavor to prescribe books and subject matter that we think no human being should miss; the second is that we want students to talk and work with each other in and out of class.

The authors are supplemented by arts, those "liberal arts" after which colleges are still named. These arts of learning are very different from the "methods" or the "critical reasoning" sometimes taught in special courses; one might say that the liberal arts, as established in a long tradition and reconceived by us, reconcile the present pedagogical quarrel known as "process versus product." These arts are really exemplary subject matters that have the property of preserving within themselves the elements of their genesis, so that in learning the matter one also learns the way. The truly paradigmatic liberal arts are mathematics (which is Greek for "what is learnable"), science (Latin for "discerning knowledge"), and the arts of thinking and speaking. We choose what we think and have experienced for ourselves as the most revealing *and* accessible axiom- and theorem-sequences and the most significant scientific theories with their crucial laboratory experiments. Of the arts of language, more below.

Here is what we do not attempt to do: We do not try to introduce our students to the "scientific (or any other) method," giving them instead the means to think out what it means to bring method to matter. We do not set out to cover the field but rather make it clear to the students that their course of study is a set of choices, that is, exclusions, and that most of the world's knowledge is left to their future learning. We do not reach sophisticated levels or do cutting-edge research; we have neither the training nor the equipment. So, for example, *all* the students can and do study the Special Theory of Relativity, but only a few tutors venture into the General Theory with their classes.

But the last omission also has a more positive cause. It is part of the liberality of the program that the teachers each teach nearly everything, on the hypothesis that what we require the students to learn we can surely learn ourselves and so teach it, and with special empathy. What justifies this venture is our conviction that liberal learning is, in its nature, elementary in a double sense. First, it begins at the beginning of a study and goes on in a leisurely, reflective way that almost everyone can follow. But besides this pedagogical lingering (which follows from the faith that, given time and the opportunity to ask every sort of question, almost anyone can learn some of anything), there is our wish to dwell on beginnings because they are also foundations, and we want students to be well-founded in their thinking. So we look for learning matter that is simple, elegant, and fraught with consequence. Our classes, while disciplined occasions for detailed learning, are always ready to burst into philosophic flame, to raise questions of the deepest and most naive sort. For example, a class in the freshman geometry sequence may suddenly be wondering in what sense a geometric figure is transportable and can be made to "coincide" with another, how timeless geometry seems to require a sort of matterless motion.

What I have just described is readily recognizable as related to the traditional quadrivium, the arts by which products of reason are applied to the world of nature. The trivium, which consists of the complementary arts of thinking itself and its expression, is exercised through the study of two languages. They happen to be Greek and French, but as six decades of debate show, they could be Latin and German or any other two languages—such curricular discussions always supply reasons not only why the subjects chosen are best but also why something similar is good in another way. These languages are not, however, studied with any expectation of real competence (which some students nevertheless achieve), but in order that students have the wherewithal to reflect on their own language and on language simply, on how thoughts become sounds, how words catch things, how sentences are grammatically structured, how grammar cooperates with or diverges from logic, how the same thing can or cannot be said in two languages (we do a lot of translating), how speech becomes persuasive or beguiling, and how a poem may both mean and be.

Our students also sing together and later study the elements of music so as to be able to make sense of a score, and to treat a composition, such as the *St. Matthew Passion* or *Don Giovanni*, as a work on which the liberal arts may be brought to bear. But the main object here is to consider how the passions can be brought into play by high artifice.

All these arts are, however, plied mainly in aid of the central activity, the reading of the chosen texts and their discussion in the seminar. Difficult philosophic works are read. In the junior year, for example, our students study Descartes, who founded the method of devising methods that captured learning and is now central to modern practice. Also read for the seminar are the long novels that students labor through and never forget, such as *Don Quixote, War and Peace,* and *Middlemarch.*

The way of the seminar is simple and direct. There are two tutors to prevent the students from directing their contributions to an authoritative teacher figure. On alternate seminar nights (seminars happen at night because that is when young people talk) each tutor asks an opening question. It is an art to devise a good question—not a "teacher's question," that parody of our most human activity where the answer is all too well known to the inquisitor, nor a dogma with a question mark, but the catalyst of an inquiry. It is an everlasting subject of tutors'

conversation whether such a question requires some prior interpretation; it certainly requires engaged reading. Once started,
the seminar conversation can blow where it will. The tutors'
function is to restrain the overexuberant, encourage the shy,
maintain civility and responsiveness, and, above all, make people
explain themselves. Tutors can enter their own opinions, which
carry the weight only of their persuasive rationality. Thus the
seminar is the most egalitarian of grounds, where even the
greatest—or most sacred—of books is confronted with respect-
ful directness. To me the "great books seminar" is the incarna-
tion of liberal teaching and learning. It goes without saying that
under this dispensation both the books and tutors get almost
more than their just share of trust, and sometimes love, from the
students.

THE PLACE OF LIBERAL EDUCATION

The sort of education articulated here requires an actual place.
Neither the inter-institutional community of scholars nor "distance learning," to name two examples of placelessness in
higher education, have much to do with it. It requires conversation, human beings face to face with each other, a condition
that neither typed words nor even transmitted images can
reproduce. It requires presence (though to explain why that is
so would demand a metaphysical inquiry into the difference
between reality and virtuality). Liberal education needs classrooms, quads, and coffeeshops, all the appurtenances of a concrete community of learning. It needs residences where students, especially freshmen, may learn the ways of close conver-
sational friendship (no matter what less-approved ways they
will also learn). It needs smallness, so that people may run into
each other often for spontaneous conversation. One mark of a
liberal school is that its members carry the life of the intellect
into casual encounters without the least shame, so that a student might run up to a teacher with any question ranging from
puzzlement about some technicality in Ptolemy's epicyclic theory
to a demand to know the reason why some fellow students, who
pretend to have read the same books that this student has taken
to heart, act so irrationally. Or a tutor at the lunch table may

ask another who "they" might be "that have pow'r to hurt and will do none"—and soon there will be five tutors and a discussion in full spate.

All these conditions, or similar ones, are most likely to obtain at a small American residential college. To be sure, not all colleges are liberal arts colleges, and not all liberal arts colleges have preserved the purity of their designation. Some have been pushed by financial exigency into losing what I consider the defining features of liberal education: its nonvocational, nonpreparatory, nonutilitarian aim and its contemplatively leisured, expansively communal mode. As Aristotle turned out to be right in supposing that liberal education has a special subject matter—namely, objects inherently worthy of contemplation—so, it follows, he is right in saying that such an education cannot be narrowly tailored as a means to a practical end. The liberal arts colleges, which have a good deal of residual independence and, moreover, an old tradition of liberality, are still the last best hope for such an education. The university colleges offer, to be sure, somewhat similar conditions, but they are continually under pressure from the containing giant on whose revenues they depend and from whom come the bright ideas that galvanize liberal arts programs with spasms that turn out to be death throes.

There is something very remarkable about the American college. It belongs not only historically but in its conception to those many all-American institutions that are mundanely marginal but spiritually central to American life. Americans appear publicly devoted to the pursuit of material happiness, but as every sympathetic observer of the scene knows, they are, perhaps preeminently among humankind, filled with private longings of a nonmaterial sort. That is why I emphasized the importance of rhetoric in the beginning: If some colleges stated boldly and specifically their nonvocational aims, making it clear that their education, however structured, is an end in itself that happens incidentally to be practically useful, that their pedagogy works by indirection, that their tempo is leisurely, their means bookish, their mood contemplative, they would attract some fierce denigration but also, I am persuaded, far more outspoken support from the American public. It is a risky choice, but the situation borders on the perilous.

The very modesty of means at all but the most prestigious private colleges is an advantage in the restoration of liberal education. Two elements that are truly deleterious to a community of learning are out of the question for them. One is star professors with astronomical salaries, who disrupt collegiality and at least on occasion display the intellectual vice of vices, the notion that they know something. The other is selectivity. By one of those lucky dispensations that turns disadvantages into opportunities, most small colleges only make a brave show of being selective. In fact, they take whoever wants to come, and since this sort of education is always relatively expensive, their applicants do, by and large, want to come to this particular school. But that is just the way it ought to be. The aforementioned "best and brightest" by the normal criteria of admission are not invariably the most thoughtful and the most teachable. Small colleges are afflicted with an unfortunate *de facto* exclusivity because they are expensive; they should not add to that a harmful *de intentione* selectivity. If the matter and the teaching are in tune with the meaning of liberal education, almost anyone who wants to learn will be a profitable member of the community of learning. In fact, it is a test of a good school that its students rise not only above all the standard indices but even above all expectations; selectivity is, conversely, a blatant admission of pedagogic inability. For liberal learning, desire is the chief index of capability. Consequently, informed self-selection is a better criterion for admission than testable scholastic aptitude.

I have one final observation concerning the relevance of liberal education, which tends to be temporally cosmopolitan, to the local conditions of modernity and its afterbirth, postmodernity. Are the liberal arts colleges, as we sometimes hear, little islands of decorative antiquarianism or, worse, of traditions that enshrine superseded dominances? This kind of questioning does not come from the public so much as from opponents within the academy, and more often from the universities than from the colleges. To me the following answer seems sufficient: There is general agreement that democracy and technology are two, perhaps *the* two, phenomena that dominate our lives, and increasingly those of the whole globe, for better or worse. They have their deep roots in the Western tradition and in the very books and arts that together constitute a liberal education. Since the recovery of roots—racial, familial, religious—is a current preoccupation, the digging up (desedimentation is the technical word) of these beginnings should be congenial to consciously contemporary scholars. This recovery has nothing to do with nostalgic antiquarianism, which is the love of the past insofar as it is bygone. On the contrary, it yields "effective history," the past as it is present—the source of much of the matter particularly germane to liberal learning.

Thus, whether the enterprise is congenial or not, and whether your taste is for critique rather than appreciation or for deconstruction rather than reception, what our students surely need is to learn in some detail and with a minimum of ideological static how they came by the opinions they bring along, so that they may be able to choose whether to hold on to them or to change them. But even the possession of well-examined opinions is secondary to the sheer love of learning engendered by something that is of self-revealing intrinsic worth. That is the liberal learning for which college is the time and the place.

ENDNOTES

[1]Rev. 3:16.

[2]Aristotle *Politics* 1337b.

[3]Nietzsche, *The Use and Abuse of History*, VIII (Indianapolis: Bobbs-Merrill, 1957), 51.

[4]Mark Neustadt of Neustadt Creative Marketing.

[5]Plato *Apology* 21b ff.

It has become the fashion to level the charge of Eurocentricity at the West for ignoring our debt to the achievements of other civilizations. Yet while fully acknowledging this debt, we must still ask why the West, after the end of the Middle Ages, so rapidly overtook the great civilizations of the East.

In the venerable civilizations of the East, custom was king and tradition the guiding principle. If change came it was all but imperceptible, for the laws of Heaven existed once and for all and were not to be questioned. That spirit of questioning, the systematic rejection of authority, was the one invention the East may have failed to develop. It originated in ancient Greece. However often authority tried to smother this inconvenient element, its spark was glowing underground. It was that spark, perhaps, that was fanned into flame by the awareness that our ancestors did not have the monopoly of wisdom, and that we may learn to know more than they have if only we do not accept their word unquestioned. As the motto of the Royal Society (dating from 1663) has it, *Nullius in verba*—By nobody's word.

—E. H. Gombrich
"Eastern Inventions and
Western Response"

from *Dædalus*, Winter 1998
"Science in Culture"

Richard H. Hersh

Generating Ideals and Transforming Lives: A Contemporary Case for the Residential Liberal Arts College

I N THE FOREWORD TO THIS VOLUME, Steven Koblik states that residential liberal arts colleges "remain the best models of undergraduate education in the country." Can a case be made to support such an audacious claim? I believe so, if the ends of education—"consciousness" as meaning making, and satisfying the innate human need for coherence—are properly perceived. If ours is a "culture of neglect," as I believe, then that must have a corrosive effect on our youth, which a liberal education can help alleviate if the ends and means inherent in such an education are correctly interpreted. Too many of the country's influential publics yearn only for a "practical" and "professional" education, imagining that this is the opposite of a liberal education. As I believe this essay will show, they are mistaken.

EDUCATIONAL INCOHERENCE: ELIZA'S LAMENT

Helping young people make sense of the world has always been problematic. Each generation worries about facing an uncertain future, and struggles to construct meaning in what is perceived as a complex and ambiguous world heretofore unknown to previous generations. The current generation of stu-

Richard H. Hersh is President of Hobart and William Smith Colleges in Geneva, New York.

173

dents is no exception to this phenomenon. American society feels as if it has become a free-for-all, a social lottery with no security, not even from a lifetime of merit. Technological, economic, and social changes of the last thirty years have rendered the psychic landscape seemingly unstable.

But this is not new. At the turn of the nineteenth century, an adolescent lamented:

> I left school with a head full of something tumbled in without order or connection. I returned home with a determination to put it in more order. But I soon lost all patience, for the greater part of my ideas I was obliged to throw away without knowing where I got them or what I should do with them.
> —Eliza Southgate to Moses Porter, 1801[1]

Eliza Southgate could sense coherence even if she had not experienced it. Sent to a fashionable Boston school at the age of thirteen, she had learned a little of this and a little of that, much as secondary students and undergraduates in many colleges and universities do today. She was hungry for learning and perceptive enough to know what she had missed. She lamented the disorder as well as the shallowness of her education. She wanted to know whence came the sentiments she had been taught, how they related to each other, and what to do with them.

There is a deeper concern in Eliza Southgate's letter. She was convinced her society had not asked enough of her. Her cousin, Moses Porter, had provoked her by arguing that as a woman she did not really need the kind of education she was seeking. "Do you suppose the mind of woman the only work of God that was 'made in vain'?" she answered. "The cultivation of the powers we possess, I have ever thought a privilege (or I may say duty) that belonged to the human species."[2]

Her lament is instructive. She articulates poignantly the idea that the essence of our humanity is to discover and construct meaning in our lives, to make connections among the "something tumbled in without order." Like us, at the turn of another century, she wanted to understand the connection between where knowledge came from and where it might lead her. For Eliza, the purpose of an education was the "cultivation of the powers we possess."

The quest to make sense of our past, present, and future, especially during times of rapid and substantial change, has been important throughout history. In considering the upheaval of the Industrial Revolution, for example, Matthew Arnold admonished that "not a having and a resting, but a growing and a becoming is the character of perfection."[3] On the other hand, American higher education after World War II was a model perhaps best suited to "a having and a resting." For an America at the height of its well-earned and dearly bought influences, sustaining the status quo was the ultimate task. Teaching was conceived essentially as transmitting general knowledge and received wisdom to succeeding generations of students. As the multi-universities grew, they were, in those early years, the direct spawn of the traditional liberal arts campuses; their commitment to the same core curriculum was a way of demonstrating that they could be as good as their predecessors yet also deliver economies of scale.

But the sixties brought a new mood. The larger institutions, both public and private, dependent on state funding and massive alumni support, were forced to make an accommodation: they enlarged their support base by raising enrollments, with a promise of no loss of quality. The reverberations of this decision toward economies of scale, relaxed admissions, and rising prices have exacerbated the trends towards an increasingly less effective education system.

It is perfectly understandable that prospective students and parents should want the maximum return on their educational investment. In an economy with no long-term job security, parents impart to their children the same sort of anxieties as did survivors of the depression two generations ago. At the same time, a seductive myth prevails that large public universities are not only less expensive but, considering the price of private education, more cost-effective, offering an opportunity for large-scale networking and institutional name recognition.[4] And it is also unsurprising that the homogenizing tendencies of our mass-market culture should affect popular attitudes toward higher education—the best schools must be those that most resemble a "learning mall." Few parents or students see through the false advertising and unquestioned assumptions lurking in the pages of university catalogs: the priority of research, the prevalence of graduate students teaching the sections of high-salaried star professors too busy doing research to bother with the students who were lured by their fame.

This state of affairs is increasingly being questioned. Parents are showing growing signs of hesitancy at the idea of sending their children to campuses of twenty thousand students, where they live in dormitory towers redolent of public housing, hear lectures in cavernous halls with the assistance of a television monitor, and sign their exams with a Social Security number. It is unsatisfying and, moreover, inefficient: fewer than 50 percent of those students in such institutions ultimately graduate.[5] The point has been underscored by the report of the Boyer Commission on Educating Undergraduates, *Reinventing Undergraduate Education: A Blueprint for America's Research Universities,* which recently concluded that what most large research universities promise is not delivered.

> An undergraduate at an American research university can receive an education as good or better than anything available anywhere in the world, but that is not the normative experience. Again and again, universities are guilty of an advertising practice they would condemn in the commercial world. Recruitment materials display proudly the world-famous professors, the splendid facilities and the ground-breaking research that goes on within them, but thousands of students graduate without ever seeing the world-famous professors or tasting genuine research.[6]

The report goes on to echo Eliza's lament:

> Many students graduate having accumulated whatever number of courses is required, but still lacking a coherent body of knowledge or any inkling as to how one sort of information might relate to others. And all too often they graduate without knowing how to think logically, write clearly, or speak coherently. The university has given them too little that will be of real value beyond a credential that will help them get their first jobs. And with larger and larger numbers of their peers holding the same paper in their hands, even that credential has lost much of its potency.[7]

There are countless thousands of modern-day Eliza Southgates, graduating from colleges and universities with profound feel-

ings of incoherence, of heads "full of something tumbled in
without order or connection," ideas that they are "obliged to
throw away without knowing where (they) got them or what
(they) should do with them." This condition exists in part
because the academy, most often but not exclusively in large
universities, has poorly understood the complex nature of teaching
and learning required to truly unleash the human "powers we
possess," to use Eliza's phrase, and the necessity of coherence
in both the ends and means of a liberating education.

Acknowledging the ineffectiveness of higher education today, many recommend panaceas, the most alluring of which is
the use of technology. Indeed, we are now confronted with the
notion of "virtual universities," premised on the use of technology to transcend place and person-to-person interaction. The
University of Phoenix and its ilk are quite real, if "real" is an
appropriate notion in this context. And while most colleges
need some of what modern technology offers, it is not so true
that what technology can offer has anything that approaches
the transformative power of a genuine liberal arts education.

A CULTURE OF NEGLECT

At the close of the so-called American Century, the moral
fabric of American society is fraying from the strains of identity
politics, the celebration of victim-status, the attenuation of
community bonds, the dissolution of family structure, and the
economic pressures that make financial stability elusive. All
loyalties seem to be negotiable. Economies of scale, mass-
marketing, and technology have created a centrifugal culture
with a decreasing sense of history, community, and stability, in
flight from personal responsibility, addicted to speed, and easily
distracted.

Our culture has produced a generation of quite fragile students who come to college unsure of who they are, fearful in
their lack of identity, and without confidence in the future.
Many are ashamed of themselves and afraid of relationships,
which is too often manifested in the use and abuse of alcohol
and other drugs. This diminished sense of self has caused an
increase in acts of racism, sexism, assault, date rape, attempted

suicide, eating disorders, theft, property damage, and cheating on most campuses.[8] In a recent national study of college students, Arthur Levine, president of Teachers College, Columbia University, concluded,

> The bottom line is that students are coming to college overwhelmed and more damaged than those of previous years. Six out of ten chief student affairs officers (60 percent) reported that undergraduates are using psychological counseling services in record numbers and for longer periods of time than in the past; this is true at 69 percent of four-year schools and 52 percent of two-year colleges. Eating disorders are up at 58 percent of the institutions surveyed. Classroom disruption increased at a startling 44 percent of colleges, drug abuse at 42 percent, alcohol abuse at 35 percent of campuses. Gambling has grown at 25 percent of the institutions, and suicide attempts have risen at 23 percent.[9]

This cannot be explained as an "underclass" problem; it is found on our most privileged campuses, large and small, public and private, professional and vocational. It is happening because the generation now entering college has experienced few authentic connections with adults. This is the manifestation of what I call a "culture of neglect," and we—parents, teachers, professors, and administrators—are among its architects.

It begins at home, where social and economic factors such as declining wages and stagnating incomes require longer work hours and result in less family time. Young people have been allowed to or must take part-time jobs rather than spend time in school, on homework, or with their families. More children and adolescents are being reared in problematic family situations, with television and peers as their companions.

> Again and again, deans of students reported on the growing rate of dysfunctional families among their students. They talked of violence; instability; blended families; and emotional, sexual, and financial problems. As one dean put it, "It's hard to send a student home, when home is the problem."[10]

All along the line leading from kindergarten to matriculation, we have failed to teach an ethic of concern and to model a culture of responsibility. We have created a culture characterized by dysfunctional families, mass schooling that demands only minimal efforts, and media idols subliminally teaching disrespect for authority and wisdom.

Like most college presidents I receive angry letters and phone calls from parents demanding an acknowledgment of their child's victimization. One parent wanted to know how it was possible that her son had received an F. Another insisted that with such high tuition it was somehow the college's responsibility to provide a lawyer for students when they are arrested by city police after presenting false identification. On an admissions tour, a parent left the campus angrily upon learning that we did not provide cable-television hookups in residence halls. This is consumerism writ large; not surprisingly, we see these same attitudes in our students. As Mark Edmondson, a professor at the University of Virginia, recently observed,

> For someone growing up in America now, there are few available alternatives to the cool consumer worldview. My students didn't ask for that view, much less create it, but they bring a consumer weltanschauung to school, where it exerts a powerful, and largely unacknowledged, influence.[11]

Levine describes the same phenomenon.

> [Students] want easy, accessible parking, . . . no lines, and a polite, helpful, and efficient staff. They want high-quality education at a low cost. For the most part, they are willing to comparison shop, placing a premium on time and money. . . . Their focus is on convenience, quality, service, and cost. They believe that since they are paying for their education, faculty should give them the education they want, and they make larger demands on faculty than students in the past ever have.[12]

Colleges and universities, however, must accept some responsibility for the culture of neglect. We have succumbed to lower standards by believing we must cater to our student-consumers. Faculty members and administrators have lowered their expectations, resulting in grade inflation. The intellectual demands that are placed on students are less than students need or are capable of handling. And those who graduate are increasingly seen by employers as having learned too little.

Is it possible that in one generation America could have changed from a nation that held to its beliefs despite all pains and costs until the world was free to one that has no core beliefs besides buy low and sell high? Indeed it is possible, in large part because, along with families, the impersonal mass schooling that has largely replaced elementary, secondary, and higher education in America may be failing to impart the core human values necessary to turn the tide. A nation of individuals who cannot read or write well, with no sense of the major human questions, who cannot think critically or show interest in learning, and who are unable to act responsibly in a diverse democratic society will be ill-equipped to compete in any new world order. A culture of neglect asks very little; a culture of responsibility demands more but holds the promise of far greater rewards.

THE ENDS AND MEANS FOR A
TWENTY-FIRST CENTURY EDUCATION

We have created our own educational crisis; yet we cannot thrive without a creative, healthy, socially cohesive, educated, and hopeful citizenship. The solution is not only in the miraculously reified-by-decree nostalgia of "back to the basics" (although that is necessary) so popular among politicians but in current concerns about families, schooling, and higher education. In a sense, America has to take up the task of redefining itself as a unified polity, which cannot be achieved by the mere transmission of data and factual knowledge. It can only be done by having leaders who can and will grapple with ideas and cope with intellectual challenges—who can approach problems not only creatively but by enlarging the scope of their analytic embrace, which is comprehension in its truest sense.

Most of higher education advocates these same ends. Yet a dependence on graduate students as teachers, technology used as surrogate professors, large classes, and massed housing—none provide the appropriate educational environment in which to accomplish these ends.[13] As the research below suggests, the residential liberal arts college, by virtue of its small size, residential nature, and linkage of educational ends and means, promotes student participation in the ongoing civic life of its community. When it comes to creating the optimum educational environment in which to produce the profoundly liberating education required to redress our larger cultural conditions, not to mention the requirements of future employment and democratic civic engagement, liberal arts colleges emerge clearly as the model to embrace.

It is an evasion of adult responsibility to believe that undergraduates are anything more than physically mature. Most are in an elastic, formative stage of development. They need an education that is personalized as well as demanding, coherent, and mentored. It is a human-intensive calling, not a job for televisions, central processing units, and modems. It is extremely difficult for large universities to sustain the community dialogue necessary for liberal learning at the undergraduate level, although it is interesting to note that a number of such institutions are creating liberal arts colleges within their own larger campuses in the hope of replicating the conditions required for a transformative education. Why? Because residential liberal arts colleges are dedicated to working closely with individual students and, simultaneously, to building community. They are places that understand Emerson's admonition that "the ends preexist in the means." They recognize the need for small classes, professors who teach and form genuine relationships with students, and a campus community that demands active participation of its citizens as a condition of one's education.

With the focus solely on undergraduates, it is the faculty and administration of liberal arts colleges who understand the developmental process and the need for an environment that encourages students; that helps them develop a secure sense of their own voices; that gives them the courage to exhibit humility in seeking wisdom from others; that generates a class of citizens who hold themselves accountable for and take pride in being articulate in their writing, speaking, and social behavior; that teaches students to care about others even more as they learn to value the meaning of being themselves. Such an education requires the use of human faculties: imagination, judgment, compassion, abstract reasoning. These form the substrate of ethical and emotional intelligence on which powerful reasoning must rest. We know from research and experience that these develop best in conditions of active intellectual, social, and emotional engagement with demanding and caring mentors and with the constructive power of a peer group that shares equally in such a commitment.

Most colleges and universities promise students and parents that the students who graduate from their institutions will not only be more fit to survive in the next century but will be more fully human. This is a promise of an education that is not so much a transition as it is a dimensional transformation. Yet, as the research shows, the sort of mind that can master a technological world's challenges is one that is handcrafted, developed in an authentic, daily apprenticeship of faculty and student— small classes, tutorials, independent study and/or research with a professor, and out-of-class contact with professors.

RESEARCH SUPPORT FOR RESIDENTIAL LIBERAL ARTS COLLEGES

The best education takes place at the nexus of profound intellectual and social/emotional development. Yet most colleges and universities dichotomize the various facets of learning, as if our intellectual, emotional, and ethical lives were compartmentalized. This paradigm of compartmentalized learning is extended to "life" on most campuses—faculty take care of the intellect, student-services staff and coaches handle the rest. What goes on inside the classroom is thought of as separate and different from what takes place outside. One of higher education's fundamental tasks, and the modus operandi of liberal arts colleges, is to undo such false dichotomies and foster a more global or holistic version of education. "Higher" learning, the type expected to occur in colleges and universities, is not simply learning poured or programmed into the brain. Imaginative and creative problem solving, analysis and synthesis of data, collaborative decision making, creative or persuasive writing or speaking, moral judgment—each requires what cognitive psychologists and neuroscientists refer to as "constructed learning." The professor's primary role is therefore not simply to offer information in the traditional lecture mode but to provide a stimulating environment in which students actively engage in the construction of knowledge, alone and with others, in class and out.

What conditions are optimal for the kind of intellectual and psychosocial outcomes embedded in the concept of a "liberal education"? The research consistently points to several variables, the most fundamental of which is the quantity and quality of student effort and involvement. Pascarella and Terenzini affirm this in their comprehensive study *How College Affects Students*:

> One of the most inescapable and unequivocal conclusions we can make is that the impact of college is largely determined by the individual's quality of effort and level of involvement in both academic and nonacademic activities.[14]

But how best to optimize student effort and involvement? They do not occur by chance but are heavily influenced by the size of institutions, the nature of their residential arrangements, the faculty's commitment to students, and the amount of student-student and student-faculty interaction. It is on a small campus, with its sense of community and peer identity created by shared residence and a faculty committed to engaging students in and out of class, that the most profound positive effects on student effort and achievement occur.

While student involvement and effort are greatly influenced by the size and nature of the peer group interaction, it is important to emphasize that the faculty plays a major role. They determine the educational objectives and the structuring of student effort by virtue of their expectations, standards, commitment to teaching, and a pedagogy that purposefully engages students in and out of class. As Pascarella and Terenzini note,

> the research makes clear the important influence faculty members have on student changes in virtually all areas. There can be little doubt about the need for faculty members' acceptance of their roles and responsibilities for student learning and for their active involvement in students' lives.[15]

No single variable alone guarantees a liberating education. Whether a college or university is private or public, well endowed or not, urban or rural, is of little consequence by itself. Ultimately it is the college's culture and ethos that undergird all else. The research points to a cluster of attributes that, in their cumulative and synergetic effects, creates an institutional ethos that increases the probability of significant student cognitive and socioemotional development, retention, and satisfaction. These attributes influence and in reciprocal fashion are influenced by students and faculty:[16]

- *High expectations and standards.* The higher the expectations and standards held by professors and the institution, the greater the learning.
- *Emphasis on high academic engaged time.* The more time devoted to a learning task (if the task is at the appropriate level of difficulty), the greater the learning.
- *Frequent assessment and prompt feedback.* Learning is increased when one is assessed at frequent intervals and feedback is promptly provided. Assessment might take the form of short quizzes, oral questions in class, short or long papers, or comprehensive exams. Feedback may come from professors and/or one's peers.
- *Active student engagement.* Effective learning occurs best when students move out of a purely receptive learning mode and into one in which they actively operate in and on the environment. Classroom discussion, individual or group projects, laboratory work, significant reading and writing, research projects, tutoring and teaching others—all require active learning.
- *Frequency of faculty contact, in and out of class.* Student-faculty interaction increases academic achievement. Such interactions increase the probability of student risk-taking, useful feedback from the professor, greater clarity of the learning objectives, and a greater sense of student connection to the institution. The greater the faculty-student contact the greater sense of intellectual and personal development reported by students.
- *Collaborative learning.* Working in student teams, peer tutoring, and student study groups outside class enhance problem solving and communication skills, provide immediate assessment and feedback, and promote respect for different perspectives. Such teamwork is also active practice for future postcollege employment.

- *Residential campus.* Living on campus maximizes the potential for academic, social, and cultural involvement. The greater the connections to the institution through involvement with faculty and other students, the greater will be student retention and satisfaction.
- *Individualized learning.* Learning is enhanced when the institution and faculty respect the individualized needs of each student. Students enter college with different backgrounds, interests, and competencies, and the degree to which the institution respects such differences is the degree to which student success is enhanced.
- *Emphasis on active learning and connection to the institution during the first two years of college.* Finding one's academic and social place on a campus is crucial to ultimate college success, and institutions that help students make these connections early and often promote student success. Crucial in this task is what is called "psychological size"—the sense a student has that a college feels small enough to venture forth in making friends, faculty connections, and engage in social and cultural activities.

It is in residential liberal arts colleges that one finds these attributes most often in optimum combination. As Chickering and Gamson contend, "The selective private liberal arts college, perhaps more than any other type of American higher education institution, exemplifies much of what has come to be known as 'best' educational practice in undergraduate education."[17]

Research, experience, and wisdom converge. No matter how one asks the question, it is close working relations between students with faculty and other students, high expectations, and sustained student effort and time that make a difference. This does not happen by chance; it occurs when an institution sets out to create such conditions. It is in the residential liberal arts college that we find these conditions, that optimal mix of human ends and means conducive to a transforming and liberating education. Such a transforming process is a rare and precious gift. P. F. Kluge, in his reminiscence *Alma Mater*, quotes Ron Sharp, professor of English at Kenyon College:

> I have this romantic idea of teaching as gift exchanges. What matters is if I reach a few students at a level that transforms them and gets them to see the world in a different way. Gift exchange. Sure, teaching is method and information, but it is something else, a gift, an enrichment of your life, a transformation that you can spend the rest of your life discovering.[18]

Surely this is the best "gift" that money can buy: small classes, faculty dedicated to students, and a small residential campus community that nurtures intellectual and emotional development. Such growth is in turn crucial to the development of moral character as well.

While all of higher education espouses as one of its ends the moral development of its students, embedded in the ethos of a small college dedicated to forming a community among a diverse group of students and faculty is a commitment to such moral values as justice, mutual understanding, civility, honesty, trust, and respect for others. This ethical dimension helps bind together the ends and means of such an educational enterprise, crucial because the ethical underpinnings of character development are inextricably a part of a liberal arts education. Not only are the great moral questions debated in the classroom, they are discussed in the residence halls, cafes, and locker rooms as well.

The development of one's moral sense involves intellectual, emotional, and spiritual growth, each fueled in interaction with one's peers, faculty, family, and others. Moreover, it includes how one ultimately behaves—what one actually does when confronted by a moral dilemma. Here the classroom lessons of history, sociology, philosophy, literature, economics, and biology, for example, converge with the influences of peers, mentors, and the moral atmosphere (or lack thereof) of the community in which one is expected to participate fully. It is thus that the civic virtues taught and learned in a liberal arts college are connected in moral consequence. Harry Payne, president of Williams College, eloquently makes this point:

> So, too, when one works to create an effective residential community among a diverse group of students, one also works to nurture such virtues as mutual understanding, civility, and cooperation. Moral education is embedded in the definition of what we have always been committed to do.[19]

LIBERAL ARTS AS PRACTICAL EDUCATION?

A transforming liberal education is not currently understood by the public to be a necessity for life in the twenty-first century. Rather, the sense is that education must be practical; its mantra, "Get a job!" Thus each spring, more than one million high-school students, shouldering the anxious hopes of their parents and the larger culture, choose a college that will give them a "practical" education. Roughly four years later they test their assumptions, as well as those of their parents, about the practicality of that education in the job market.

The inherent value of a liberal education notwithstanding, the vast majority of college students enroll not in liberal arts programs but in degree programs, whose chief purpose is to land them their first job. The reasons for this are clear. Pragmatism and rationality have gained a firm grip on America's psyche. Driven by sober economic thinking, Americans are applying cost-benefit analysis to all decisions and are focusing on the bottom line, examining all expenditures in terms of "What do I get?" or "What is the payoff?"

In a review of public opinion surveys, researchers John Immerwahr and James Harvey found a consistent public belief that higher education was a necessity for employment, and that a liberal arts education was irrelevant to this purpose. "If I'm going to be an accountant," one survey respondent said, "what do I care what someone did back in ancient Egypt?"[20] But if the results of a recent national survey are any indicator, employers sharply disagree with this attitude and the fixation on a "practical" education.[21]

The survey, while verifying earlier findings that parents and college-bound students focus on the short-term value of "getting a job," surprisingly found that business leaders and liberal arts college graduates more often look to the long-term benefits of a college education. The divergence of views between parents and corporate executives is worth noting. Specifically, the survey found that an overwhelming majority of parents (75 percent) and college-bound students (85 percent) believe that the ultimate goal of college is to get a practical education and secure a first job. But only about one third (37 percent) of business leaders agree with this belief. CEOs value the long-term outcomes of a college education—those that prepare one not only for a first job but for a long and variable career.

Choosing an appropriate college or university is a serious and pragmatic decision for families. Financial considerations, preconceptions about colleges and universities, and perceptions of what employers want often point families in the direction of what they perceive to be sure-ticket schools that bestow prestige and, by implication, sure employment. One parent stated plainly, "We live in an environment that can destroy you if you are not practical." The smart choice, some say, is a professional program tailored to specific jobs in business, computer technology, engineering, law, or medicine.

Employers, represented in the study by CEOs and human resource managers, presumably are every bit as "practical" as parents. But to them, practicality means the ability of higher education to impart general skills that give people the flexibility and capacity to keep on learning what today's high-tech businesses require. Business leaders say that improving the bottom line calls for a competitive edge, and increasingly they view their human resources as a key to improved competitiveness. They insist that a college education produce people of strong character with generalized intellectual and social skills and a capacity for lifelong learning.

CEOs and human resource managers in the survey consistently asked for three clusters of skills: cognitive, presentational, and social. Cognitive skills include problem solving, critical thinking, and "learning to learn." The ability to move up each new learning curve rapidly in response to new challenges, the ability to see things in a new light and make sense of ideas in new contexts, and an intellectual agility and playfulness are desired. Presentational skills include oral and written communication about oneself, ideas, and data, in a coherent, clear, persuasive, and articulate manner. The ability to communicate, to make sense of and present clearly what appears to others as information chaos across many disciplines is, they say, crucial if one is to advance in a career. Social skills include the ability to work with other people cooperatively in a variety of settings. Intercultural understanding, as well as the ability to work with people regardless of race, gender, and age, is important. International experience and foreign language facility are considered very desirable.

These are the "well rounded" and "practical" skills business executives want and for which in the study they cited a liberal arts education as the best "practical" preparation. Parents, however, reject what they perceive to be those charming ivory-tower liberal arts colleges (and their counterparts within large universities) that profess to turn out "well-rounded" graduates. To parents, looking through the lens of our culture's mass-consumer orientation, "practicality" means getting a college degree as quickly, efficiently, and as cheaply as possible. Ironically, the very global conditions seeming to fuel such parental concerns are understood quite differently by corporate leaders. To them "practical" means liberally educated.

There is evidence to suggest that the corporate leaders are right, as reflected in a decade of social trends regarding the nature of the future workplace, our culture's preoccupation with value, the quest for a higher quality of life, and the movement away from a focus on the self.[22] Business has grown more international, more competitive, and more susceptible to technology-driven change. In such a climate, rigid specialists limited to one specific skill are quickly left behind. In the workplace of the future, graduates must be capable of independent thought, creativity, risk taking, perseverance, and entrepreneurship as well as open to new ideas and willing to express unpopular points of view. They must be comfortable with different cultures and possess foreign language aptitude.

The past decade has witnessed a national obsession with securing value and making every nickel count in tangible ways. This helps to explain parents' and students' emphasis on getting a job. But employers, too, are preoccupied with value, and they see a college education as a necessary and valuable long-term investment that enhances one's imagination, communication skills, values, and ethics—all attributes for a productive career, not to mention a lifetime. Simultaneously, Americans are turning away from material expressions of success toward a definition that emphasizes achievement of a better quality of life—less stress; better health; a safe, clean, living environment; and the appreciation of art and culture. The notion of a "well-rounded" person is making a comeback. Interestingly, this is an outcome most parents and employers identify as a unique purpose of a liberal arts education. Finally, the sharp focus on the self that has fed hedonism, moral relativity, and overpersonalization is beginning to blur. Concern for the community, more attention to spiritual life, a greater focus on concepts of right and wrong, a search for meaning in life, and a hunger for idealism are all on the rise. These are identified by parents, students, and employers as outcomes most associated with the liberal arts.

Such trends point to a possible narrowing of the "practicality gap." The culture is beginning to value liberal education outcomes. Simultaneously, liberal arts colleges have been redefining their sense of practicality as well, placing increasing emphasis on internships, international education, higher writing and speaking standards, foreign language skills, and computer literacy. Colleges also understand that it is not business alone that drives the need for such change. Graduate schools, non-profit agencies, and state and federal governments are all searching for people who are passionate of spirit, independent yet team players, less preoccupied with their own self-expressiveness, and capable of coping with a complex world. Given social and workplace changes, liberal arts colleges may be closer to what parents and prospective students desire in a "practical" education than they realize.

LIBERAL ARTS AS PROFESSIONAL EDUCATION

Lee Shulman, president of the Carnegie Foundation for the Advancement of Teaching, cogently makes the connection between liberal and professional education. The ends of professional education, suggests Shulman, center on: 1) an education for a moral purpose—service to others using knowledge and skills not readily available to those not so trained; 2) academy-based knowledge and practice; 3) knowledge that is not only theory-based but also field-tested in practical settings; 4) professional judgment—knowledge applied appropriately and ethically; 5) reflective practice in which one learns from experience and modifies theory, knowledge, and skills; and 6) membership in a professional community in which there are publicly shared standards, values, and knowledge.[23]

These lofty professional education attributes encompass the very essence of a liberal arts education and represent the best of what parents, students, employers, and our larger society value. Shulman delineates the conditions required for such professional education: students are engaged with professors, with each other, and with practitioners in the field (by reading, writing, arguing, diagnosing, problem solving, questioning, and student reflection informed by feedback from caring mentors); collaborative work is valued and required as a means of encountering others who represent a diversity of knowledge, skills, values, and perspectives; faculty and student passion and commitment are valued and nurtured; and finally, a genuine sense of community, the idea that we are all in this together and share both the joys and disappointments inherent in profound learning. These, Shulman suggests, are also the conditions best created in liberal arts colleges.[24]

In a world that is fragmented yet drawn ever closer together by technology, there is a need to better educate for the nourishment of the human spirit. The real bottom-line issue for parents, students, and our society is not whether today's undergraduate education is affordable but whether we can afford not to have it done well. The wish to have it on the cheap is understandable, but the defining quality of a college education is not something that lends itself to mass production. Indeed, the "savings" in cost on a large scale, if there is a savings at all, is reflected by a loss in real and lasting value. Our current higher education system, oriented toward mass education that breeds impersonal, passive, and incoherent learning, is not sufficient to the task. Higher education can and ought to be pivotal in the revitalization of our society and preparing students for the complex and international dimensions of the twenty-first century. The key to a stable and humane society is the education of citizens whose concern for justice, community, and democracy is at the moral center of life. In short, higher education's role is to generate ideals and transform lives.

Residential liberal arts colleges—by virtue of their primary focus on teaching, their small size, residential nature, quest for genuine community, engagement of students in active learning, concern for a general and coherent education, and emphasis on the development of the whole person—provide the most important kind of undergraduate education for the twenty-first century. Because of their exclusive focus on undergraduates and the priority given to a teaching faculty, residential liberal arts colleges have become the benchmark for undergraduate education. They are sui generis, themselves a special kind of pedagogy. They not only properly concern themselves with the appropriate ends of education—the skills, knowledge, and competencies derived from the study of the arts, humanities, social sciences, mathematics, and sciences—but so, too, the means, by creating authentic communities of learning that focus more clearly on *how* all such study coheres into templates of consciousness, of what it means to be fully human and humane, and what it means to be a good person and a good society.

In a world that is increasingly fragmented by fear of difference and specialization of knowledge, a world that has lost a sense of connection between the individual and community, and a world of "McUniversities" or learning malls catering to the whims of their customers, liberal arts colleges stand as a bastion of handcrafted education that best nurtures individual growth and the development of competence and confidence.

How, then, to convince society to embrace an educational model that now enrolls only 5 percent of this country's undergraduates? By making the case that a liberal arts college education offers people exactly what they claim they are seeking— the most professional and practical education possible. No invention is needed; America already has the patent.

ENDNOTES

[1]Nancy F. Cott, *Root of Bitterness: Documents of the Social History of American Women* (New York: E. P. Dutton & Co., 1972), 106.

[2]Ibid., 107.

[3]Matthew Arnold, *Culture and Anarchy* (New York: The Macmillan Company, 1911), 11.

[4]George Dehne, "A Look at the Future of the Private Colleges," *Trinity Magazine* (Summer 1995): 16–17.

[5]Thomas G. Mortenson, "Institutional Graduation Rates, 1983 to 1998," *Postsecondary Education Opportunity* (July 1998): 1.

[6]*Reinventing Undergraduate Education: A Blueprint for America's Research Universities* (New York: Carnegie Foundation for the Advancement of Teaching, 1998), 5.

[7]Ibid., 6.

[8]Arthur Levine and Jeanette S. Curetin, *When Hope and Fear Collide: A Portrait of Today's College Student* (San Francisco: Jossey-Bass, 1998), 95–96.

[9]Ibid., 95.

[10]Ibid.

[11]Mark Edmondson, "On the Uses of a Liberal Education," *Harper's Magazine* (September 1997): 40.

[12]Arthur Levine, "How the Academic Profession is Changing," *Dædalus* 126 (4) (Fall 1997): 7.

[13]*Reinventing Undergraduate Education,* 6.

[14]Ernest T. Pascarella and Patrick T. Terenzini, *How College Affects Students: Findings and Insights from Twenty Years of Research* (San Francisco: Jossey-Bass, 1991), 611.

[15]Ibid., 655.

[16]This list of critical attributes is a synthesis of research findings from the following sources: Ernest L. Boyer, *College: The Undergraduate Experiences in America* (New York: Harper & Row, 1980); Alexander W. Astin, *What Matters in College: Four Critical Years Revisited* (San Francisco: Jossey-Bass, 1993); Pascarella and Terenzini, *How College Affects Students*; Richard J. Light, *The Harvard Assessment Seminars: Explorations with Students and Faculty about Teaching, Learning, and Student Life* (Cambridge, Mass.: Harvard University Press, first report 1990; second report, 1992); Wilbert J. McKeachie et al., *Teaching and Learning in the College Classroom: A Review of the Research Literature* (Washington, D.C.: National Center for Research to Improve Postsecondary Teaching and Learning, 1988); George D. Kuh, "Ethos: Its Influence on Student Learning," *Liberal Education* (Fall 1993): 22–30; Education Commission of the States, *Making Quality Count in Undergraduate Education* (Denver: ECS, 1995); and Arthur W. Chickering and Zelda F. Gamson, eds., *Applying the Seven Principles for Good Practice in Undergraduate Education* (San Francisco: Jossey-Bass, 1991).

[17]Arthur W. Chickering and Zelda F. Gamson, "Seven Principles for Good Practice in Undergraduate Education," *The Wingspread Journal* (9) (June 1987): 2.

[18]P. F. Kluge, *Alma Mater* (Reading, Mass.: Addison-Wesley, 1993), 44.

[19]Harry C. Payne, "Can or Should A College Teach Virtue?" *Liberal Education* (Fall 1996): 2.

[20]John Immerwahr and James Harvey, "What the Public Thinks of College," *The Chronicle of Higher Education,* 12 May 1995, B1.

[21]Richard H. Hersh, "Intentions and Perceptions: A National Survey of Public Attitudes Toward Liberal Arts Education," *Change* (March/April 1997): 16–23.

[22]These trends are drawn from DYG SCAN, a trend-identification program developed by Daniel Yankelovich and used by his research firm DYG. Since 1986, SCAN has tracked attitudes on many values and issues directly relevant to the question of the status of liberal arts education. Used with permission of DYG, Inc.

[23]Lee S. Shulman, "Professing the Liberal Arts," *Education and Democracy: Reimagining Liberal Learning in America,* ed. Robert Orrill (New York: College Entrance Examination Board, 1997), 151–173.

[24]Ibid.

Thomas R. Cech

Science at Liberal Arts Colleges: A Better Education?

I T WAS THE SUMMER OF 1970. Carol and I had spent four years at Grinnell College, located in the somnolent farming community of Grinnell, Iowa. Now, newly married, we drove westward, where we would enter the graduate program in chemistry at the University of California, Berkeley. How would our liberal arts education serve us in the Ph.D. program of one of the world's great research universities? As we met our new classmates, one of our preconceptions quickly dissipated: Berkeley graduate students were not only university graduates. They also hailed from a diverse collection of colleges—many of them less known than Grinnell. And as we took our qualifying examinations and struggled with quantum mechanics problem sets, any residual apprehension about the quality of our undergraduate training evaporated. Through some combination of what our professors had taught us and our own hard work, we were well prepared for science at the research university level.

I have used this personal anecdote to draw the reader's interest, but not only to that end; it is also a "truth in advertising" disclaimer. I am a confessed enthusiast and supporter of the small, selective liberal arts colleges. My pulse quickens when I see students from Carleton, Haverford, and Williams who have applied to our Ph.D. program. I serve on the board of trustees of Grinnell College. On the other hand, I teach undergraduates both in the classroom and in my research laboratory at the University of Colorado, so I also have personal experience with science education at a research university.

Thomas R. Cech is Distinguished Professor of Chemistry and Biochemistry at the University of Colorado, Boulder, and an Investigator of the Howard Hughes Medical Institute.

195

Thus, recognizing that I may be too close to this subject to be completely unbiased, I have attempted to broaden my view in several ways. I have gathered statistics that quantify some aspects of the success of science education in liberal arts colleges versus research universities, although interpretation of these numbers is not unambiguous. I have also interviewed scientists who have achieved the highest levels of success in academia and government to obtain their perspective on the relative strengths and weaknesses of the preparation afforded by liberal arts colleges. I did so knowing that those interviewed had excelled in their profession, so one would expect them to be generally enthusiastic about the education that had preceded their success. Finally, I have sought the counsel of some of the country's best college science teacher-scholars, those who are truly immersed in the subject. Others who have analyzed the subject of science education at liberal arts colleges have independently come to similar conclusions, providing some confidence that this shared view must not be too far off the mark.[1]

The aim of this essay is to explore three questions regarding undergraduate science education. First, how successful are those graduating from liberal arts colleges compared to their contemporaries at large universities? This analysis is based on objective measures of success, including the percentage of graduates who go on to obtain Ph.D. degrees. Second, how does the education at liberal arts colleges compare with that encountered by undergraduates at large universities? Both classroom education and research experiences will be considered. Third, why are the top liberal arts colleges so successful in training successful scientists? Here we confront a vexing conundrum: are these colleges successful because they do a great job training students, or are the students who enter their programs already so highly selected that they are destined to be successful no matter what sort of education they receive?

HOW SUCCESSFUL ARE LIBERAL ARTS COLLEGES AT EDUCATING SCIENTISTS?

Before examining the question of what it is about liberal arts colleges that makes them so successful at training future scientists, it is useful to review the objective data that indicate that they are indeed successful. Only about 8 percent of students who attend four-year colleges or universities are enrolled in baccalaureate colleges (a category that includes national liberal arts colleges).[2] Among the students who obtain Ph.D.'s in science, 17 percent received their undergraduate degree at a baccalaureate college.[3] Thus, these colleges are about twice as productive as the average institution in training eventual Ph.D.'s. On the other hand, these same schools trained only 4 percent of the eventual Ph.D.'s in engineering, so their productivity is half the average in that field. This is unsurprising, as few liberal arts colleges have engineering programs.

A more detailed view is provided by considering students trained by the top national liberal arts colleges. The institutions listed alphabetically in table 1 are representative of the best in the United States. Examination of table 1 indicates that most of the nation's top colleges educated one to three hundred of the students who obtained Ph.D.'s during the five-year period from 1991–1995. These numbers put several of the liberal arts colleges in the top hundred of all institutions in Ph.D. production (see "Rank" in table 1). However, most of the institutions ranking in the top hundred are research universities with typical enrollments of twenty to thirty thousand students, whereas the liberal arts colleges typically enroll thirteen to twenty-six hundred, roughly tenfold fewer. Thus, to compare relative Ph.D. productivity of institutions of different size, the ratio of Ph.D.'s per hundred enrolled has been calculated. Note that this ratio is approximately equal to the percentage of baccalaureate degree recipients from the college who eventually obtain a Ph.D. in science or engineering. (Because it integrates five years, it would exactly equal the percentage if one-fifth of a college's total enrollment graduated in any given year; considering attrition and the number of students who take more than four years to graduate, this is a reasonable approximation.) Thus, most of the top liberal arts colleges see between 5 percent and 18 percent of their graduates going on to obtain a Ph.D. in science or engineering (table 1, last column). Considering that their graduates majored in English, history, art, and other humanities disciplines as well as in science, this represents an astounding percentage.

Table 1. Top National Liberal Arts Colleges: How many of their baccalaureate degree students go on to receive Ph.D.'s (1991–1995)?[a]

Institution	Number of Ph.D.'s[b]	Rank[c]	Ph.D.'s/100 enrolled[d]
Amherst	118	169	7
Barnard	133	143	6
Bowdoin	89	205	6
Bryn Mawr	121	165	9
Carleton	260	69	15
Claremont McKenna	12	741	1
Colgate	132	145	5
Davidson	76	231	5
Grinnell	128	151	10
Haverford	114	174	11
Middlebury	82	219	4
Mount Holyoke	124	160	6
Oberlin	266	68	10
Pomona	135	138	10
Smith	153	120	6
Swarthmore	248	73	18
Vassar	125	158	6
Wellesley	137	137	6
Wesleyan	189	96	7
Williams	155	119	8

[a]Students who received an undergraduate degree at the listed institution and went on to receive a Ph.D. in science or engineering.
[b]Number of former graduates who received a Ph.D. from 1991–1995 (NSF 96-334).[2]
[c]Rank among all universities and colleges, based on raw numbers from previous column; the top 820 institutions were ranked.
[d](Number of Ph.D.'s) x 100/(Number of undergraduates enrolled).
Source: NSF 96-334.

For comparison, let us examine the extent to which baccalaureate degree recipients from the nation's top research universities go on to receive science and engineering Ph.D. degrees. After all, these are the institutions that grant most of the Ph.D. degrees, so one might expect their undergraduates to be oriented towards graduate education. Indeed, as shown in table 2, undergraduates from each of the nation's top research universities accounted for three hundred to more than one thousand Ph.D.'s in the recent five-year period. (The criterion of federal contract and grant money favors larger institutions and underrates those not associated with a medical school; e.g., CalTech did not make this particular list.[4] Yet the institutions on this "top twenty" list mostly remain on the list when other criteria of research success are substituted.) Most of these research universities rank among the fifty-largest producers of undergraduates who go on to obtain science and engineering Ph.D.'s (see "Rank" column). When normalized to the size of the undergraduate population, as few as 1 percent or as many as 22 percent of these undergraduates go on to obtain Ph.D.'s (see "Ph.D.'s/100 enrolled").

Table 2. Top Research Universities: How many of their baccalaureate degree students go on to receive Ph.D.'s (1991–1995)?

Institution[a]	Number of Ph.D.'s[b]	Rank[c]	Ph.D.'s/100 enrolled[d]
Columbia U.	270	65	2
Cornell U.	1090	3	9
Harvard U.	752	9	11
Johns Hopkins U.	324	50	10
M.I.T.	1000	5	22
Penn State U.	865	7	3
Stanford U.	519	23	8
U. of Colorado	500	26	3
U. of Michigan	1060	4	5
U. of Minnesota	712	10	3
U. of No. Carolina	354	43	2
U. of Pennsylvania	535	21	6
U. of So. California	192	94	1
U. of Washington	560	19	2
U. of Wisconsin, Madison	995	6	4
UC Berkeley	1590	1	7
UC San Diego	535	22	4
UCLA	781	8	3
UCSF	0[e]	-	-
Yale U.	495	27	10

[a]Alphabetical listing of institutions with the greatest federally financed research and development expenditures, 1989–1996. These twenty institutions accounted for 36 percent of the total research expenditures of the 493 institutions ranked.[4]
[b]Number of former graduates who received a Ph.D. from 1991–1995 (NSF 96-334).[2]
[c]Rank based on raw numbers from previous column; the top 820 institutions were ranked.
[d](Number of Ph.D.'s) x 100/(Number undergraduates enrolled); relative values are more precise than the actual numbers.
[e]UCSF has no undergraduate degree programs.
Source: NSF 96-334.

Table 3. Top twenty-five institutions in terms of fraction of undergraduates who go on to receive Ph.D.'s in science and engineering (1991–1995).

Institution	Ph.D.'s/100 enrolled[a]	Number of Ph.D.'s[b]
CalTech	42	368
M.I.T.	22	1000
Harvey Mudd	19	124
*Swarthmore	18	248
*Carleton	15	260
*Reed	14	182
U. of Chicago	13	435
Rice U.	12	324
Princeton U.	12	544
Harvard U.	11	752
*Haverford	11	114
Johns Hopkins U.	10	324
*Oberlin	10	266
*Pomona	10	135
*Grinnell	10	128
Yale U.	10	495
*Kalamazoo	9	115
*Bryn Mawr	9	121
Rensselaer Polytech. Inst.	9	370
Cornell U.	9	1090
Case Western Reserve U.	8	296
Stanford U.	8	519
Brown U.	8	469
*Williams	8	155
*Amherst	7	118

[a](Number of Ph.D.'s) x 100/(Number undergraduates enrolled). The Ph.D. degree is usually obtained at an institution different from the baccalaureate institution listed.
[b]Number of Ph.D.'s who obtained their baccalaureate at the listed institution (NSF 96-334).[2] Only institutions graduating more than 110 future Ph.D.'s in the five-year period are included here.
*Liberal arts colleges.
Source: tabulated by the author.

At the risk of belaboring the statistics, there is yet another useful way to compare liberal arts colleges with other institutions in terms of their training of Ph.D. scientists and engineers. All U.S. colleges and universities can be listed according to the percentage of their baccalaureate recipients who eventually receive science and engineering Ph.D.'s (table 3). With the calculation now done such that size is no longer an advantage, liberal arts colleges make an even more impressive showing.

Swarthmore, Carleton, and Reed College rank below only three very specialized science-intensive schools—CalTech, M.I.T., and Harvey Mudd—in terms of producing eventual Ph.D. scientists. This is astounding, because many of the students at these liberal arts colleges have limited interest in science, often viewing the science building as a healthy shortcut between a humanities class and an art class during the cold winter. In contrast, the top three technical schools specialize in training scientists and engineers. Perhaps it is fairer, therefore, to compare these liberal arts colleges to Chicago, Rice, Princeton, Harvard, Stanford, and Brown, which have a more similar distribution of chemistry, English, and fine arts majors. Yet the conclusion remains the same: the science students graduating from the liberal arts colleges stand up well in comparison to those graduating from the Ivy League schools and other top research universities.

The leadership of U.S. science also benefits from a disproportionate representation of liberal arts college undergraduates. Considering those elected to membership in the National Academy of Sciences in a recent two-year period who were educated in the United States, 19 percent obtained their baccalaureate degree from a liberal arts college.[5] Thus, liberal arts college graduates not only obtain Ph.D.'s but go on to excel in their field of research at a rate at least two-times greater than bachelor's degree recipients in general.

THE LIBERAL ARTS COLLEGE EXPERIENCE AND
ITS INFLUENCE ON THE DEVELOPMENT OF YOUNG SCIENTISTS

In the previous section, I concluded that liberal arts colleges are remarkably successful in training eventual Ph.D.'s. They account for only a minor fraction (17 percent) of the science Ph.D. population of the nation, but when the data are normalized to the number of students these colleges enroll, it becomes clear that they are exceedingly successful on a per-student basis. The ultimate question will be one of causality: are the liberal arts college graduates successful *because of* their college experience, or independent of that experience, or perhaps even in spite of that experience? We must now, therefore, look at the experience of a liberal arts college science major—both curricular and extracurricular—and compare it to the experience of a science major at a research university. In the extreme case that the two experiences were identical, any difference in outcome would have to be ascribed to a difference in the quality of the two student populations rather than a difference in the quality of the training. Alas, as described in this section, the two environments are distinct, leaving us to grapple with the question of causality in the final section of this essay.

Formal Coursework

First, how does the science curriculum differ between liberal arts colleges and research universities? The names of the undergraduate courses and their content are similar. The differences occur in the manner in which the courses are taught. At the colleges, lecture sections rarely exceed fifty students in an introductory class and drop to perhaps a dozen in the upper-level science courses inhabited mostly by junior and senior science majors. At research universities, the numbers are typically much higher, with sometimes as many as five hundred students in a single classroom for an introductory class and as many as one hundred students in an upper-level course. In such large classes, it is difficult to avoid having students become passive recipients of information. Small classes provide the opportunity for students to engage actively in the learning process.

The teachers in the two sorts of institutions also have a very different orientation towards education. Many university professors enjoy teaching, or at least take satisfaction in their teaching, but rarely is it their first love. They were trained primarily as researchers, their promotion and tenure decisions were (or will be) based heavily on their research accomplishments, and their national and international reputations are almost totally dependent on the papers they publish and the invited research talks they present. Their peers outside their own institution will rarely know how well they teach, or perhaps even *if* they teach. In contrast, liberal arts college faculty are committed to teaching by their career choice. Their satisfaction with their own career and their reputation are heavily tied to teaching, and teaching that is simultaneously rigorous, innovative, and popular is especially prized. They are also committed to research, which at the top colleges constitutes one major criterion for promotion, but the expectations are appropriate: the research program is expected to be active and scholarly, producing publishable work and contributing to the full education of science majors (Grinnell College), in contrast to helping establish a new field, bringing in half a million dollars per year in federal funding, and resulting in several publications per year, with one in *Science* or *Nature* at least occasionally (UC Berkeley). Because of their different orientation towards teaching, the liberal arts college faculty are more accessible to students inside and outside class. The students respond by being much more interactive with faculty—willing to explore questions in depth, stopping by the office, calling faculty at home.

Given these expectations for faculty, one might expect that good or excellent teaching is *sine qua non* at liberal arts colleges, whereas it occurs almost as an afterthought at many large research universities. Such a view is overly simplistic. University science teaching also has features in which it excels. Teachers who are working at the leading edge of their field, perhaps even defining the leading edge, can bring a special type of excitement to their teaching. In some cases they share their new discoveries or those of their colleagues with their undergraduate class. They are more likely than their liberal arts college counterparts to know what material in the textbook is of current interest, and what has remained there through inertia. Thus, in some respects college teaching and research university teaching should be considered different, and not just a matter of superior versus inferior. Yet the much lower student-to-faculty ratios in the colleges are very much to their advantage, as anyone who has taught in a wide range of class sizes will attest.

The science courses taken by science majors usually have associated laboratory sessions, and here the contrast between a student's experience at a liberal arts college and a large university is even more distinct. Many liberal arts colleges integrate more open-ended, less predictable laboratory projects even in introductory courses, making them more like miniresearch experiences. While the research universities are moving in the same direction, they are severely constrained by large class sizes and low budgets, so the inquiry-based laboratories tend to be reserved for science majors in their junior and senior years. Furthermore, university lab sections are almost always supervised by TAs (teaching assistants), who are usually graduate students. While TAs are typically hard-working and enthusiastic, few of them have much teaching experience or more than a week's training, and many of them are teaching primarily because it provides their stipend. In contrast, college lab sections are typically taught by the same full-time faculty who teach the classroom sessions, which assures continuity between lecture and lab. Even more importantly, the college professor is more experienced, more committed to education, and probably more patient than a typical graduate TA.

How about courses taken outside the science building? Students choose to attend liberal arts colleges because they have broad interests, and, once there, the colleges encourage that predisposition through advising or formal requirements. As a student at Grinnell College I talked my way into Joe Wall's advanced constitutional history course, for which I lacked the prerequisites. Harold Varmus majored in English at Amherst.[6] Jennifer Doudna enjoyed medieval history and French at Pomona. Kathy Friedman was torn between majoring in English or biology at Carleton. In contrast, research universities provide students the option of focusing heavily on their favored discipline, and most science majors concentrate on the sciences. At the University of Colorado, I talk to many students who are double majors, with a typical one being biochemistry plus molecular biology. Double majors in biochemistry plus English or history are a rarity.

What impact does a liberal arts curriculum have on a career in science? In brief, the classroom and laboratory sessions are more personal, while the broad distribution of nonscience courses promotes the development of critical thinking skills and facility with written and oral communication. The influence of these features of a liberal arts education will be analyzed in a subsequent section of this essay.

Undergraduate Research

At both colleges and research universities, science majors are strongly encouraged to undertake an independent research project under the guidance of a faculty mentor. In some institutions, independent research is even a requirement for all majors. These experiences differ markedly from the laboratory sections that accompany regular courses. The problems are open-ended; typically, it is not clear how long the project will take, how accurate or even self-consistent the data will be, whether the approach and methods being used are really optimal, or whether the data will provide convincing support for or evidence against the hypothesis. In addition, the equipment and computers available for the project are typically sophisticated, up-to-date instrumentation, and expensive reagents may also be used. This is in contrast to laboratory sections, where a fixed schedule, limited budget, and constraints of having to provide a similar experience to multiple students encourage simpler, more straightforward exercises with more predictable outcomes. In short, an independent research project provides most students with their first direct experience of the life of a practicing scientist. They gain skills in identifying and solving problems, reasoning, organizing scientific data, and presenting their results and interpretations, and along with these they gain state-of-the-art technical skills. Students typically rate this experience as the most important and most memorable of their college education, and they correctly perceive it as the most relevant in terms of future employment.

> During my junior and senior school years at Pomona College, I built a high-speed photometer for astronomy research, and actually got to use it at Palomar Observatory. The profs at Pomona gave me a place in the basement to work. It was a great environment. In the basement, there was a little electronics shop with a full-time technician, and a machine shop with a full-time machinist, with both facilities there expressly for people like me.[7]

Given the importance of independent research, we next need to explore how this experience at liberal arts colleges compares to that at research universities. Two questions will be considered:

how does the quality of the research compare, and how does the value of the research experience to the student compare?

Someone unfamiliar with undergraduate research in the sciences might feel quite safe in predicting that the quality of the research would be far better at research universities than at liberal arts colleges. After all, the amount of research-grant funding, the availability of state-of-the-art instrumentation, the research reputation of the faculty, the quality of the library, and the frequency with which highly successful scientists visit to give seminars and share research ideas all weigh heavily in favor of the research universities. More specifically, while successful college professors might raise tens of thousands of dollars a year to support their research programs, successful university professors often raise half a million dollars per year. While a college would be justifiably proud to have a 400 MHz NMR (Nuclear Magnetic Resonance) spectrometer costing perhaps $400,000, research universities vie for 800 MHz NMRs that cost around $2 million. Finally, while top colleges might host an internationally known scientist to their campus for a day or two each month, top research universities are stimulated by several such seminar speakers every week, in each field of science.

Yet in spite of these obvious advantages of conducting research at a research university, there is no compelling evidence that their undergraduates end up doing better research. At both types of institutions, successful undergraduate research culminates not infrequently with a publication in a peer-reviewed journal with the student as a co-author. Such publication sets a very high standard, and certainly many good research projects do not generate publications. But publications provide a universally appreciated, objective measure of quality. With respect to the current argument, the frequency with which undergraduate research is published is not so different between colleges and universities as to mandate the conclusion that one or the other set of research projects is generally of higher quality. Furthermore, in interviews with professional scientists who are familiar with undergraduate research in both types of institutions, there was no consensus that research was generally better in one type than the other. To the contrary, most rated them to be of similar quality.

Why then do the large grants, expensive equipment, and famous laboratories available at research universities not lead to overwhelmingly superior undergraduate research opportunities? The answers are not so difficult to fathom. University research labs survive on the productivity of their graduate students, postdoctoral fellows, and technical staff. The grant money, the access to multimillion-dollar instrumentation, and typically the best projects go mainly to these more advanced scientists. Undergraduate research is promoted because of its educational value, but it does not determine the research productivity of the laboratory. In contrast, the research at liberal arts colleges is carried out almost entirely by undergraduates and faculty members, and the productivity of the undergraduates largely determines the research productivity of the laboratory. As a result, the faculty member spends more time organizing each project, more time training the students, more effort in troubleshooting the technical problems that inevitably hinder progress. At research universities, these time-consuming tasks are delegated to postdoctoral fellows or graduate students who are heavily occupied with their own research projects. The greater investment in time and effort spent with undergraduates at liberal arts colleges more or less compensates for the fact that research universities are better set up to carry out research.

In fairness, superiority of research facilities in large universities does make an impact on some undergraduates. For example, some university undergraduates participate in research in structural biology, a field dedicated to the determination of atomic-resolution pictures of biological macromolecules such as proteins. The high-field NMRs, x-ray diffraction systems, computer workstations, and synchrotron light sources required for such work can be found at many universities but are beyond the reach of liberal arts colleges, unless their students gain access by engaging in off-campus research. As another example, undergraduates at research universities occasionally participate in a "hot" project that becomes internationally acclaimed and is published in *Science* or *Nature* because of its impact and broad interest. Such an outcome is very rare for undergraduate research at a small college. Yet the fraction of undergraduate research projects that are so exceedingly successful is small even at research universities. The general situation is that there is a wide range in the quality of undergraduate research at both colleges and research universities, and that the two distributions overlap extensively.

We now move from the quality of the research itself to the quality of the research experience—how well does it promote the development of the scientist-in-training? The special feature of undergraduate research at colleges is that it is much more personal. The college professor guides the research of a small number of students at a time, and therefore spends much more time with them than a typical university professor. The quality of mentoring of undergraduates can be very high when it is direct, faculty to student, rather than mediated through a postdoctoral fellow or graduate student.

> [My] physics research was not as intense or cutting-edge as at a university, but I think I had much more attention from my advisor than I would have at a university. For instance, I remember calling him at home one evening to tell him of an important paper I had found; he walked back to campus to talk with me about it that night.[8]

Other liberal arts graduates speak of the high level of responsibility and independence engendered by their undergraduate research experience. In the absence of roomfuls of graduate students or postdocs with expertise in every imaginable technique or procedure, the student needs to be self-reliant and innovative. Furthermore, a senior undergraduate may be called upon to help mentor and train the new undergraduate entering the lab. In a university lab, that same senior undergraduate would be near the bottom of the hierarchy in terms of level of experience.

In summary, the personal attention given by the professor often leads to an intense and highly focused research experience in a liberal arts college. Those who have had such an experience prize it greatly and consider it to have been highly influential in their development as scientists.

WHY ARE LIBERAL ARTS COLLEGE SCIENCE STUDENTS SO
SUCCESSFUL?

A Nurturing Environment

Many of the features of a liberal arts education already mentioned above combine to create a very comfortable and supportive environment for learning. These features include the
low student-faculty ratio and the involvement of faculty in the
whole education of the students—laboratory sections as well as
classes. The faculty are much more available for casual interactions with undergraduates than are university professors,
whose time is fragmented by expectations that they contribute
to the diverse missions of a university: undergraduate education, graduate education, creation of new knowledge, developing a national and international presence, protection of the
university's intellectual property through patents, public service, and perhaps even aiding the economic development of
their state.

> There were only two of us in the lab, so we received a great deal
> of personal attention from our professor. She was always there for
> us. We have great students here at Yale, too, but they are handed
> off to a graduate student or postdoc for their research. It doesn't
> compare with the quality of the research experience I had at
> Pomona.[9]

There may also be students at universities who see their
professors as such giants that they cannot imagine themselves
attaining such heights. The more approachable faculty at liberal arts colleges provide less intimidating role models. The
students are encouraged to maintain their interest in science
during the critical period when their maturity—both intellectual and personal—is growing to the point where they can
envision themselves obtaining a Ph.D. Speaking more generally, at a liberal arts college the undergraduates are the center
of attention, the reason for the existence of the institution. This
can engender confidence and a feeling of self-worth.

Cross-training in the Humanities and Arts

Athletes often incorporate a variety of exercises not directly
related to their sport to improve their overall strength and

conditioning. For example, swimmers and soccer players cross-train by lifting weights. The cross-training may exercise key muscle groups more effectively than spending the same amount of time working out in the sport of interest. Analogously, a liberal arts education encourages scientists to improve their "competitive edge" by cross-training in the humanities or arts. Such academic cross-training develops a student's ability to collect and organize facts and opinions, to analyze them and weigh their value, and to articulate an argument, and it may develop these skills more effectively than writing yet another lab report.

What is the value of such intellectual cross-training? Just as mathematics is considered to be good exercise for the brain even for those who will never use calculus in the future, so the study of great books, history, languages, music, and many other nonscience fields is likely to hone a scientist's ability to perceive and interpret the natural world. More specifically, in history, literature, and the arts one is presented with diverse, often mutually contradictory "data"—different points of view due to incomplete knowledge or the different backgrounds of those doing the viewing. One learns to distill the critical elements from the irrelevant, synthesize seemingly discordant observations, and develop a strong argument. While scientific data are commonly thought to exist on a different plane— absolute, precise, unambiguous, and above reproach—such is rarely the case. Random error and systematic deviations must be taken into account. Choices of experimental design inevitably affect the results obtained. Interpretations are often heavily influenced by expectations, which in turn are heavily influenced by earlier conclusions published in the research literature. Scientists need the same skills as humanists to cut through misleading observations and arrive at a defensible interpretation, and intellectual cross-training in the humanities exercises the relevant portions of the brain.

Another obvious value of humanities classes for a scientist is the development of communication skills. Success in science, like many other endeavors, is highly dependent on the scientist's ability to write manuscripts and research-grant applications that are well organized, clear, and persuasive. Oral communication skills are equally important, including the ability to present one's research in a manner that is not only convincing but also exciting and perhaps even entertaining. The most brilliant research accomplishments make no impact unless they can be communicated to an external audience.

> My present ability, such as it is, to distill the results of structural analysis into paragraphs of text I attribute directly to the hours spent in the analysis of English verse. A strong emphasis on performance on the stage and in oral interpretation of text has also helped with science lectures.[10]

Writing papers for humanities classes allows students to develop skills in stating their position, evaluating it critically, presenting evidence (internal, such as quotations from the work being analyzed, and also external, from other authors), and organizing their argument. Sketching, painting, and sculpting help a student to develop skills in perception and in the construction of visual aids that illustrate scientific observations or models. Like cross-training in sports, exercising one's communication skills in areas unrelated to science may be more advantageous than taking yet one more science course.

The value of the broadening experience of a liberal arts education is unlikely to be quantifiable, and verifying its impact is therefore problematic. Nevertheless, many of us who have enjoyed such an education are convinced that it has benefited us as scientists. This practical benefit is in addition to the stated goal of a liberal arts college education: to enhance one's whole life.

Counterpoint: Some Disadvantages of a Liberal Arts College Education

Two educational features in which liberal arts colleges cannot match research universities have already been mentioned: some undergraduates at research universities have access to equipment and reagents that enable more sophisticated research projects than are possible even at well-equipped colleges, and the special thrill of being present when important discoveries are being made is much more likely to be encountered at a research university. Neither of these experiences is common, so the number of university undergraduates who derive these benefits is limited.

Two other areas in which liberal arts colleges may fall short of research universities deserve discussion. First, it was noted by one liberal arts college graduate that there may be a real danger of setting one's goals too low. If world-class discovery research is not being carried out in the same building, it may make it more difficult for talented students to appreciate what such research involves and to picture themselves engaged in it. Yet this may be more of a concern for liberal arts colleges that draw many of their students from local communities; the top national colleges such as those listed in table 1 are very successful in placing their students in the most competitive graduate programs. A second possible shortcoming of colleges was mentioned by many of those interviewed: the colleges are very sheltered, and their students generally have no concept of the "real" research world of million-dollar research grants, press releases, and cutthroat competition. The counterargument is that premature exposure to these practical issues could actually discourage many students from pursuing a career in science. In any case, it may be inconsistent to extol the virtues of the friendly, supportive, nurturing environment found at colleges and simultaneously bemoan their isolation from the politics of big science.

Cause or Effect?

The top liberal arts colleges are highly selective in their admissions, and they turn out very successful scientists. Are they successful because they do a great job, or because the input is of such high quality? We do not have the luxury of being able to take two identical groups of students, place one group in liberal arts colleges and the other in research universities, and return four or more years later to evaluate their relative success. However, it is noteworthy that the most selective private research universities (Harvard, Princeton, Stanford, Columbia, and Yale) are more selective than any of the liberal arts colleges, and their students taken as a group have higher SAT test scores than the entering classes of any of the liberal arts colleges. Yet their efficiency of production of Ph.D.'s, while excellent, lags behind that of the top liberal arts colleges (table 3). Clearly the liberal arts institutions are doing much more than simply recruiting talented students and hoping for their eventual success. On a more subjective note, in interviews with successful liberal arts college science graduates, none of them chose to attribute the success of the colleges primarily to their high selectivity. Instead, they commented that the quality of the incoming students and the quality of the education must both contribute.

Further confounding this question of nature versus nurture is the tendency for talented students to be encouraged to achieve ever more when surrounded by other high achievers. There has recently been renewed discussion of the influence of peers relative to parents in determining a child's values, aspirations, and ultimate success.[11] Perhaps there is also a tendency to underestimate the effect of the peer group on the quality of education. In this regard, the colleges may be successful because they surround a student not simply with other bright students who performed well on standardized tests but with students who are excited about learning, who are confident but not overconfident about their own abilities, and who enjoy working hard.

Thus we arrive at the conclusion, perhaps obvious from the outset, that innate talent and a quality education both contribute to the success of science students graduating from liberal arts colleges. Intelligence, creativity, and hard work can take a student far, but they constitute an even more powerful combination when channeled, guided, and motivated by excellent teachers in an environment supportive for learning.

SUMMARY AND OUTLOOK

Liberal arts colleges as a group produce about twice as many eventual science Ph.D.'s per graduate as do baccalaureate institutions in general, and the top colleges vie with the nation's very best research universities in their efficiency of production of eventual science Ph.D.'s. On a more subjective note, when highly successful scientists compare their liberal arts college education to what they likely would have received at a large research university, most rate their college experience as a substantial advantage to their career. Distinguishing characteristics of liberal arts college science education include small classes, a faculty that is available to the students and focused largely on undergraduate education, and the incorporation of courses in the humanities and arts that promote intellectual "cross-training." Independent research at liberal arts colleges does not approach the leading edge of scientific fields as often as that carried out at research universities, but it benefits from highly personal one-on-one interactions between students and faculty mentors, making for an overall experience that often surpasses that at large universities. Reinforced by these features, the liberal arts college science education is highly valued by its graduates and contributes to the nation's strength in science at a level disproportionate to its size.

Will science education at the liberal arts colleges continue to thrive in the next century? After all, scientific supplies are increasing in cost more quickly than the general rate of inflation. Instrumentation of an ever-increasing variety and technological sophistication is essential for scientific research, and it can be argued that at least some of it must be made available to students lest their training become dated. However, the national liberal arts colleges have been very successful in garnering internal resources, federal and private foundation grants, and donations to obtain supplies and equipment that are more up-to-date than those available in undergraduate laboratories at many major universities; given their demonstrated success in using these resources to enhance the education of successful students, the colleges have built a firm foundation for continuing to obtain the scientific resources they desire. Furthermore, if funds for supplies and equipment tighten, imaginative faculty will find ways to substitute less expensive laboratory exercises that have similar pedagogical value. What the colleges cannot change without compromising their very heart and soul is their personalized approach to education and their committed faculty, which add up to a very expensive approach to higher education. The challenge to continue to make such an education available to students with diverse economic backgrounds cuts across disciplines, and is not specific to the sciences. This is the challenge of the liberal arts college in the twenty-first century.

ACKNOWLEDGMENTS

I am grateful to the following educators for their comments on an early draft of this essay: John Burke, Ron Capen, Luther Erickson, Tass Kelso, Ted Lindeman, Jerry Mohrig, Kathryn Mohrman, Libby Rittenberg, and Barbara Whitten. I have incorporated many of their suggestions, much to the benefit of this work.

ENDNOTES

[1] David Davis-Van Atta, Sam C. Carrier, and Frank Frankfort, *Educating America's Scientists: The Role of the Research Colleges* (Oberlin, Ohio: Oberlin College, 1985); Sam C. Carrier and David Davis-Van Atta, *Maintaining America's Scientific Productivity: The Necessity of the Liberal Arts Colleges* (Oberlin, Ohio: Oberlin College, 1987); Sophie Wilkinson, "Liberal Arts Colleges are Good Ph.D. Incubators," *Chemical & Engineering News* (3 August 1998): 45–46.

[2] The remainder attend research universities (the 125 leaders in federal funding), doctoral universities (e.g., Iowa State University, University of South Florida, Howard University, and Rensselaer Polytechnic Institute), master's colleges and universities (e.g., Glassboro State College, Old Dominion University, and Creighton University), or specialized institutions that focus primarily on technical or professional programs (e.g., New Jersey Institute of Technology, Princeton Theological Seminary, and Teacher's College of Columbia). These categories are taken from the 1994 Carnegie Classification as described in NSF 96-334 [National Science Foundation, *Undergraduate Origins of Recent (1991–1995) Science and Engineering Doctorate Recipients, Detailed Statistical Tables,* NSF 96-334 (Arlington, Va.: NSF, 1996)].

[3] These data concern 1991–1995, the most recent five-year period for which data have been compiled (NSF 96-334, p. 6); data for the previous five-year period are similar.

[4] National Science Foundation, Division of Science Resources Studies, *Academic Research and Development Expenditures: Fiscal Year 1996,* NSF 98-304, ed. M. Marge Machen (Arlington, Va.: NSF, 1998).

[5] Data for 114 members elected in 1997 and 1998, compiled by Judith Harrington, Membership Director, National Academy of Sciences.

[6] Scientists interviewed were David Baltimore (B.A. in Chemistry, 1960, Swarthmore), President, Cal Tech, Nobel Prize in Medicine (1975); David P. Corey (B.A. in Physics, 1974, Amherst), Professor, Harvard Medical School; Jennifer A. Doudna (B.A. in Chemistry, 1985, Pomona), Assistant Professor, Yale, Markey Scholar, Searle Scholar, Packard Fellow; Katherine L. Friedman

(B.A. in Biology, 1990, Carleton), Postdoctoral Fellow, HHMI Predoctoral Fellow at the University of Washington; Richard H. Gomer (B.A. in Physics, 1977, Pomona), Associate Professor, Rice University; John Kuriyan (B.S. in Chemistry, 1981, Juniata), Haggerty Professor, Rockefeller University; Joan A. Steitz (B.S. in Chemistry, 1963, Antioch), Henry Ford II Professor, Yale; and Harold E. Varmus (B.A. in English, 1961, Amherst), Director, National Institutes of Health, Nobel Prize in Medicine (1989). In addition to their academic appointments, Corey, Doudna, Gomer, Kuriyan, and Steitz are Investigators of the Howard Hughes Medical Institute.

[7]Gomer, interview.

[8]Corey, interview.

[9]Doudna, interview.

[10]Kuriyan, interview.

[11]M. Gladwell, "Do Parents Matter?" *The New Yorker* (17 August 1998): 54–64, discusses the work of J. R. Harris, *The Nurture Assumption: Why Children Turn Out the Way They Do* (New York: Free Press, 1998).

Priscilla W. Laws

New Approaches to Science and Mathematics Teaching at Liberal Arts Colleges

> ... *the power of instruction is seldom of much
> efficacy, except in those happy dispositions where
> it is almost superfluous.*
> —Edward Gibbon, 1737–1794[1]

INTRODUCTION

RECENTLY, HIGH-SCHOOL STUDENTS were polled about which regional institution was most likely to have an award-winning introductory science program. The majority selected the state research university with a nationally ranked football team rather than the liberal arts college that created the program. People unfamiliar with four-year liberal arts colleges believe that one studies philosophy and classics at these institutions rather than science or mathematics.

Although liberal arts college faculty are justifiably proud of their role in nurturing prominent research scientists, only a small percentage of undergraduates actually major in science. Even in outstanding science programs, 70 percent or more of students enrolled in science and mathematics courses are nonmajors seeking to satisfy general studies requirements.[2] Participants at a recent Pew Higher Education Roundtable characterized traditional courses as primarily serving the needs of potential science majors. They felt that this approach ne-

Priscilla W. Laws is Professor of Physics at Dickinson College.

217

glects the needs of the majority of students for whom a basic knowledge of science is a primary tool for citizenship, future employment, personal enlightenment, precollege teaching, and parenthood.[3]

My own experience shows that basic science knowledge can have unforeseen value to nonscience majors. Take the case of the Dickinson College classics major who took a few computer science courses and put off the dreaded lab science requirement until her senior year. As a computer system manager for a midsized company, she found herself removing ceiling tiles and checking continuity in cables with an ohmmeter—a task for which she was prepared by her hands-on physics course sequence. She is now a global Internet consultant for Arthur Anderson. And about twenty years ago, two nonscience majors' career plans were altered by a project-based land-use course that a geology colleague and I taught. One is now a public interest lobbyist, the other specializes in environmental law.

In this essay, I augment Thomas Cech's account by highlighting the leadership role in science-education reform played by liberal arts colleges. This reform movement, which rests upon a set of fundamental principles, has been made possible by new federal funding strategies. Traditional liberal arts science and mathematics programs have unique strengths and weaknesses that can be judged in the context of fundamental reform principles. A new field of discipline-specific, science-education research has moved beyond general reform principles and has greatly enhanced the effectiveness of science curricula. Liberal arts colleges have taken a leading role in developing, implementing, promoting, and facilitating the use of reform-based curricula.

TRENDS IN SCIENCE-EDUCATION REFORM

Since 1983, over five hundred reports have been published dealing with the problems of science and mathematics education. These reports are so similar that one can easily extract a set of principles that define current trends. The principles of reform call for all students to have the opportunity to: learn science and mathematics actively by doing them in collaboration with peers and instructors; engage in extended research projects with faculty mentors; explore fewer topics in more depth; achieve scientific literacy by being able to ask and answer questions such as "How do we know . . . ?" and "What is the evidence for . . . ?";[4] relate scientific and mathematical understandings to contemporary social issues; and develop written and oral communication skills.

The reform community agrees with the view expressed by Edward Gibbon in the epigraph, that "instruction is seldom of much efficacy." Reformers believe that instruction should be replaced by active learning opportunities. They feel that a conceptual understanding of science and the processes of experimentation and theory-building are more important than a broader knowledge of accepted facts and theories. Since fewer topics can be covered, reformers believe that the topics selected should provide a foundation for self-actuated learning and be relevant to social issues and the workplace. These educators feel that collaborative work and the development of oral and written communication skills not only enhance learning but are also important ends in themselves. Their major goal is to help students "learn how to learn."

Multiple factors have shaped these principles, the primary one being the wisdom of experience developed by teachers about "what works" and what knowledge and skills seem most important. However, these principles have been influenced by understanding how students learn vital concepts in science and mathematics, an understanding that has emerged from educational philosophy, cognitive psychology, and discipline specific educational research. Finally, social and political agendas that exist in federal funding agencies and programs such as the National Science Foundation and the U.S. Department of Education's Fund for the Improvement of Postsecondary Education have contributed to the formulation of these principles.

Intellectual Precedents of Reform Trends

Precursors of many of the current ideas in science-education reform are found in the writings of several educators. Philosophers Alfred North Whitehead and John Dewey promoted education that guides the self-development of students through experiential learning.[5] Social psychologist Kurt Lewin believed that learning was best facilitated in a collaborative environment where active dialogue by members of a group is used to resolve tensions between immediate, concrete experiences and previously held conceptions.[6] Cognitive psychologist Jean Piaget focused on identifying stages of intellectual development in children and the role of experience in promoting intellectual growth.[7]

Since 1960, a number of cognitive psychologists have extended earlier work on the abstract reasoning abilities of children to college-age adults and beyond.[8] These extensions have been pivotal in helping educators identify common learning difficulties of undergraduate students in mathematics and science, and have contributed to the articulation of reform principles.

Arnold Arons has had a profound influence on trends in science and mathematics education. He taught physics at Amherst College from 1952 to 1968 as part of a required interdisciplinary studies program that he helped to develop. He had a deep understanding of the history of science and was a keen observer of the intellectual development of several generations of Amherst physics students. He wrote about the learning difficulties shared by a large percentage of introductory physics students in light of new research in cognitive development, and has been a relentless advocate of helping students achieve scientific literacy. Arons's notion of scientific literacy has much more to do with students understanding the basis of knowledge than with knowing facts. He spoke of the importance of allowing students to grapple with important concepts over and over again in new guises rather than being forced to study too many topics. His textbooks, expository books for physics teachers, and journal essays have served as the foundation for educational reform in science and mathematics.[9]

Recent History of Federal Funding for Undergraduate Reform

High quality educational research and research-based curriculum development is expensive. For this reason, federal funding is a major determinant of new trends in undergraduate science and mathematics teaching. There were no notable twentieth-century science-education reforms of any kind until the Soviet Union's 1957 *Sputnik* launch. The notion that the United States was behind in the space race inspired dozens of federally funded projects to develop instructional materials. Although many of the post-*Sputnik* curricular materials were inquiry oriented and involved students as active learners, most were designed for precollege students. Thus, these new programs did not directly influence undergraduate programs or have much lasting effect on teaching practices in primary or secondary education. Oft cited reasons include the lack of teacher training, the lack of detailed knowledge on how students at various grade levels learn specific topics, and a complacency that set in by 1969 when the United States landed astronauts on the moon.

During the early post-*Sputnik* era, undergraduate science programs at both liberal arts colleges and universities were growing rapidly without serious consideration of changes in the curriculum or teaching practices. College and university instructors based course offerings and teaching methods on those they had encountered in the research university programs where they served as graduate teaching assistants. The small amount of federal funding that existed in those years ended in 1981 when the Reagan administration greatly reduced funding for education.

The current wave of science and mathematics reform at the undergraduate level began in 1987, when the National Science Board's "Neal Report" on undergraduate science, mathematics, and engineering education was released.[10] The major goal of the report was to help the National Science Foundation make the programmatic changes needed to achieve excellence in science, mathematics, and engineering education. A social agenda was presented that envisioned implementing and expanding programs that would benefit "students in all types of institutions," improving "public understanding of science and technology," and mounting efforts to "increase the participation of women, minorities, and the physically handicapped in professional science, mathematics, and engineering." In addition, for the first time there was recognition that cognitive issues might be important. The Neal Report cited the need to stimulate creative activities in teaching and learning and to perform "research on them," analogous to basic disciplinary research.

Since World War II most federal funding for undergraduate science and mathematics education has come from the National Science Foundation (NSF). In 1986, the NSF expended almost $36 million to provide undergraduate departments with instructional equipment and to promote undergraduate research. By 1989 the Neal Report had helped stimulate the NSF to add several new programs, including one for course and curriculum development and another for the professional development of faculty. Since 1986 the NSF's annual budget for the support of undergraduate education programs increased fivefold. Thus, in the past twelve years, a number of major undergraduate reform initiatives in the basic sciences, mathematics, and engineering have been funded.

Back in 1986 the NSF seemed most interested in using funding to increase the number of college students majoring in science. Officials used a leaky pipeline analogy to describe the drastic decline of students interested in studying science and mathematics at each level of education. For example, at present fewer than half the students who enter college intending to major in science, mathematics, or engineering actually do. To add insult to injury, statistics show that the percentage of freshmen interested in majoring in the sciences declined from 12 percent in 1966 to 6 percent in 1988.[11] Significantly, the NSF's focus has shifted in the past twelve years from the leaky pipeline to the idea of improving the quality of education in science and mathematics for all students, especially women and minorities—not just for students majoring in science and mathematics. The fact that the pipeline is leaky is no longer deemed the principal challenge. The overall number of scientists and mathematicians now seems adequate, although there are shifts in student interest occurring among the disciplines. The medical sciences, electrical engineering, and computer science are currently in vogue. Thus, the number of physics majors is decreasing at the same time that undergraduate chemistry and biology departments are scrambling to develop new major programs in biochemistry.

The new focus of federal programs involves developing scientifically literate citizens, reducing science and mathematics phobias among students, and increasing the chances for success of all students who choose to take college-level courses in science and mathematics. It can be argued that this new science-for-all focus may benefit science majors more than would developing rigorous programs for committed science majors. In 1997, Elaine Seymour and Nancy Hewitt published an ethnographic study of 335 students majoring in science, mathematics, and engineering at seven undergraduate institutions.[12] The goal of the study was to determine why over half of these students do not complete their intended majors. The authors conclude that it is extremely important ". . . to improve the quality of the learning experience for all students—including those non-science majors who wish to study science and mathematics as part of their overall education."[13]

TRADITIONAL SCIENCE EDUCATION AT LIBERAL ARTS COLLEGES

Educators at liberal arts colleges frequently cite the many advantages they enjoy over large institutions: smaller classes; an emphasis on teaching, rather than research, that frees faculty for class preparation and attention to individual students; laboratory sessions led by faculty rather than graduate students; undergraduate research opportunities; and interdisciplinary courses relating science to social issues.

How does the quality of learning experiences in science and mathematics at liberal arts colleges stack up against those at larger universities? Do liberal arts colleges realize the full potential from their advantages? Would the application of reform principles enhance learning in the liberal arts setting?

Strengths

Liberal arts colleges have been national leaders in promoting undergraduate research. Extended senior research is often used as a capstone for highly motivated science majors; this experience has inspired many students to pursue graduate studies. Liberal arts colleges, especially the most selective, take great pride in the many students sent on to graduate school. Compared to other institutions, a larger proportion of liberal arts college graduates earn Ph.D.'s in science and mathematics.[14]

Faculty at liberal arts colleges often work closely with colleagues in other departments. For this reason, many liberal arts colleges have developed interdisciplinary general studies programs that include science and mathematics. One such program, at Drury College, is described below. The focus on interdisciplinary work is strongest at a handful of distinctive experimental institutions such as Hampshire College, the College of the Atlantic, and Evergreen College. The emphases on student research and interdisciplinary course work typical of liberal arts institutions are clearly consonant with the educational reform principles. Both highly motivated science majors and nonscience majors can benefit from these program elements.

Weaknesses

Science and mathematics pedagogy at the majority of liberal arts colleges mirrors that at large research universities. The content and teaching methods used center on the use of standard textbooks. Introductory science students typically attend several large-group lectures and one laboratory session each week. Upper-level courses, while smaller in size, still rely heavily on the lecture format. In mathematics, students attend small-group lectures each week. It is difficult to incorporate reform principles into traditional lecture and laboratory courses. Formal lectures do not provide opportunities for active learning, collaboration, investigation, or research. Lecturers often cover more topics than students can assimilate. Textbook expositions are boring and incomprehensible. Laboratory activities, rarely based upon outcomes of educational research, involve complicated procedures in which students "can't see the forest through the trees."

The disadvantages of traditional pedagogy more than offset the advantages of small class size when it comes to reaching nonscience majors. How often does the typical liberal arts college nonscience major talk about getting his science requirement "out of the way?" Liberal arts colleges also fail to retain their less-motivated science majors for the same reasons large universities do. Seymour and Hewitt identified reasons why approximately 50 percent of potential majors eventually leave the sciences. The students interviewed cited loss of interest, poor teaching, conceptual difficulties, and the overwhelming pace and load of required courses as primary reasons for switching majors. Seymour and Hewitt found that

> ... in the small private liberal arts college where we expected to find conditions more conducive to good educational experiences in science and mathematics, the main concerns of switchers and non-switchers differed little from those of students at other institutions. Although some aspects of the teaching emphasis traditional in liberal arts colleges were discernable, they were more in evidence in the non-sciences than in the sciences.[15]

It appears that the liberal arts colleges are not succeeding at reaching nonscience majors or at retaining potential majors. Assessments of curricula based upon reform principles in a number of disciplines show enhanced student learning and improved attitudes towards science. Given the correlation between the application of reform principles and the quality of student learning, it is disturbing that many liberal arts colleges fail to embrace the principles of reform. This is particularly ironic since the liberal arts college environment is ideal for experimenting with and implementing new curricula and programs.

Curriculum developers at liberal arts colleges and elsewhere have incorporated the principles of reform into their work. Those who have been most successful in enhancing student learning have also taken advantage of developments in a new discipline-specific field of scholarship known as science education research. In the following sections, I will describe the emergence of physics and mathematics education research and exemplary reform efforts mounted by college faculty.

SCIENCE AND MATHEMATICS EDUCATION RESEARCH

Some of the most effective new curricula, especially in physics and mathematics, are based on a new style of discipline-specific educational research. It is helpful to understand the origin of this type of research and how it is used as a basis for effective curriculum development.

In 1968, Arnold Arons, whose work contributed to many of the principles of science-education reform, moved to the University of Washington to develop a course in the physics department for prospective elementary school teachers.[16] Lillian C. McDermott collaborated with Arons on this project, extending it to the development of a course for prospective middle- and high-school teachers.[17] This collaboration led to the formation of the Physics Education Group at the University of Washington. As part of McDermott's early work on teacher preparation courses, she began to investigate student thinking about certain physical phenomena in order to identify conceptual difficulties that interfere with learning. For example, most physics students believe that a ball tossed in the air hovers at the top of its path before descending, so that its velocity, acceleration, and net force are all zero. Mature physicists understand that the ball's position is changing continuously under the influence of a constant downward gravitational force exerted by the Earth. It never hovers; its net force and acceleration are never zero. Students who believe that the ball hovers have a difficult time understanding Newton's second law of motion and using it to explain common, everyday motions.

To identify student conceptual difficulties like that of the "ball toss," McDermott and other physicists often begin with individual student interviews. The results from these interviews are used to guide the design of written questions that are administered to large numbers of students. The information obtained from the interviews and written questions can then be used to develop curricular materials that enhance student understanding of various topics. The effectiveness of these instructional materials is assessed by comparing student performance on conceptual questions before and after the use of the curriculum.

McDermott's systematic research on learning difficulties was the genesis of a new field of scholarly inquiry for physicists: Physics Education Research. In 1973, McDermott began a new program in which graduate students could earn doctorates in physics for research on the learning and teaching of physics.

Under McDermott's guidance, the Physics Education Group has served as a model for discipline-specific educational research and curriculum development and has produced numerous trailblazing articles.[18] Similar physics education research Ph.D. programs have been set up at the University of Maryland, San Diego State University, Kansas State University, and North Carolina University. Basic research is also taking place at the University of Oregon and Tufts University. Related research, focusing on the differences between how experts and naive students solve physics problems, is being conducted by groups at the University of Massachusetts and Carnegie Mellon University.[19]

Discipline-based educational research is a bit newer in mathematics than it is in physics. Alan Schoenfeld at the University of California is a leading proponent of using the outcomes of cognitive psychology in mathematics education.[20] Ed Dubinsky from Georgia State University, a pioneer in mathematics education research, began his research as an extension of Piaget's work.[21] Dubinsky's work involves exploring the subconcepts students need to acquire in order to understand key mathematics concepts, and then designing activities, often computer-based, that help students acquire these subconcepts.

Commonly held notions that result in student's learning difficulties have been identified in other disciplines. Astronomy students often think that the weather is cold in the winter months because the Earth is farther away from the Sun. Even if they are taught that the Earth is closer to the Sun in the winter in the northern hemisphere, they will revert to thinking the opposite is true soon after the exam is over. Biology students typically believe that plant biomass is made primarily from material gathered up from the soil. Unless these students complete a well-designed activity such as growing plants using hydroponics, they will probably cling to their belief even if told otherwise. Many students who complete chemistry forget how to balance equations because they have not made a connection between the balancing procedures they have memorized and the law of multiple proportions, which states that the relative number of atoms of each type must be the same before and after a reaction. If they are asked to use this law to design a method for deciding how many molecules of each compound are needed for a given reaction, they will be more likely to remember equation balancing. Mathematics students have difficulty understanding the functional relationships between the linear dimension of an object and its area. In the absence of direct experience paying for and eating pizzas of various sizes, they cannot answer questions such as: "If the diameter of a pizza is doubled and its price tripled, should you buy the big pizza or three small ones?"

Discipline-based science-education research is an extraordinary tool for curriculum development; it is commonly used in new physics curriculum development and to a lesser extent in mathematics curricula. The Physics Education Group at the University of Washington has created an extensive body of research-based supplementary curricular materials for science and engineering students enrolled in introductory physics courses.[22] It has also developed a laboratory-based curriculum for the preparation of prospective and practicing teachers to teach physics and physical science as a process of inquiry.[23] Widely disseminated physics and mathematics curricula—based, in part, on physics education research—have also been developed at a number of institutions. Workshop Physics and Workshop Calculus developed at Dickinson College are of particular interest in the context of this essay and will be discussed in more detail in the next section.[24]

Although many astronomy, biology, chemistry, and geology curriculum developers are guided by the principles of reform, the notion of doing research on specific learning difficulties to refine curricular materials has not yet spread to these disciplines. There is no substantive science education research literature that developers in these disciplines can draw upon.

LIBERAL ARTS COLLEGE EDUCATORS AS LEADERS IN REFORM

Liberal arts college educators are having a profound impact on the course of reform throughout the science and mathematics education community. Educators have helped to create influential national organizations and served as leaders in curricular reform. Institutions such as Drury College and Hope College have implemented comprehensive science programs that embody the educational reform principles.

National Organizations

In 1979 Michael Doyle, a chemist from Trinity University, along with several other liberal arts college professors, founded the Council on Undergraduate Research to develop federal programs that promote summer research for undergraduates and help institutions acquire modern laboratory equipment. The Council also organizes national conferences and publishes a journal that allows students to present the results of their research. The Council has been instrumental in spreading interest in undergraduate research programs to universities and two-year colleges. In twenty years, membership in the Council has grown to more than 3,500 members representing over 850 institutions.

Jeanne Narum founded Project Kaleidoscope (PKAL) in 1989 for the purpose of strengthening science and mathematics education in the nation's liberal arts community. PKAL was initially led by a committee of liberal arts college presidents, deans, and science educators. Over the past nine years it has expanded to serve undergraduate science educators from all kinds of institutions through publications, workshops, seminars, and national conferences. PKAL facilitates faculty and administrators in almost every conceivable manner: designing new facilities, promoting undergraduate research, attracting women and minorities to the study of science, mentoring new faculty, and developing curricula based on reform principles.[25]

Curricular Reform

Liberal arts colleges are ideal environments for the development, classroom testing, and evaluation of curricular materials. The leadership taken by scientists and mathematicians from liberal arts institutions is not accidental. It flows from the confluence of many streams—the intellectual heritage of educational philosophers and cognitive psychologists, the by now widely known guiding principles of science education reform, a new wave of federal funding, the emergence of discipline-based educational research, and the availability of new computer technologies and instrumentation. It is an interesting coincidence that leading curricula in the four major sciences were developed at only two small colleges, Beloit College and Dickinson College. These curricula, examined below in detail, have been widely adopted at institutions of many different types.

The BioQUEST Curriculum Consortium (Beloit College). BioQUEST is a group of educators and researchers committed to providing students with biology research and research-like experiences. This project, deeply rooted in the liberal arts, was founded by John Jungck, editor of *The BioQuest Library.* The Consortium began with an initiative of the Commission on Undergraduate Education in the Biological Sciences, established by liberal arts college biologists in the 1960s. Since its inception in 1986, the Consortium has grown to a community of more than 4,500 educators representing a diverse range of subject areas and educational levels.

The BioQUEST philosophy emphasizes the acquisition of scientific literacy through the collaborative intellectual activities of problem posing, problem solving, and the persuasion of peers (the "three P's" of science education). A major project has been the development of computer simulations that help students understand fundamental biological concepts. For example, students studying genetics can breed fruit flies and observe the inheritance of characteristics such as eye color. They can then augment their laboratory experience with software that simulates the breeding of thousands of virtual fruit flies, leading the student to discover the laws of genetics. In addition, computer tools have been developed that help students transfer data, graphics, hypotheses, and analyses into word-processing, spreadsheet, and graphics software. Students then build scientific manuscripts that can be reviewed by student editorial boards and published in student-run journals.

To build the collection of computer tools, the Consortium established *The BioQUEST Library,* an electronic, peer-reviewed academic journal.[26] The BioQuest software collection received an EDUCOM award for distinguished curriculum innovation in 1992. The Consortium also conducts faculty-development workshops and distributes a free newsletter, *BioQUEST*

Notes, three times a year to interested members of the education community.

The ChemLinks Project (Beloit College). The ChemLinks project was initiated by Brock Spencer of Beloit College and developed with members of the Midstates Science and Mathematics Consortium. After receiving startup grants from the Pew Charitable Trust, the ChemLinks Coalition became one of five NSF-funded systemic initiatives in chemistry education. Chemistry educators at forty institutions collaborate to develop topical modules for introductory and intermediate college chemistry curricula. The majority of these institutions are Midwestern liberal arts colleges, including Beloit, Carleton, College of Wooster, Grinnell, Hope, Kalamazoo, Knox, Lawrence University, Macalester, Rhodes, and St. Olaf. The ChemLinks Coalition has recently collaborated with The Modular Chemistry Consortium centered at the University of California at Berkeley. Between the two projects, over a hundred faculty from more than forty two-year colleges, four-year colleges, and universities have developed and tested modules dealing with chemistry, the environment, technology, and life processes.[27]

ChemLinks modules cover topics relevant to contemporary issues and take three to five weeks to complete. Students are guided to develop the chemistry knowledge needed to deal with these complicated issues. Modules incorporate collaborative activities and inquiry-based laboratory projects that replace traditional lectures, exams, and laboratories. All of these approaches are consistent with the reform principles.

It is unlikely that ChemLinks could have been developed at a large research university. After overseeing the development of ChemLinks at institutions of all sizes, Spencer has become "acutely aware of how difficult it is for a large university with large lecture . . . and lab sections to experiment."[28] He points out that faculty in liberal arts programs can make significant changes without waiting for funding, and cites several examples of rapid, modestly funded projects initiated at liberal arts colleges: Grinnell's recent success in testing ChemLinks modules, Franklin and Marshall College's unfunded Middle Atlantic Discovery Chemistry Project, College of the Holy

Cross's development of Discovery Chemistry, and Merrimack College's microscale organic chemistry laboratory system.

The Workshop Physics Project (Dickinson College). Development of the Workshop Physics curriculum began at Dickinson College in 1986 with a grant from the U.S. Department of Education's Fund for the Improvement of Postsecondary Education (FIPSE). The curriculum was designed to provide activities for a two-semester course in calculus-based physics. In Workshop Physics courses, lectures and traditional laboratory sessions have been abandoned in favor of activity-based sessions that last for two hours and are held three times each week. The structure of these courses is based on a program of guided inquiry embodied in a workbook-style activity guide.[29] A major objective of Workshop Physics courses is helping students understand the basis of knowledge in physics as a subtle interplay between observations, experiments, definitions, mathematical description, and the construction of theories. Whenever appropriate outcomes of Physics Education research were available, they were used to inform the development of activities. Curriculum refinements were based on the results of pre- and post-tests on known student learning difficulties.

The Workshop Physics curriculum makes extensive use of computer software and hardware tools for the collection, graphing, analysis, and mathematical modeling of data. These tools have been codeveloped by educators at Dickinson College, Tufts University, and Millersville University. They include a computer-based laboratory system,[30] tools to enhance spreadsheet performance,[31] and video analysis software.[32] Educational research by Ronald Thornton, David Sokoloff, and others has demonstrated that computer-based laboratory tools used with curricular materials based on educational research can help students achieve dramatic learning gains.[33]

Since the fall of 1987 over five hundred Dickinson College students have completed Workshop Physics courses. Research has shown improvements in student attitudes toward the study of physics; mastery of critical concepts; student performance in upper-level physics courses and in solving traditional textbook problems at a level as good as or better than that of students taking traditional lecture courses; and confidence working in a laboratory setting.[34] The Workshop Physics curriculum is now used at approximately fifteen residential liberal arts colleges as well as at thirty-five other institutions including universities, two-year colleges, and high schools. The computer tools that have been developed for use with the curriculum have been distributed to hundreds of institutions. Major portions of the Workshop Physics curriculum have been incorporated into RealTime Physics Modules designed for use in university and college laboratory programs.[35]

The Workshop Mathematics Program (Dickinson College). Nancy Baxter-Hastings, Allan Rossman, and Priscilla Laws began developing Workshop Mathematics courses in 1991 with grants from FIPSE and the Knight Foundation. Additional support has come from the NSF and FIPSE. Workshop Mathematics courses embody the reform principles. The courses are distinguished by their emphasis on active learning, conceptual understanding, real-world applications, use of computer and/or graphing calculator technology, and motivation of underserved populations. Students work in small groups to examine the behavior of mathematical systems in much the same way that science students explore natural phenomena. They are invited to make connections, pose questions, explore, and learn from mistakes. The Workshop Mathematics program was chosen by PKAL as one of ten "programs that work."

Workshop Mathematics contains four entry-level courses: Quantitative Reasoning, Statistics, and Calculus with Review I & II. Activity guides are being developed for all of the courses. The Workshop on Quantitative Reasoning teaches students to interpret and assess quantitative arguments. Topics are presented in the context of practical applications to motivate students, for example, estimating gasoline-tax revenues and interpreting the results of AIDS tests. Workshop Statistics is intended primarily for social-science and prehealth students. Students analyze genuine data, both from available sources and generated by the students themselves, on real-world problems. Workshop Calculus: Guided Explorations with Review is a two-course sequence for students unprepared to enter the regular calculus program. It integrates a review of basic precalculus concepts with the study of fundamental ideas encountered in a traditional first semester calculus course: functions, limits, derivatives, integrals, and an introduction to integration techniques.[36]

With no competing activity-based statistics curricula, more than thirty thousand copies of the Workshop Statistics activity guide have been distributed.[37] Approximately thirty institutions have adopted the Workshop Calculus program. Workshop Calculus and Workshop Physics share the distinction of being the only curricula described here that are explicitly shaped by outcomes of discipline-based educational research. Rigorous assessments of Workshop Calculus students have shown substantial improvements in their attitudes, learning, and retention of concepts.[38]

Other National Curriculum Projects

Several other well-known curriculum development projects are worthy of mention. Larry Marschall at Gettysburg College leads a group that has developed laboratory exercises illustrating modern astronomical techniques using digital data and color images (Project CLEA). Arnold Ostebee and Paul Zorn of St. Olaf College have authored a very successful two-volume set of calculus books entitled *Calculus from Graphical, Numerical, and Symbolic Points of View*. These books make creative use of symbolic algebra systems and graphing calculators to help students learn basic calculus concepts by engaging in innovative graphing activities. Several mathematics educators from liberal arts colleges were members of the consortium that contributed to the extraordinarily popular Project Harvard Calculus effort.[39]

Programmatic Reform in Science and Mathematics

Although many colleges are revitalizing their science and mathematics programs, PKAL and the NSF have identified a number of exceptionally successful institutions. Two, Hope College and Drury College, are especially noteworthy.

Holistic Reform at Hope College. In 1998 Hope College was chosen by the National Science Foundation as one of ten liberal arts colleges to receive a prestigious award for the integration of research and education. Hope's Division of Natural Sciences has developed an innovative curriculum that intertwines student learning and faculty development. Students are given the opportunity for collaborative work, and upper-level students mentor younger students. Approximately 85 percent of Hope's science majors undertake extended undergraduate research projects. For the 70 percent of students not majoring in science, Hope has developed a strong core curriculum of interdisciplinary courses that promote an understanding of science and technology. This is intended to help students excel in a technological culture. Courses in science and mathematics are taught in an experiential, hands-on mode that includes in-course research projects.

As a result of their institutionwide revitalization efforts, Hope College's program in science and mathematics is particularly successful at reaching nonscience and less-motivated science majors. About 30 percent of Hope's science majors enter graduate programs, much higher than the national average for liberal arts colleges. The faculty also benefits; it has an enviable record of producing quality publications in collaboration with students. With seventy-six NSF grants awarded since 1989, Hope science faculty rank third among more than 160 liberal arts colleges in the number of grants received.

Drury College's Integrated Math and Science Program. With a major grant from the NSF in 1995, Drury implemented a new integrated science and mathematics curriculum as part of its general education program.[40] The major goal was for students to achieve science and mathematics literacy, defined as "understanding how science and scientists work." The core program begins with a course entitled Mathematics and Inquiry, which is designed to develop quantitative and abstract reasoning abilities. Next, students take a longer interdisciplinary course, Science and Inquiry, taught by a physicist, chemist, and biologist. A case-study approach, involving real-world problems, is used. These courses prepare students for the culminating Undergraduate Research course, where students engage in a research project and present their results orally, in writing, and at a public poster session.

The program has a strong assessment component that focuses on both student attitudes toward and understanding of
science. This assessment has shown a significant enhancement
of attitudes toward the study of science, self-esteem, and self-
confidence as scientific investigators. The college has recently
received a second grant from the NSF to integrate its science
and math curriculum with the rest of the general-education
program. And there is evidence that Drury has applied its
innovative philosophy towards its program for science majors;
the physics department has successfully adopted Dickinson's
calculus-based Workshop Physics curriculum.[41]

PROBLEMS AND CHALLENGES

Science curricula at many liberal arts colleges are still dominated by traditional textbooks and the lecture method. There is
an urgent need for high-quality curricular materials developed
according to the reform principles and refined with reference to
the outcomes of systematic, discipline-specific educational research. This requires continued funding for both science education research and curriculum development in all disciplines.
This blend of development and educational research presents
exciting opportunities for collaboration between colleges and
universities. At liberal arts colleges, small student-faculty ratios, teaching-oriented philosophies, and modern laboratory
equipment provide a fertile environment for the development of
new teaching methods and curricula. University graduate programs in the basic sciences, with graduate students specializing
in educational research and access to large undergraduate populations, provide an ideal setting for educational research.

Ideally, every liberal arts college in the country would spend
the time, effort, and money to develop or adapt exemplary
programs for students completing general science requirements
as well as for its science majors. Such programs would have
innovative interdisciplinary courses linking science to social
concerns, state-of-the-art equipment and facilities, and integrated undergraduate research programs. Faculty would take
advantage of new principles of teaching and discipline-specific
educational research outcomes.

But ideal programs are beyond the reach of mortal faculties. "First tier" liberal arts colleges, such as Oberlin, Carleton, Swarthmore, and Reed, have outstanding records when it comes to recruiting, retaining, and educating future research scientists and mathematicians. "Second tier" liberal arts colleges have collaborated with large universities to take national leadership in curricular revitalization based on reform principles and, where possible, research on student learning difficulties in the sciences. Still other liberal arts colleges have taken local leadership in revitalizing their own institutions. The creative ideas and successes of these institutions provide models to inspire colleagues to revamp their own programs.

Liberal arts colleges share common problems. Good teaching and conducting undergraduate research in student-centered programs is labor intensive. The time to keep abreast of new teaching methods and educational research and the money to maintain computer systems and apparatus are perpetually in short supply. Faculty become isolated from communities that could stimulate them to seek excellence in teaching based on educational principles and research, the supervision of undergraduate research, or participation in interdisciplinary courses. A balanced institution with experts in several disciplines in each of these areas would be able to mount a truly outstanding science and mathematics program.

ACKNOWLEDGMENTS

I am grateful to Phil Thompson who helped with the background research for this essay, and to Lillian McDermott for her perspectives on the development of physics education research and for insightful comments. I would also like to thank George Allan, Arnold Arons, Ken Laws, and Scott Franklin for helpful advice on revisions, and Gail Oliver for suggestions in revising and straightening out the references.

ENDNOTES

[1] Edward Gibbon, *The History of the Decline and Fall of the Roman Empire*, vol. 1 (New York: Harper & Brothers, 1831), chap. 4.

[2]Susan T. Hill, *Science and Engineering Degrees: 1966–95*, NSF 97–335 (Arlington, Va.: NSF Division of Science Resource Studies, 1997). These data show that only one out of every sixteen bachelor's degrees goes to a student studying science or engineering. The proportion of science majors at liberal arts colleges varies from 8 to 30 percent, which is quite a bit higher than the national norm.

[3]Pew Higher Education Roundtable, "A Teachable Moment," *Policy Perspectives* 8 (1) (June 1998): 1–10.

[4]Arnold B. Arons, "Achieving Wider Scientific Literacy," *Dædalus* 112 (2) (Spring 1983): 91–122.

[5]Alfred North Whitehead, *The Aims of Education* (New York: Macmillan, 1929; Free Press, 1967); John Dewey, *Experience and Education* (New York: Macmillan Publishing Co., Inc., 1938, 1997).

[6]Kurt Lewin, *Field Theory in Social Sciences* (New York: Harper & Row, 1951).

[7]Jean Piaget, *Genetic Epistemology* (New York: Columbia University Press, 1970).

[8]This work has been summarized by Chickering and Gamson. See A. W. Chickering and Z. F. Gamson, eds., "Applying the Seven Principles of Good Practice in Undergraduate Education," *New Directions for Teaching and Learning*, no. 47 (San Francisco: Jossey-Bass Publishers, 1991).

[9]Arnold B. Arons, *Development of Concepts of Physics* (Reading, Mass.: Addison-Wesley, 1965); Arnold B. Arons, "Cultivating the Capacity for Formal Reasoning," *American Journal of Physics* 44 (1976): 834; Arnold B. Arons, "Critical Thinking and the Baccalaureate Curriculum," *Liberal Education* 71 (1985): 141; Arnold B. Arons, "Guiding Insight and Inquiry in Introductory Physics Laboratory," *The Physics Teacher* 31 (1993): 278–282; Arnold B. Arons and R. Karplus, "Implications of Accumulating Data on Levels of Intellectual Development," *American Journal of Physics* 44 (1976): 396; and Arnold B. Arons, *Teaching Introductory Physics* (New York: John Wiley & Sons, Inc., 1997).

[10]The National Science Board, *Undergraduate Science, Mathematics and Engineering Education*, NSF 86–100 (Washington, D.C.: NSF, 1987), vols. I, II.

[11]Elaine Seymour and Nancy M. Hewitt, *Talking About Leaving: Why Undergraduates Leave the Sciences* (Boulder, Colo.: Westview Press, 1997).

[12]Ibid.

[13]Ibid., 319.

[14]Thomas R. Cech, "Science at Liberal Arts Colleges: A Better Education?" in this issue of *Dædalus*.

[15]Seymour and Hewitt, *Talking About Leaving*, 41.

[16]Arnold B. Arons, *The Various Language: An Inquiry Approach to the Physical Sciences* (New York: Oxford University Press, 1977).

[17]Lillian C. McDermott, "Combined Physics Course for Future Elementary and Secondary School Teachers," *American Journal of Physics* 42 (1974): 668–676.

[18]Lillian C. McDermott, "Research on Conceptual Understanding in Mechanics," *Physics Today* 37 (7) (1984): 24–32; Lillian C. McDermott, "A View from Physics," in *Toward a Scientific Practice of Science Education,* ed. Marjorie Gardner et al. (Hillsdale, N.J.: Lawrence Erlbaum Associates, 1990); Lillian C. McDermott, "Bridging the Gap between Teaching and Learning: The Role of Research," in *The Changing Role of Physics Departments in Modern Universities: Proceedings of the International Conference on Undergraduate Physics Education* (ICUPE), ed. Edward F. Redish and John S. Rigden, AIP Conference Proceedings, 399 (Woodbury, N.Y.: American Institute of Physics, 1997).

[19]Current research in Physics Education has been summarized by Lillian C. McDermott and Edward F. Redish, "Resource Letter on Physics Education Research," *American Journal of Physics* (in press).

[20]Alan H. Schoenfeld, ed., *Cognitive Science and Mathematics Education* (Mahwah, N.J.: Lawrence Erlbaum Associates, Inc., 1987).

[21]Ed Dubinsky, "Teaching Mathematical Induction I," *Journal of Mathematical Behavior* 5 (1986): 307–317; Ed Dubinsky, "On Helping Students Construct the Concept of Quantification," in *Proceedings of the Twelfth Annual Conference of the International Group for Psychology of Mathematics Education I,* ed. A. Borbas (Veszprem, Hungary: OOK Printing House, 1988), 255–262; E. Dubinsky and G. Harel, "The Nature of the Process of Function," in *The Concept of Function: Aspects of Epistemology and Pedagogy,* eds. G. Harel and E. Dubinsky (Washington, D.C.: Mathematical Association of America, 1992), 85–106.

[22]Lillian C. McDermott, Peter S. Shaffer, and the Physics Education Group at the University of Washington, *Tutorials in Introductory Physics,* prelim. ed. (Upper Saddle River, N.J.: Prentice Hall, 1998).

[23]Lillian C. McDermott and the Physics Education Group at the University of Washington, *Physics by Inquiry* (New York: John Wiley & Sons, Inc., 1996).

[24]Leading developers of research-based curricula in mathematics include David Smith at Duke University and Nancy Baxter-Hastings at Dickinson College. David A. Smith, "Renewal in Collegiate Mathematics Education," *Documenta Mathematica,* extra volume ICM III (1998): 777–786; Nancy Baxter-Hastings, "The Workshop Mathematics Program: Abandoning Lectures," in *Student-Active Science,* ed. Ann P. McNeal and Charlene D'Avanzo (Orlando, Fla.: Harcourt Brace & Company, 1997), 355–381.

[25]The Project Kaleidoscope web site is at <http://www.pkal.org>; Project Kaleidoscope, *What Works: Natural Science Communities,* vol. I (Washington, D.C.: The Independent Colleges Office, 1991); Project Kaleidoscope, *Structures for Science: A Handbook on Planning Facilities for Undergraduate Natural Science Communities,* vol. III (Washington, D.C.: The Independent Colleges Office, 1997).

[26]*The BioQUEST Library* is currently published by Academic Press. The BioQUEST web site is at <http://www.academicpress.com/bioquest>.

[27]John Wiley & Sons is publishing a preliminary edition for use in 1999–2000, and the first commercial edition is scheduled for release in the fall of 2000.

240 *Priscilla W. Laws*

The ChemLink web site can be found at <http://www.pkal.org/resources/other/nsf/chemlink.html>.

28Brock Spencer et al., "The ChemLinks and ModularCHEM Consortia: Using Active and Context-Based Learning to Teach Students How Chemistry is Actually Done," *Journal of Chemical Education* 75 (March 1998): 322–324.

29The author has collaborated with colleagues at Dickinson College and with educators from the University of Oregon, Tufts University, and Millersville University to create a Workshop Physics activity guide. Priscilla W. Laws, *Workshop Physics Activity Guide* (New York: John Wiley & Sons, Inc., 1997).

30The microcomputer-based laboratory system tools are available from Vernier Software, 8565 S.W. Beaverton-Hillsdale Highway, Portland, OR 97225-2429; telephone: (503) 297-5317.

31WPTools are available at <http://www.physics.dickinson.edu>.

32The VideoPoint web site is at <http://www.lsw.com/videopoint>.

33Ronald K. Thornton and David R. Sokoloff, "Learning Motion Concepts using Real-Time Microcomputer-based Laboratory Tools," *American Journal of Physics* 58 (1990): 858–867.

34Priscilla W. Laws, "Calculus-Based Physics Without Lectures," *Physics Today* (1991): 24–31.

35David R. Sokoloff, Ronald K. Thornton, and Priscilla W. Laws, *RealTime Physics* (New York: John Wiley & Sons, Inc., 1998).

36Nancy Baxter-Hastings, *Workshop Calculus*, vol. I (New York: Springer-Verlag, 1997); vol. II (in press).

37Allan J. Rossman and J. Barr Von Oehsen, *Workshop Statistics* (New York: Springer-Verlag, 1997).

38Hastings, "The Workshop Mathematics Program," 355–381.

39These include Jeff Tecosky-Feldman of Haverford College, Patti Frazer Lock of St. Lawrence University, Eric Connally of Wellesley College, and Carl Swenson of Seattle University.

40Supported in part by the National Science Foundation Course and Curriculum Development Program under Grant 95–54960.

41Drury chemist Rabindra Roy must surely rank as one of the most productive undergraduate research mentors in history, averaging over four papers and ten conference presentations *per year* for over thirty years. He has copresented talks and coauthored papers with hundreds of his undergraduate students.

Christina Elliott Sorum

"Vortex, Clouds, and Tongue": New Problems in the Humanities?

Y COLLEAGUES AND I AT UNION COLLEGE are bemused when we hear humanists at other liberal arts colleges lament the "preprofessionalism" of students, which they perceive as a new phenomenon causing shrinking interest and enrollments in the humanities. We teach in a school that long ago played a major role in displacing the traditional classical curriculum—ancient languages and literatures, philosophy, history, and religion—from its dominant role in higher education. In 1827, Eliphalet Nott, then the president of Union, moved "to afford a choice between the ancient and modern languages and also between the branches abstract and scientific and branches practical and particular." In the optional "Scientific Course" he instituted, classical studies were omitted after the freshman year, and one third of the curriculum was given over to science (including optics, physiology, and mineralogy), one third to mathematics, and the rest to modern languages (French or Spanish), social studies, law, English composition, and oratory. This curriculum, which led directly to the professions of engineering, medicine, law, and mining, was soon selected by a third of the students.[1]

In fact, questions about the utility of the traditional classical curriculum with its emphasis on the humanities arose long before pragmatic Americans joined the debate. In fifth-century Athens, the discussion was enough of a commonplace for Aristophanes to mock it in his plays. In the *Clouds*, for example,

Christina Elliott Sorum is Dean of Arts and Sciences and Frank Bailey Professor of Classics at Union College.

241

Strepsiades, an old bumbling countryman, wants his son Pheidippides to be educated by Socrates in the techniques of persuasion—in rhetoric—in order that the family might evade the lawsuits brought on by the son's excessive expenditures on horses. When Pheidippides refuses to enroll in Socrates' school, Strepsiades himself decides to attend. The ensuing drama is a conflict of generations, religion (where "Vortex, Clouds, and Tongue" replace Zeus and the traditional gods), and educational theories. The curriculum offered in the Socratic "Thinkery" was rhetoric, the ability to argue a case successfully. This was indeed a useful skill in a city in which political power depended upon success as a speaker in the democratic assembly. In the play, two characters, "Right Argument" and "Wrong Argument," make their cases against and for the teaching of rhetoric and such allied innovative topics as cosmology, biology, and grammar. "Right Argument," a representative of an older generation, insists that education should focus on traditional music and poetry and instill a reverence for established religion and parental authority, as well as a sense of individual and civic honor, probity, and modesty; "Wrong Argument" dispenses entirely with both the traditional content and the moral and civic function of education and insists instead that students should learn clever argument, by which they can exploit conventional beliefs and moral standards in order to win the day. "Wrong Argument," a moral relativist, appeals especially to the young with hints of the pleasures of all manner of dissipation.

Amidst the ribald nonsense, the question emerges: do we study the literary and philosophical works of the past to learn virtue and truth from them, or to utilize them by means of "scientific methodologies" in service of our contemporary concerns and preoccupations? The ideas attributed to Protagoras in Plato's *Theatetes* are similar if more serious than those of "Wrong Argument." He too indicates that absolute truth is unknowable and that rhetoric must be used to determine the truth approximate to each time and place—in other words, "Man is the measure of all things."[2] In the *Republic*, the Platonic Socrates makes a different sort of complaint against the traditional curriculum of the poets propounded by "Right Argument." He describes its practitioners as "imitators of images of excellence and of the other things" and hence unable to reveal any truth.[3] Poets further undermine their educational value because they appeal to the emotions rather than to reason. Thus Plato snatches truth and virtue away from the jurisdiction of poetry and relocates it in the study of logic and dialectic. Only with these tools is it possible to discover the truth that is absolute and knowable, the truth essential to live a good life both as a citizen and a person.

In American colleges, the golden age of the humanities may have been the time before the Revolution when the fundamental disciplines were Greek, Latin, Hebrew, logic and rhetoric, natural and moral philosophy, metaphysics, and mathematics. This curriculum, like that of Strepsiades and Plato, was designed to produce good men and loyal citizens, but it also offered the training necessary for law, medicine, and theology. In the late 1700s the other liberal arts were introduced, including modern languages and, in some cases, astronomy, physics, and chemistry. By the early 1800s, navigation and surveying had crept in—courses to which we humanists in liberal arts colleges would object today. Next, requirements in the ancient languages became the focus of change. Between 1796 and 1806 Princeton experimented with substituting scientific subjects for the Latin and Greek requirement.[4] In 1796, a student at Union College could take four years of French instead of Greek, although by 1802 French was dropped from the catalog, a change explained by Eliphalet Nott as due to a lack of patronage but that his biographer views as a move to accommodate parents who had a conservative dislike of the revolutionary ideas espoused in that tongue. In this period, however, students attending Union or similar colleges for the most part studied a modified classical curriculum.[5]

Then, in 1827, Nott introduced at Union the preprofessional "Scientific Curriculum" discussed above, which severely limited traditional studies in the humanities and challenged their authority as sufficient education for the contemporary world.[6] These and similar changes elsewhere did not go unremarked upon. In 1828, Jeremiah Day, the president of Yale, affirmed the classical common curriculum and argued that undergraduate colleges should not include discrete professional studies, for the mission of higher education should be directed to acquiring the arts of living.[7] In 1850, however, Francis Wayland of Brown University lamented that with the traditional curriculum colleges were producing an article for which demand was diminishing.[8] Subsequently, in 1869, Charles Eliot at Harvard challenged the old order head on with a declaration of the value of a broad elective curriculum that could appeal to students' individual abilities and tastes.[9] This new educational order was contrasted with the old in 1890 by the president of DePauw, who said, "Old Education ascribed the virtue to the subject, the New Education ascribes it to the process," thus echoing the Aristophanic debate and foreshadowing later controversies of content versus methodology.[10]

Inside and outside the academy the debate continues today over the proper subject of study in the humanities, the appropriate methodology to carry out that study, and the particular value of studying the humanities. In order to acquire a contemporary perspective on these issues, I asked six undergraduates whether and why they should study the humanities, and where this study should fit into a liberal arts education at an undergraduate residential college.[11] Their answers were inclusive; they did not perceive a split between the transcendent and the pragmatic, nor between the study of texts to comprehend their truths and to master their techniques for their own purposes. Five students—agreeing with "Right Argument"—spoke of the importance of reading the great works of literature, history, and philosophy (both Western and Eastern) in order to answer the perennial questions of mankind that are important for individual and human development: "Literature presents imaginative and exploratory uses of language; reading, talking about, and writing about these uses not only exposes us to different ways of conceiving and expressing human experience, but also requires us to integrate them into our own lives," or, more simply, "The humanities are the only place to turn when we want to study ourselves, to know how and why we live."

Then, sounding more like Protagoras than Plato, they presented a utilitarian argument for the study of the humanities as "language." One said with great assurance, "The most important skill students can learn is taught by the study of literature.

The study of literature is a study of manipulations of language. The humanities, in general, concern themselves with the use of language, teaching us skills like persuasion through reading and writing about novels, philosophical treatises, and historical documents." Another who studies Greek and Latin said that reading these languages had taught her to integrate "symbols (or data) into something meaningful." A third described the critical thinking that is learned through the study of the humanities as a tool that he and other scientists should use in evaluating their research traditions as well as the values and implications of their research projects.

In response to the particular question of the virtue of studying the humanities in a liberal arts college, they viewed the answer as self-evident. Said one, "The only authentic approach to the humanities can occur in a liberal arts college because the institution itself (ideally) is governed by the same belief as the humanities in the importance of dialogue." They stressed that the small classes and seminars on which colleges pride themselves are the breeding grounds for such explorations and creations of language and that "Humanities students at liberal arts colleges emerge having been participants of vigorous discussions about and examinations of texts—how they construct stories or arguments or ideas to form beautiful and convincing works." They noted that the teacher in small classes engages the students so that they are compelled to grasp the difficult messages about thought, experience, and knowledge and averred that this was unlikely to happen in another educational format.

In light of these affirmations, it is difficult to believe that the humanities are considered to be in dire straits. But we regularly hear, even at liberal arts colleges with their long traditions in the humanities, that enrollments are shrinking, that humanities teachers are demoralized, and that students resent studying topics that seem irrelevant to their future careers. Furthermore, the press, members of the government, and academics themselves perceive that the humanities are "suffering from a failure of confidence, of coherence, and particularly of the nerve to defend and disseminate the great traditions of philosophy, literature, and the arts."[12] It is clear to me—as a classicist, faculty member, and dean—that there are, in fact, major problems with regard to the faculty, students, and curricula that must be addressed so that the humanities can continue to flourish at liberal arts colleges.

The students quoted above regard the close interaction of faculty and students in small classes as an essential part of studying the humanities and as one particular virtue of a liberal arts college. This is what we all speak of in our catalogs and mission statements and what we tell prospective students and parents.[13] The students believe that they will be or are engaged in a common learning experience with the faculty in which they read, discuss, and write about significant ideas and texts. Yet while I believe most faculty at liberal arts colleges endorse the ideal, seldom do I hear faculty rejoice in this opportunity—or even discuss it as the activity in which they are engaged. Rather, many perceive themselves as assailed by a variety of forces both internal and external to their institutions that prevent them from fully achieving this ideal.

Primary among these forces are the increased specialization and professionalization of the faculty of liberal arts colleges. Almost all of these faculty have trained at a research university, where specialization is the mode of study. These universities owe much to the vision of Daniel Coit Gilman, the founder of Johns Hopkins, who in the 1870s spoke of creating a university based on a scientific view, emphasizing discovery of knowledge and encouraging narrowly focused research rather than broad learning. This approach, Gilman believed, would provide every scholar "the unique experience of having contributed some tiny brick, however small, to the Temple of Science, the construction of which is the sublimest achievement of man."[14] Students trained in such institutions as Johns Hopkins emerge into the profession as specialists in one area in which they continue to work, for they understand that if they are to be successful they must contribute something new to the discussion, and this requires the close examination of a topic, of learning more about it than is already known. These graduates comprise the pool from which liberal arts colleges hire.

In a recent article in the *Chronicle of Higher Education*, Leonard Cassuto observed that the "most highly professionalized and accomplished graduate students and incoming faculty members that anyone has ever seen are applying for jobs."[15] While one might think the academy would rejoice in this, the truth is otherwise. In the rapid expansion of higher education that occurred between the late 1950s and the mid-1970s, in which the number of Ph.D.'s nearly quadrupled, the ever increasing number of scholars led to a further narrowing of specialties.[16] Because of the sudden collapse of the academic job market in the 1970s, many young scholars who had expected to be employed at major research universities became candidates for jobs at liberal arts undergraduate colleges. The competition for these positions as well as for those at research institutions has led would-be faculty members to present themselves at hiring time not as apprentice scholars, but rather as professionals with publications in hand or detailed plans for their publishing future. Over the years, as more and more of these young scholars have accepted jobs at liberal arts colleges, they have brought with them not only their talent but also the professional mode and expectations acquired in graduate school at research universities. This mode defines excellence in terms of peer-reviewed publications in scholarly journals or with scholarly presses. And the peers are specialists.

This situation has special implications for Liberal Arts I college faculty.[17] It certainly does not mean that these scholars are not good undergraduate teachers; most whom I have known consider their teaching of primary importance, are successful at it, and enjoy it.[18] But there is an underlying tension or sense of dissatisfaction in many of these men and women, who have been trained to locate their definitions of success in scholarly achievements that are necessarily specialized. They begin their new job eager to profess their topic but immediately learn that the special skill of a college teacher is to be able to translate the significance of the topic—presumably of a topic that he or she loves—into a context that is meaningful for the undergraduate. This takes a reorientation of scholarly values, for the details and complexity that are the essence of scholarly work must be put aside and the grand scheme—which as scholars they have learned to distrust—must be put forward. Furthermore, many in the humanities will not be teaching their particular topics to upper-level students in seminars. Rather, they will teach introductory or core courses with large enrollments that cover a broad area in a brief time and in which they must emphasize not only content but also basic reading and writing skills. Finally, many students may not be planning to continue study in the discipline or may be present only because the course is required. Successfully teaching these students can be both exciting and rewarding, but the constant pressure to publish created by the brutal reality of the job market and the tenure process and the message of the low status of teaching such "service courses" intrude with nagging persistence on the pleasure.

The typical faculty member in the humanities at a liberal arts college must teach not only introductory material but also a wide variety of topics within the discipline—often four to six different courses a year. In addition, the faculty member may be called upon to teach in multidisciplinary general-education programs. Such are the exigencies of small departments and general-education programs. Where generalists are needed, specialists are provided who, upon beginning the job, find themselves called upon immediately to develop a repertoire of courses in areas they may have only briefly or never studied.[19] For example, Union College requires all freshmen to take the Freshman Preceptorial, an intensive reading and writing seminar with a common reading list that is designed to introduce students to varieties of good writing and types of argument. Faculty from across the college teach the course, although almost half come from the humanities. The eclectic reading list, which is arranged in clusters designed to generate discussion, includes works and authors as diverse as the Koran and the Bhagavad Gita, Voltaire and Ibsen, Shakespeare, and Frederick Douglass. Newer faculty, even those in the humanities who are used to teaching primary texts, have been increasingly reluctant to teach the course, not only because of their commitment to their area and to the belief that authority is vested in specialization, but also because of a fear that they will not teach as "well" and hence will be evaluated poorly by their colleagues or the students, which in turn can affect their success in the tenure process.

The problems posed in teaching by specialization do not, however, have the same impact on morale and behavior as those posed by the demand—real and imagined—of remaining a productive scholar in a liberal arts college. As Ernest Boyer noted, "Research per se was not the problem. The problem was that the research mission, which was appropriate for *some* institutions, created a shadow over the entire higher learning enterprise—and the model of a 'Berkeley' or an 'Amherst' became the yardstick by which all institutions would be measured."[20] The inclusion of "Amherst" in Boyer's remark is both notable and ironic. Amherst is a liberal arts college—a wealthy and top-ranked school to be sure, but still a liberal arts undergraduate college and not a research university. Should even an Amherst have the same research expectations as a Berkeley? The question is to a large degree irrelevant, for faculty at the highly selective liberal arts colleges have aligned themselves with the research universities in terms of their research expectations; the rest of the four-year and two-year colleges fall into a group with lesser expectations and demands.[21] This alignment is not unexpected, for the candidate pool for jobs at research universities and Liberal Arts I colleges is the same. It is, however, a fact of critical importance when considering the ethos and self-expectations of Liberal Arts I faculty in the humanities, expectations that run afoul of two major obstacles—time and money.

For professors, the time available for research is to a large degree dependent upon the number of courses they teach. The teaching load at liberal arts colleges is normally higher than that of a research university. The thirty-two schools with which Union College, for example, chooses to compare itself have for the most part teaching loads of five or six courses a year, although a very few—the wealthiest—have a four-course load. Research university faculty, however, may have only three or four courses a year, at least one of which will be in their research area, and they may have graduate assistants to help with grading or to lead discussion sessions of their undergraduate courses. Furthermore, for humanists, the load can be especially time consuming because a number of their courses will be introductory, hence larger and entailing considerable amounts of graded writing, a time-consuming task. An additional demand upon the time of all liberal arts college faculty is the expectation that they will participate in the intellectual life of the students outside of the classroom with extensive office hours and attendance at language tables, poetry readings, and philosophy colloquia. Many also are regularly asked to talk to student groups, join student-faculty panels, plan trips to museums and theaters, attend student productions, plan film series, and entertain students in their homes.

Money, or its lack, exerts a further pressure upon the scholar-teacher in the humanities. Humanities faculty need funds to support time away from teaching and for travel. Frequently the materials they need for research are not in undergraduate libraries. National Endowment for the Humanities money available for research has been shrinking as scholarly expectations have been rising. Funds for four-year colleges and their affiliated scholars were 13.6 percent of the NEH budget in 1982, 10.5 percent in 1987, and 7.6 percent in 1992. Furthermore, the humanities receive less than 1 percent of all foundation giving—and those amounts, too, are falling. Cumulatively, according to John D'Arms, the total number of fellowships in the humanities awarded by the American Council of Learned Societies, the National Humanities Council, and the Guggenheim Foundation was just over 150 in 1994, a fall of nearly 40 percent from the early 1980s; simultaneously, purchasing power has been seriously eroded.[22] Yet the prevailing university value system, in which personal and institutional legitimacy is obtained predominantly through research activities, has moved full-blown with young scholars to liberal arts colleges, where these scholars must in many cases compete with those at universities who have more time, more money, and more support for obtaining grants.[23]

Scarce money for grants for humanities faculty in liberal arts colleges can also contribute to lower salaries. Frequently salary increases depend upon research productivity, not because teaching is disregarded, but because publications are easier to evaluate in terms of their number and venue and because there are more good teachers than money available for salary allocation. Moreover, the oversupply of job candidates and the undersupply of jobs, exacerbated by the absence of employment opportunities outside of the academy for humanists, have led to lower starting salaries and a lack of bargaining power. In addition, lower salaries may be attributed to the "feminization" of the humanities (33 percent of the faculty in humanities are women) and to the humanities' position at the forefront of the culture wars, from which they have suffered disproportionate decreases in public funding and support.[24] This salary differential is another source of demoralization for humanities faculties.

The inevitable question arises: should humanists at liberal arts colleges reduce their research expectations? It is not the new Ph.D.'s alone who would argue against this; many faculty trained during or after the 1960s would also agree.[25] In 1969, according to a report of the Carnegie Foundation for the Advancement of Teaching, in Liberal Arts I and II colleges traditionally known for their emphasis on teaching 6 percent of the faculty strongly agreed that it was difficult to achieve tenure without publishing. By 1989, the number had risen to 24 percent while another 16 percent agreed with reservations. At the same time, 22 percent considered that the pressure to publish reduced the quality of teaching, but 76 percent agreed either strongly or with reservations that teaching effectiveness should be the primary criterion for promotion. Furthermore, 83 percent indicated that their interests either lay primarily in teaching or leaned toward teaching. When asked what they actually had published, 32 percent reported having published no articles while 42 percent reported having published one to five, and 67 percent had not published a book or monograph, while 30 percent had published one to five. These liberal arts faculty—who, in most cases, create and apply the standards for reappointment, tenure, and promotion—seem to support a reward and status system that is at odds with their primary interests and activity. Thus it is not surprising that over half find their job a source of considerable personal strain and anxiety.[26]

Nevertheless, as both a humanist and a dean of arts and sciences, I believe that research expectations for humanists at liberal arts colleges should be encouraged. In fact, I have become increasingly committed to the idea that liberal arts college faculty must be active scholars, not least because providing research opportunities for faculty makes these colleges appealing to the most competitive job candidates. Equally importantly, scholarship can and does inform teaching in a variety of ways, including exposing the teacher to new ideas, methods, and information. Furthermore, most of us became faculty members because we were intensely interested in our fields and wanted to pursue them; this is an important part of our identity and our happiness. It is as critical to respect and nurture this motivation at a liberal arts college as at a research university, for frequently in a liberal arts college a faculty member will be the only person in his or her area; this makes it easy to suffer not only from intellectual loneliness but also from intellectual sloppiness or even arrogance. By engaging in scholarly activity and submitting work for consideration by their peers, teachers of undergraduates are able to maintain a high level of engagement and performance in their disciplines. Consequently, the administration must find ways to enable faculty to concentrate on their teaching without abandoning their research, and faculty in judging each other must take a broad and generous view of what constitutes appropriate research and productivity. Only in this way will the faculty of liberal arts colleges thrive as teachers and scholars and realize the goals of a liberal arts college education.

STUDENTS

Although the students with whom I spoke clearly expressed a belief in the importance of studying the humanities, they do not appear to be a representative sample. In 1966, humanities degrees were 20.7 percent of the total degrees awarded nationally; by 1993 they were only 12.7 percent. In Liberal Arts II colleges, there was a drop from 26 to 10 percent of the total in the absolute number of humanities B.A.'s, and a corresponding decrease in each of the major humanities disciplines. At Liberal Arts I colleges, however, the total degrees awarded in the humanities dropped only 10 percent, from 40 percent in 1966 to 30 percent in 1993.[27] These statistics must be considered in the context of changing enrollments. For example, in the 1950s and 1960s the numbers of humanities degrees may have been temporarily swollen by the women who attended college in increasing numbers, and who initially chose to study the fields tradi-tionally identified with women.[28]

The most frequently cited scapegoat for this state of affairs is preprofessionlism; students, like faculty, have been soiled by the mundane reality of getting and keeping jobs. In 1993, 85 percent of students reported that they had come to college with a specific career in mind for which they wished to prepare, and more than one-third admitted that, if they thought attending college was not helping their job chances, they would drop out. In 1996, 72 percent said they went to college in order to make more money—an increase of 18 percent since 1976. At the same time, the number of students who reported that they came to college to gain a well-rounded education and to formulate their values and goals declined from 71 to 57 percent. This pattern applies to all groups of students, regardless of age, race, gender, full-time or part-time attendance status, or the type of institu-tion attended. The same careerism is apparent in the choice of majors. Nationally, majors leading to jobs in business, educa-tion, and health professions are benefiting; on a liberal arts campus, business and health professions translate into econom-ics, biology, and psychology majors (up 70 percent nationally between 1985–1986 and 1993–1994). Nevertheless, although English, foreign languages, philosophy and religion, and visual and performing arts had all dropped in the number of degrees awarded between 1975–1976 and 1985–1986, they began to recoup their losses between 1985–1986 and 1993–1994.[29]

This preprofessional attitude is moderated, according to Alexander Astin's latest surveys, in students who attend private independent, Protestant, or Roman Catholic colleges, a set that includes Liberal Arts I colleges. These institutions have the strongest "humanities orientation," a measure he defines by the importance given to teaching the classics of Western Civiliza-tion, using essay exams, offering general-education courses, and encouraging the use of multiple drafts of written work. Small highly selective colleges exhibit the strongest humanities orientation, whereas the larger, nonselective institutions show the weakest.[30] This is reflected in the frequent inclusion of English among the top three majors at those Liberal Arts I colleges usually regarded as among the most elite.[31] Students' self-reported increases in both writing and critical-thinking skills also correlate positively with the humanities orientation, while the view that the principal benefit of a college education is to increase one's earning power or to improve job skills correlates negatively. There is also an indirect positive effect of the humanities orientation on self-reported growth in overall academic development and cultural awareness, in preparation for graduate school, listening ability, participation in protests, attending recitals or concerts, liberalism, and a diversity orientation. Clearly, in spite of the prevalence of preprofessional attitudes among the college-bound, liberal arts colleges are in an optimal position to engage students in the study of the humanities.

Even at liberal arts colleges, however, factors other than careerism pose significant and potentially more long-term problems for the humanities. The very styles of learning that seem best suited for today's students are not those of the typical humanities course. Humanities are text-based, but our students, we fear, are losing the ability to read, or as Denis Donoghue writes, "giving up that ability in favor of an easier one, the capacity of being spontaneously righteous, indignant, or otherwise exasperated."[32] The impairment of literacy—and hence verbal expression—becomes an impediment not only in the *reading* of texts but also in the interchange of ideas, both oral and written, that is fundamental to the *teaching* of texts.[33] Furthermore, a study by Charles Schroeder indicates that more than half of today's students perform best in a learning situation characterized by "direct, concrete experience, moderate-to-high degrees of structure, and a linear approach to learning." These students "value the practical and the immediate, and the focus of their perception is primarily on the physical world."[34] Three-quarters of faculty, on the other hand, prefer the global to the particular; are stimulated by the realm of concepts, ideas, and abstractions; and assume that students, like themselves, need a high degree of autonomy in their work.[35] Students prefer concrete subjects and an active mode of learning; faculty prefer abstract subjects and passive learning.[36] The implications for the humanities seem especially significant. No matter how many active and cooperative learning projects we invent, much of our students' learning must come through reading, a slow and solitary act, and much of our discussion must involve ideas and abstractions.

The mismatch of student learning styles and disciplinary methods in the text-based humanities is apparent in the difficulty humanities faculty and students have in benefiting from the current enthusiasm for undergraduate research. The National Council on Undergraduate Research, the Council on Undergraduate Research, and admissions literature tout such research as the pinnacle of the undergraduate experience. Indeed, active, hands-on learning, with faculty and students working closely together, and not infrequently publishing together, is well suited to the sciences.[37] The social sciences, too, with their emphases on data collection and manipulation, present to students opportunities of discovery and active learning in collaboration with faculty. Furthermore, funding is available for scientists and social scientists to support research with students through National Science Foundation programs such as "Research at Undergraduate Institutions" and "Research Experience for Undergraduates," as well as through student assistantships included in standard research grants.

In the humanities, however, although many students do serious work on senior projects and theses, and although this work entails meetings and discussions with the advisor, most of it is done alone, in reading, taking notes, and writing, and there is seldom external funding available to support either faculty or students. Furthermore, most seniors in the humanities are not able to produce original work because their language skills are inadequate or because they lack sufficient literary, philosophical, historical, or theoretical background. I do not wish to denigrate the achievements of humanities students or faculty; many of us have had wonderful intellectual experiences working with students on their senior theses, and many students have found the experience transformative. But the appeal is not to the scientific method of active discovery that is the model for student learning and undergraduate research today.

CURRICULUM

The humanities curriculum has attracted the most attention in public discussion of problems in higher education. Faculty are held responsible for its perceived disarray and blamed for failing to declare with one voice what students should learn— something that neither fifth-century Athenians nor nineteenth-century Americans could do. On occasion, they are even blamed for the moral breakdown of American society as a whole (which should at least boost the morale of those who think the humanities do not receive proper recognition of their centrality).[38]

Certainly, the curricula in the humanities have changed since the 1960s, and the increased discussion of literary theory and the politics of multiculturalism, the causes of most controversy, have contributed to this. Most noticeable is the tremendous increase in course offerings with a shift in course descriptions away from period or genre to thematic topics, the inclusion of interdepartmental and interdisciplinary programs, a globalization of the curriculum, and the proliferation of course offerings pertaining to minority populations, ethnic groups, and women and gender-related issues.[39] The average number of undergraduate courses listed in catalogs has increased by a factor of almost five since 1914 and almost doubled between 1964 and 1993; but this trend has been especially pronounced in the humanities where, with all types of institutions counted together, in 1914 there were an average of 156 courses in the humanities; in 1939, 263 courses; in 1964, 394; and in 1993, 788. This contrasts with mathematics and the natural sciences where the change between 1914 and 1993 was from 106 to 293.

An increase in course offerings does not, however, indicate the degree of true curricular change. The proliferation has had little effect upon majors in the humanities, for the new courses have not replaced the traditional required offerings, but rather have been added as electives.[40] Furthermore, in reading descriptions of majors in college catalogs, it appears that there are few schools in which new theoretical approaches are actually shaping programs. As Francis Oakley points out, "The bulk of the critical commentary on the current state of teaching in the humanities—frequently characterized by sweeping and sensationalist claims and a species of disheveled anecdotalism—has been based on what is supposed to be going on at probably no more than a dozen of the nation's leading research universities and liberal arts colleges."[41]

The increased number of courses, however, has made the designation of general education or core requirements a more contentious issue—an issue that often thwarts the development of general-education curricula entirely. This situation is the result both of a changing world and of an uncertainty about priorities in teaching the humanities. First, in an environment that is increasingly multicultural and global in orientation and experience and in which knowledge is expanding in all areas, it is difficult to set dates or geographical boundaries on the content of the humanities, or to ignore the interactions between the curriculum and the changing social, moral, political, and economic structures of society. Just as the introduction of French at Union in 1796 and its deletion in 1802 reflected social and political realities, so do current topics and emphases. Today enrollments are soaring nationally in Spanish and Chinese— both of which have a pragmatic appeal and an immediacy for our students—while those in Russian, French, and German are either barely maintaining their hold or falling.[42] Greater numbers of women and minorities are attending colleges, and courses that address their concerns and locate them within the intellectual conversation are flourishing. Second, today's students expect to study the humanities as a way to discover the "other," as well as to uncover shared values. Finally, we cannot with any degree of intellectual honesty refuse to recognize the existence of new methodologies for studying texts any more than we can refuse to recognize new techniques in science.

The inevitability of curricular change in a changing world appears to have uncoupled three obligations that traditionally motivated many humanities faculty. The first is to teach students those works that we regard as significant in our field, the works that have created our disciplinary traditions and, in many cases, our intellectual environment; the second is to teach ways of reading or methods of interpretation that will enable our students to make reasoned aesthetic, philosophical, or political judgments about texts; and the third is to engage students through consideration of verbal and visual texts in an exploration of universal human questions and concerns. The increased number of texts available to teach and the explosion of a variety of critical theories and approaches seem to present us with a series of choices that necessitate making significant decisions about literature and language, culture, and politics, and, in fact, about ourselves as scholars. Fortunately, as faculty teaching undergraduates in the humanities know, we can take the inclusive view that a course exists and that learning takes place not through the composition of a reading list or the explanation of a theoretical approach, but through the interactions of the teacher, the students, and the text. "Great works" can be taught from subversive perspectives, perspectives that make immediate what seems antique; "alternative" works can be taught "traditionally;" and few classes take place without at least oblique comments upon the basic human condition. Moreover, just as Aristophanes dramatizes opposing arguments, we should, to borrow Gerald Graff's phrase, "teach the conflict," for it is in responding to and evaluating alternative models and texts that students discover the excitement, urgency, and value of the humanities.

Most research on the state of the humanities in liberal arts colleges focuses on the degrees granted, that is, the number of majors. Naturally, faculty want majors in their departments not only because they wish to teach upper-level courses but also because they consider their subjects to be of great interest and hence worthy of study in depth. Yet, if humanists truly believe what they profess—that study in the humanities is an essential element in the creation of "educated persons," that it is important for the development of individuals apart from their professional training, that it enables people to lead their lives with an understanding of themselves and others, with rational purpose and sympathetic response—they must take general-education curricula or distribution requirements seriously, for they have been and will continue to be the way most liberal arts college students encounter the humanities.

Yet humanists have failed to convince their colleagues of the importance of general education for all undergraduate students. In 1914, an average of 55 percent of credits necessary to earn a B.A. were taken within the general-education requirement; in 1939, it was 48 percent; in 1964, 46 percent; and in 1993, 33 percent.[43] This occurred in spite of the Carnegie Foundation's 1977 report that declared general education a "disaster area."[44] Furthermore, general-education programs usually exist within a college as orphans without a department, budget, or dedicated faculty advocates. Faculty convey this low status both directly and indirectly to students, who perceive general-education courses as something that should be "gotten out of the way" before embarking on the serious project of the major. Humanists, therefore, must put aside their distaste for teaching students who are in classes because they are required to be, finding ways to engage them in these subjects and leading them to recognize the importance of such study. They must also put aside the arguments over content that frequently prevent the implementation of general-education courses in the humanities, and create coherence in the discussion that arises from inclusiveness. It is not, according to Astin's research, the formal curricular content and structure that determine how students approach and how faculty deliver general-education courses but the extent to which students interact with student peers, and the extent to which students interact with faculty. These are the types of interactions that can be fostered in the discussion format of humanities classrooms in small liberal arts colleges and that can attract students to our disciplines.[45]

Union College, a Liberal Arts I college with an enrollment of slightly over two thousand students, illustrates the resilience of the humanities. The school has a strong and unabashedly professional engineering program, a long history of strength in the sciences, and did not become coeducational until 1970. Yet both the humanities orientation Astin identifies with liberal arts colleges and the power of a general-education program to attract more students to the humanities are demonstrated in our enrollment patterns. The curriculum, a modified core introduced in 1988–1989 that promotes the idea that context is necessary for understanding, requires that, in addition to a Freshman Preceptorial, all students enroll in an ancient, European, or American "history sequence." Within each sequence, students take two history surveys and two aligned courses, one of which must be in literature. In addition, students must take three language courses, or three courses dealing with a non-Western culture, or participate in a term abroad. Many of these courses are also in the humanities. Significant enrollment increases that can be directly attributed to the general-education program have occurred in history, classics, and modern languages. The overall increase in humanities enrollments is 10 percent.[46] Furthermore, since the introduction of the general-education program, majors in the humanities (including history), which had fallen to a low of 14 percent in 1988, have risen to 21 percent in 1998, which just exceeds the high of 1969.[47]

In the conclusion of the *Clouds*, Pheidippides, who eventually learned the technique of clever argument, attempts to convince Strepsiades that it is proper for the son to beat the father. Strepsiades, not surprisingly, rejects the newfangled learning and gods and falls upon Socrates' school with ax and torch. Although vigorous attacks upon new methodologies are not unknown among humanists today, the use of brute force obviously undermines our claim that studying the humanities encourages us to act with rational purpose and to enter into understandings with others that acknowledge difference while reaching for a commonality. Consequently, we must find our inspiration not in the *Clouds*, but nearer at hand—even, I dare propose, in the current situation of the humanities at liberal arts colleges. We can note the slowly increasing number of students in our courses, the positive effects that general-education programs can have on majors, the excitement and interest generated by new texts and approaches, and, most importantly, the persistent belief of a number of students in liberal arts colleges that it is important to study the humanities. Nevertheless, we must continue to make our case for the humanities not only to the public but also to our colleagues in other disciplines. We need to realize that the preprofessionalism of the students mirrors our own careerism, and we must through our own attitudes reassert and sustain for all students the significance of the humanities. The strong presence of the humanities in general-education programs is one means of doing this. General education acts as a prism for the goals of the humanities; through a multiplicity of formats, it introduces students to a conversation that encourages young people to formulate a conception of the good that transcends their specific, if honorable, utilitarian ends, and begins for them the process of answering and re-answering the questions that confound us. And it is in the discussion of verbal and visual texts in the humanities class-rooms of liberal arts colleges that the potential for this sort of learning most obviously resides.

ACKNOWLEDGMENTS

I am grateful to my colleagues Thomas McFadden, Felmon Davis, and Kimmo Rosenthal for their helpful comments and insights.

ENDNOTES

[1]Codman Hislop, *Eliphalet Nott* (Middletown, Conn.: Wesleyan University Press, 1971), 223.

[2]Plato *Theatetes* 152A1.

[3]Plato *Republic* 600E.

[4]Christopher J. Lucas, *American Higher Education: A History* (New York: St. Martin's Press, 1994), 131.

[5]Hislop, *Eliphalet Nott*, 114–116, and T. G. McFadden, "Introduction," *Laws of Union College* (Schenectady, N.Y.: Friends of Union College, 1998). Freshmen studied Latin, Greek, and English languages, arithmetic, and elocution; sophomores, geography, algebra, geometry, trigonometry, surveying, navigation, and logic; juniors, Kames' elements of criticism, astronomy, higher mathematics, and natural and moral philosophy; and seniors, ancient and modern history, Locke, philosophy, Virgil, Cicero, and Horace.

[6]Hislop, *Eliphalet Nott*, 227.

[7]"The Yale Report of 1828," in *American Higher Education: A Documentary History*, ed. Richard Hofstadter and Wilson Smith (Chicago: University of Chicago Press, 1961), 2:275–291.

[8]Francis Wayland, "Report to the Brown Corporation, 1850," in Hofstadter and Smith, eds., *American Higher Education*, 478.

[9]Charles William Eliot, "Inaugural Address as President of Harvard, 1869," in Hofstadter and Smith, eds., *American Higher Education*, 601–624.

[10]Lucas, *American Higher Education*, 169.

[11]Ann Blankman (English), Tania Magoon (Biology and Classics), Courtney Randall (English), Jeremy Newell (English), Eve Sorum (English), and Eric von Wettberg (Biology).

[12]George Levine et al., *Speaking for the Humanities*, American Council of Learned Societies, Occasional Paper, No. 7 (New York: ACLS, 1989), 2; for a longer discussion of the woes of liberal education see Francis Oakley, "Discontents in American Higher Education," in *The Politics of Liberal Education*, ed. L. Darryl, J. Gless, and Barbara Herrnstein Smith (Durham, N.C.: Duke University Press, 1992), 267–289.

[13]"Third, the College believes that the close relationship between its faculty and students motivates students to learn," mission statement from the *Union College Academic Register*, 1997–1998.

[14]"G. Stanley Hall Describes Gilman's Policies at the Hopkins in the 1880's," in Hofstadter and Smith, eds., *American Higher Education*, 650. On the necessity of specialization, see Levine et al., *Speaking for the Humanities*, 5–8.

[15]Leonard Cassuto, "Pressures to Publish Fuel the Professionalization of Today's Graduate Students," *Chronicle of Higher Education*, 27 November 1998, B4–B5.

[16]National Research Council, *Summary Report 1986: Doctorate Recipients from United States Universities* (Washington, D.C.: National Academy Press, 1987), 78.

[17]According to the Carnegie classification, Liberal Arts I colleges are primarily undergraduate, highly selective institutions that award more than half of their baccalaureate degrees in arts and science fields. Liberal Arts II colleges are less selective and award more than half of their degrees in liberal arts fields.

[18]For a similar perspective, see Oakley, "Discontents in American Higher Education," 275.

[19]Bruce Kuklick, "The Emergence of the Humanities," in Darryl, Gless, and Smith, eds., *Politics of Liberal Education*, 201–212.

[20]Ernest L. Boyer, *Scholarship Reconsidered: Priorities of the Professoriate* (Princeton, N.J.: The Carnegie Foundation for the Advancement of Teaching, 1990), 12.

[21]Oakley, "Discontents in American Higher Education," 276, and endnote 10; and Levine et al., *Speaking for the Humanities*, 28–29.

[22]John H. D'Arms, "Funding Trends in the Academic Humanities," in *What's Happened to the Humanities?* ed. Alvin Kernan (Princeton, N.J.: Princeton University Press, 1997), 38–41.

[23]On the function of research in the university, see Jonathan R. Cole, "Balancing Acts: Dilemmas of Choice Facing Research Universities," *Dædalus* 122 (4) (Fall 1993): 23–24.

[24]Lynn Hunt, "Democratization and Decline? The Consequences of Demographic Change in the Humanities," in Kernan, ed., *What's Happened to the Humanities?* 17–31, esp. 20–21. She reports average humanities salaries in 1993–1994 as $41,038 in foreign languages, $41,346 in English, $43,489 in

philosophy and religion, and $45,337 in history, versus $44,390 in mathematics, $45,000 in physics, and $52,660 in economics.

[25]William J. Bennett, *To Reclaim a Legacy* (Washington, D.C.: National Endowment for the Humanities, 1984), quoting Dean Robert Berdahl of the University of Oregon, 17.

[26]Boyer, *Scholarship Reconsidered*, Tables A-1, A-5, A-6, A-23, A-30, A-31.

[27]Kernan, ed., *What's Happened to the Humanities?* 247 and Figure 7.

[28]Oakley, "Discontents in American Higher Education," 280–281.

[29]Arthur Levine and Jeanette S. Cureton, *When Hope and Fear Collide* (San Francisco: Jossey-Bass, 1998), 115–133.

[30]Alexander W. Astin, *What Matters in College?* (San Francisco: Jossey-Bass, 1993), 45.

[31]For example, Amherst, Bowdoin, Pomona, Swarthmore, Oberlin, Carleton, Grinnell, Smith, Wellesley, and Bryn Mawr as listed in *The Princeton Review: The Best 311 Colleges*, ed. E. T. Custard et al. (New York: Random House, 1999). The other two most popular majors vary among biology, history, economics, political science, and psychology.

[32]Denis Donoghue, "The Practice of Reading," in Kernan, ed., *What's Happened to the Humanities?* 123; see also Jane Tompkins, *A Life in School: What the Teacher Learned* (Reading, Mass.: Addison-Wesley, 1996), 133.

[33]See Leon Botstein, "Damaged Literacy: Illiteracies and American Democracy," *Dædalus* 119 (2) (Spring 1990): 55–84.

[34]Charles Schroeder, "New Students—New Learning Styles," *Change* (September/October 1993): 25.

[35]Arthur Levine and Jeanette S. Cureton, "Colleagiate Life: An Obituary," *Change* (May/June 1998): 17; see also Levine and Cureton, *When Hope and Fear Collide*, 128–130.

[36]Levine and Cureton, *When Hope and Fear Collide*, 128.

[37]For example, between 1994 and 1997, Union students in the basic sciences authored or coauthored with faculty forty-eight poster and paper presentations at regional, national, and international conferences, and coauthored with faculty forty-one articles in refereed journals.

[38]Levine et al., *Speaking for the Humanities*, 2.

[39]For more specific data see Oakley, "Ignorant Armies and Nighttime Clashes," in Kernan, ed., *What's Happened to the Humanities?* 71.

[40]See Levine et al., *Speaking for the Humanities*, 19.

[41]Oakley, "Ignorant Armies," 65; for an examination of a curriculum strongly influenced by theoretical approaches, see Margery Sabin, "Evolution and Revolution," in Kernan, ed., *What's Happened to the Humanities?* 84–101.

[42]Between 1990 and 1995 enrollments in Spanish rose 13.5 percent (an increase of 72,000 students) and in Chinese 35.8 percent; in Russian they fell 44.6

percent, German 27.8 percent, and French 24.6 percent. "Foreign Language Enrollments in United States Institutions of Higher Education," Modern Language Association, Fall 1995.

[43]National Association of Scholars, *The Dissolution of General Education: 1914–1993* (Princeton, N.J.: National Association of Scholars, 1996), Figure 1.1, p. 5.

[44]Carnegie Foundation for the Advancement of Teaching, *Missions of the College Curriculum* (San Francisco: Jossey-Bass, 1977).

[45]Astin, *What Matters in College?* 424.

[46]Enrollments in Humanities at Union:

Year	Arts	Cls	Eng	His	ML	Phil	Total Hum	Total Enroll	% of Total Enroll
1978	673	326	1485	1217	987	499	5,187	17,458	30%
1988	970	415	1739	1397	1057	787	6,365	19,181	33%
1995	1035	526	1737	1981	1444	600	7,323	18,453	40%

[47]Degrees Awarded at Union:

Year	Arts	Cls	Eng	His	ML	Phil	Hum	Total	% of All Degrees
1969	8	0	17	27	6	0	3	61	20% (302)
1978	4.5	1	25	23.5	20	7	5	86	16% (536)
1988	3.5	3	26.5	13.5	11	7	9	73.5	14% (536)
1998	22	4.5	31.5	25.5	15.5	6	0	105	21% (492)

Departments awarding the most degrees at Union in 1969 were Science (35), Political Science (30), History (27), and Electrical Engineering (22) ; in 1978, Political Science (48), Biology (44), Electrical Engineering (53), and Mechanical Engineering (51); in 1987, Political Science (61), Mechanical Engineering (61), Electrical Engineering (76), and Economics (44); in 1998, Psychology (77), Biology (57.5), Political Science (52.5), and Economics (48).

Susan C. Bourque

Reassessing Research: Liberal Arts Colleges and the Social Sciences

O BSERVERS OF THE LIBERAL ARTS COLLEGES have for some
time noted their leading role in producing the nation's
Ph.D.'s. This pattern occurs in the social sciences as
well as the humanities and natural sciences. The question of
why these institutions should have such remarkable success has
not received a great deal of scholarly attention, though the
figures naturally provoke speculation about the kind of instruction that occurs in the best of these colleges and the experience
of their undergraduates.[1] The 1998 Higher Education Data
Service (HEDS) figures report on the baccalaureate origins of
doctorate recipients in the social sciences.[2] With data weighted
for size of institution, the top ten Ph.D.-producing institutions
are, in order: Swarthmore, Thomas Aquinas, Reed, Bryn Mawr,
the University of Chicago, Beloit, Shimer, Oberlin, Harvard,
and Haverford. There are only six research universities in the
top thirty Ph.D. producers—the University of Chicago (5),
Harvard (9), Yale (14), Princeton (17), Brandeis (25), and the
University of California Santa Cruz (26).[3]

One explanation for this phenomenon—which is even more
marked in the sciences and for women—may be the high percentage of undergraduates in liberal arts colleges who are
involved in original research projects. These may be individual
projects, such as an undergraduate thesis or special project in
a course, or, more significantly, they may be engaged as research assistants to faculty members. This latter opportunity

*Susan C. Bourque is Esther Booth Wiley Professor of Government at Smith Col-
lege.*

simply may not be available to the same degree for undergraduates in the research institutions. There, graduate students quite appropriately get first claim on research assistant positions. Moreover, faculty members at the research institutions undoubtedly see their first responsibility to be research training for their graduate students. That is not the case in the liberal arts colleges, where the sole focus of attention is the undergraduate and a faculty member's only real hope of getting research assistance is a well-trained undergraduate. As a result, the bright and curious undergraduate has an opportunity for firsthand experience in the intellectual life of a social scientist and potentially will experience the enormous gratification that comes from the systematic pursuit of an intriguing question. These students might more readily imagine themselves as social scientists or become interested in further work in the social sciences.

Liberal arts colleges have long been noted for their commitment to teaching and for the quality of that teaching. Recently, Robert McCaughey has demonstrated that the leading liberal arts colleges have faculties who strongly support those principles.[4] The faculty ranks of the liberal arts colleges more often than not hold Ph.D.'s from the leading research universities and B.A.'s from the leading liberal arts colleges. Many of these individuals intend to pursue careers that will integrate scholarly research with a commitment to undergraduate education.

Moreover, faculty members at the leading liberal arts colleges today are well aware that their reviews for promotion and tenure will include a review of scholarship as well as teaching. The balance in the formula for weighing research and teaching will vary from one college to the next; the more selective liberal arts colleges will weigh research more heavily and many more will weigh both factors equally. Thus for a young scholar aspiring to a faculty position in a leading liberal arts college, a research program will be essential. The new attitude towards research reflects another important change in the liberal arts colleges and, as I will discuss below, presents both opportunities and challenges to their faculties and administrators.

The convergence of events that led to a revaluing of research has also resulted in a new style of hands-on teaching and research training in the leading liberal arts colleges, with felicitous results for undergraduates. As the liberal arts colleges have come to appreciate their success in producing Ph.D.'s, they have also recognized the unique experience they offer to their students. The question has become, how can the liberal arts colleges maximize their special contribution? For some institutions this has led to discussions of how to reconfigure the faculty workload to encourage independent work with students on hands-on research projects. Colleges today routinely make funds available to the faculty to hire student assistants, both during the academic year and for summer research and internship projects. Many now include a faculty member's work with honors theses, research projects, or internship supervision as part of a faculty member's teaching load. Many will include "one-on-one" teaching in their faculty-development workshops, and in the future we will look to these institutions for guidance and leadership on how faculty can be prepared to take on this responsibility. All of this will redound to the benefit of the undergraduate. Thus, even as the leading liberal arts institutions have realigned themselves with respect to faculty research, they have done so in a unique fashion that relates research to undergraduate teaching.

My thoughts on this topic are formed less by hard data than by my own observation of the opportunities afforded to the talented undergraduate and the productive dynamic that arises between students and faculty in those settings. At my own institution, when a group of faculty members received a grant in the late 1970s to organize an intensive interdisciplinary research effort, they included student research assistants in the project. They designed a summer seminar with a leading scholar who cut across the disciplinary boundaries. Although the faculty severely underestimated the amount of time that would be needed to train and work with the undergraduate research assistants that first summer, the results for the students were spectacular. Early on in their academic careers they became part of a team engaged in the heady experience of "creating new knowledge" and "crossing disciplinary boundaries." Many of those student assistants went on to graduate study and, as the HEDS data would suggest, eventually to receive a Ph.D.

For the faculty member, using an undergraduate in a research project usually means that the project must be redesigned with that goal in mind. For the new faculty member, fresh from his own Ph.D. project, that can mean a considerable investment in start-up time. On the other hand, the experience may be liberating—forcing him to stretch beyond the traditionally narrow confines of a dissertation to engage a question with a broader or more accessible focus.

To use an undergraduate effectively, that is, to give the student more than the role of gopher or xeroxer, it is often necessary to adapt the questions posed in the research design to the skills of an undergraduate. That said, even the mundane tasks of locating books and references, finding relevant articles, and conducting library and Internet searches will produce some excellent research skills. When done as part of a larger project this can be an exciting endeavor, and especially so for someone entirely new to academic life. Moreover, in the context of a liberal arts college it is possible to watch a student progress from learning basic research skills to serving as a skilled assistant to designing and completing a high-level project on her own. It is no longer unusual—though still noteworthy—for my colleagues at Smith to list their undergraduate research assistants as coauthors of articles and to bring them to professional meetings. At those meetings, undergraduates may have an opportunity to present their own work in poster sessions and receive professional responses to their work. Again, this may be an important contributory factor in the decisions of such students to pursue graduate study and scholarly careers.

The liberal arts colleges are characterized by their size—they are smaller than the research universities, and the scale of what they undertake is necessarily more limited. This can be a great advantage for their students, particularly in the institutional ethos and structure that is geared to meeting their needs. That means a faculty that must be accessible and committed to teaching undergraduates. The disadvantage for the undergraduate is that the offerings and major programs may be more limited. A faculty of 150 to 200 simply cannot offer the same range of courses available from a faculty three or four times that size. Nevertheless, the liberal arts colleges tend to have far better student to faculty ratios than the research universities, and thus a narrower selection of courses may be balanced by greater individual attention.

For the liberal arts colleges the challenges of size are twofold. First, important choices must be made about what can be taught, what can be covered adequately so that resources are not squandered or spread too thinly. This can be a blessing in disguise, leading an institution to set priorities and focus its energies. It can also lead to interdisciplinary sharing and creativity. On a relatively small faculty the sociologists, economists, and political scientists may not all live in separate buildings or on separate floors. The smaller size of a liberal arts college may facilitate cross-disciplinary conversation, making disciplinary boundaries less rigid and interdisciplinary collaboration easier. This is, of course, not to claim that disagreements, conflicts, and disputes will be any less intense.

While scale and size may force faculty members in the liberal arts colleges to move beyond the constraints of the traditional disciplinary boundaries, there can be professional risks in such moves. Often those risks are compensated for by the intriguing questions one can pursue. Moreover, the professional risk involved has been greatly diminished by the impact of interdisciplinary work on the traditional disciplines, making the disciplines much broader. The point is to keep a faculty member part of the disciplinary conversation, and this can be accomplished through well-placed faculty-development funds.

Another consequence of the smaller size and scale of the liberal arts colleges is that if they are to maintain their quality, they must make major investments in faculty development. Recognizing that they have much to gain from a faculty that is actively engaged in scholarly research, the leading liberal arts colleges will facilitate the professional involvement of the faculty, supporting research projects as well as attendance at professional meetings. Moreover, the liberal arts colleges pay serious attention to assisting faculty members to improve their teaching—both by helping graduate students at the beginning of their careers make the transition to teaching in an undergraduate setting and also by keeping the teaching of experienced colleagues vigorous and innovative.

The contributions of the liberal arts colleges to the social sciences go beyond what happens at the individual campuses of these institutions. They are also found in the roles their faculty members play in national professional organizations. For instance, the American Political Science Association makes an explicit effort to include professors from the liberal arts colleges in the governing structure of the association. Part of this is representational, since a great number of political scientists teach in schools that are not classified as research universities. But it is also presumed by many that some of the best teaching in political science—or the other social sciences—is likely to be found in the liberal arts colleges.[5]

Future Ph.D.'s in the social sciences—most of whom will be trained in the research institutions—will not all teach in research universities. They will need to be competent and inspired teachers as well as producers of new knowledge. Since teaching is explicitly not a secondary or peripheral activity for liberal arts colleges, when professional organizations look to improve the quality of teaching within the profession—in particular, the quality of programs that teach graduate students how to teach—they look to their colleagues in the liberal arts colleges.

Most professors from the leading liberal arts colleges stay professionally active and engage in research, and thus they make regular varied contributions to national debates in the social sciences. McCaughey's study of the select liberal arts colleges demonstrated that faculty at these leading schools often have records of scholarly productivity that are comparable to, if not exceed, those of many research institutions. Furthermore, his study suggests that this is not done at the expense of good teaching; rather it appears to be linked to it. In the social sciences, it is not unusual to find academics from select liberal arts colleges with the respect and visibility that allows their counterparts from the leading research universities to regard them as peers.[6]

Continued success for the liberal arts colleges, as well as their role in the social sciences, is intimately tied to maintaining their ability to attract the best graduate students for their faculties. Candidates for jobs at the leading liberal arts colleges must be certain that they wish to make a major professional commitment to teaching. And they must have the confidence that they will be able to combine effectively a healthy research program with their teaching. If they are graduates of liberal arts colleges (as many of them are, according to the HEDS data and as McCaughey confirmed), they are already aware of the attractiveness of these institutions.[7] On the other hand, the HEDS data are weighted, so there are many social science Ph.D.'s who lack such experience. If their graduate training did not emphasize teaching, or if it was communicated that the preferred position is in a research institution, then many talented young social scientists will not become candidates for positions in liberal arts colleges. In my experience, this has been an especially acute problem for us when approaching highly sought-after candidates with no prior experience in a college setting. Often research institutions could offer packages that we could not touch, for example, a two-year postdoctoral research position, followed by a tenure-track position. The comparable offer at a liberal arts college would have been a four- (or five-) course load with student research support. If you are not already committed to a liberal arts college environment, or even familiar with it, there is no comparison between the two offers.

Graduate programs often emphasize research to the exclusion of teaching, without explaining the synergism between the two. And it is still the case that too few of the leading liberal arts colleges make clear their commitment to facilitate both research and teaching for their faculties. Perhaps in the current climate of renewed attention to teaching and accountability, it is time for the public to be more fully apprised of the benefits for students of this combined emphasis.

ENDNOTES

[1]Pathbreaking work on the role of liberal arts colleges has been done by M. Elizabeth Tidball and Vera Kiskiakowsky, "Baccalaureate Origins of American Scientists and Scholars," *Science* 193 (20) (August 1976): 646–652 and "Women's Colleges and Women Achievers Revisited," *SIGNS* 5 (Spring

1980): 504–517, and Robert A. McCaughey, *Teachers and Scholars: The Faculties of Select Liberal Arts Colleges and Their Place in American Higher Learning* (New York: Conceptual Litho Reproductions, 1994).

[2]Social sciences in this classification scheme include economics, political science, international relations, anthropology, sociology, and other social sciences—not history.

[3]The 1998 HEDS data reports on "the total number of Ph.D.'s received by the baccalaureate graduates of institutions from 1986–1995 and the ratio of Ph.D.'s earned from 1986–1995 by these graduates to bachelor's degrees conferred by the listed institutions from 1980 to 1989." McCaughey found a similar pattern using the HEDS data from Ph.D.'s earned from 1980 to 1989. McCaughey, *Teachers and Scholars*, 94.

[4]McCaughey identified and studied the faculties of two to three dozen liberal arts colleges that included Amherst, Barnard, Beloit, Bryn Mawr, Carleton, Colgate, Haverford, Hobart, Grinnell, Knox, Lawrence, Mount Holyoke, Oberlin, Pomona, Reed, Smith, Swarthmore, Vassar, Wellesley, Wesleyan, and Williams. He labeled these the Select Liberal Arts Colleges and noted that they had undergone transformations since the 1970s that made them the intellectual homes of a new category of scholar-teacher: faculty members committed to both research and undergraduate teaching.

[5]My thanks to Catherine Rudder, executive director of the American Political Science Association, for this observation and for other insightful comments on the contributions of liberal arts colleges to political science.

[6]McCaughey, *Teachers and Scholars*, 65–88, 105–116.

[7]Ibid., 51.

Peter W. Stanley

At Home in Our World: The Place of International Studies in Liberal Arts Colleges

L IBERAL EDUCATION IS INHERENTLY SUPRANATIONAL. Its focus upon the foundations of knowledge and inquiry and its aspiration to foster intellectual resilience cannot be confined within national boundaries or individual cultural traditions. Though we engage in spirited combat over the centrality of great texts or the cultural inclusiveness of curricula, almost everyone who advocates liberal learning believes in its cosmopolitan character.

In the past, American liberal arts colleges often oriented themselves toward the canonical mainstream of Western civilization. They typically justified this in cosmopolitan terms, however, arguing that the evolution of Western thought and practice was universally relevant. Such an approach to the rest of the world may strike some modern critics as ethnocentric, but it was consistent with the evangelical faith of the Protestant churches that founded most of America's liberal arts colleges. Interest in foreign countries and cultures began at many of our colleges with missionaries, because the aspiration to convert others had in time translated itself into a need to understand them and their ways. Returning missionaries fueled this interest and helped colleges respond to it by lecturing or teaching. In this spirit, they and the churches and foundations that spon-

Peter W. Stanley is president of Pomona College.

sored them put in place many of the building blocks that still support international studies at our colleges today. Pomona's Asian studies program, for example, was created in 1936 with support from the Rockefeller Foundation at the initiation of President Charles K. Edmunds, who had previously served for seventeen years as head of Canton Christian College in China.

The challenge of introducing a universal faith to particular foreign cultures epitomizes the tension between the general and the particular that complicates all discussions of the place of international studies in the liberal arts curriculum. International education is necessarily organized at least in part around the study of nation-states, their institutions, histories, policies, languages, and cultures. For an American college student to learn more about individual foreign countries is valuable in many ways. By itself, however, this orients one's education not toward general truths but toward multiple particularisms, because each foreign country, institution, culture, or language deserves to be understood first of all on its own terms. If an American student learns a great deal about, say, France or Japan, is this an international education? If so, how do liberal arts colleges draw from these particular encounters general principles that deepen liberal learning?

AREA STUDIES AS AN ORGANIZING PREMISE

One answer to this question is to be found in the organizational premises that structure, frame, and unify a college's curricular offerings in international studies. As religion ceased to play this role in the middle years of the century, the development of area studies offered an alternative by grouping countries or cultures together in larger units of study defined by geographic proximity or cultural affinity. Though area studies were not invented by or for liberal arts colleges, they opened great possibilities for us. Small colleges that could not justify hiring faculty specialists on dozens of different countries—let alone a historian, a political scientist, an economist, language teachers, literary scholars, an art historian, an ethnomusicologist, and a religious studies expert for each such country—*could* aspire to create a critical mass of faculty broadly conversant with a region of the world.

Defining the intellectual premises that made any given area or region a legitimate unit of study also helped to frame international education as more than detailed knowledge about individual states.

Asian studies is probably the most prevalent and deepest-rooted area studies field in American liberal arts colleges. This was true even before pundits started speculating about a "Pacific century." The field is a natural for liberal arts colleges for several reasons. The high cultures of the region—its literary, artistic, religious, and institutional traditions—fit nicely in traditional curricula and invite comparisons with the Western canon. Many liberal arts colleges followed (and some anticipated) the logic of Columbia University by introducing the study of Asian high cultures as a curricular complement to Western civilization. Over time, the study of Asia gained additional impetus from the growing sense of America's economic and strategic stake there. World War II broadened interest in what had been, until then, still a fairly esoteric subject, introducing an urgent "need to know" that shaped the careers of scholars such as Edwin O. Reischauer and journalists such as Frank Gibney, who later played critical roles interpreting Asians and Americans to each other. The return of veterans from places such as Japan, Korea, the Philippines, and Vietnam deepened this interest in later years. More recently, students eyeing business careers have seen Asian studies as the key that might open the door to exciting and lucrative employment. Whatever the reasons, by 1998–1999 5.4 percent of all Pomona College enrollments were in Asian studies courses.

Area studies have also enabled small colleges to develop offerings in other parts of the world, such as Latin America, the Middle East, and Africa. Until recently, however, the study of Western Europe has remained focused upon individual countries. Although Britain, France, Germany, and Russia are no more different from one another than Japan, China, Korea, and Indonesia, individual European traditions remain deeply embedded in liberal arts colleges' curricula. This has created an asymmetry in the curricular architecture of international studies, one that is both the legacy of a time when the rivalries of individual European nations set, or appeared to set, the (Western) world's agenda and a reflection of historic interest in intellectual lineages within the Western tradition. It remains to be seen whether this asymmetry will survive America's changing demography and Europe's movement toward political and economic integration. The European Union's recent support for EU centers in the United States, including one joining the University of Southern California and the Claremont Colleges, may signal a new interest in Europe as an area studies field.

In liberal arts colleges, as at universities, area studies grew under the patronage of the great foundations—especially Ford, Rockefeller, Mellon, and Luce. Beyond funding programs, teaching positions, and sometimes facilities or collections at individual colleges, beyond promoting collaboration through consortia, these funders additionally created or deepened the scholarly infrastructure of area studies fields in general through their support for research centers, graduate training, and professional bodies. Notable examples include the Association for Asian Studies, the Joint Committees of the American Council of Learned Societies, and the Social Science Research Council. This support for training, networking, scholarly travel, and publication in the area studies fields was especially valuable to faculty teaching in liberal arts colleges. Without it, professors teaching in relative isolation from other specialists might easily have lost touch with the main currents of scholarship in their fields.

In recent decades foundation support has declined, at least relatively, while the role of the federal government and individual and corporate donors has grown. Where the foundations once sought to build basic institutional capacity, today's funders typically favor more instrumental investments targeted to yield specific programmatic outcomes desired by the donor. Liberal arts colleges have been disadvantaged by this trend, because they are not as well situated as universities to respond to government or corporate interest in preparing students for specific careers, shaping policies, or promoting economic development. They exist to teach undergraduates and to build in them the capacity to reason. This has made the continuing interest in liberal arts colleges and liberal arts education expressed by foundations such as Luce and Mellon extraordinarily valuable. I shall return later in this essay to a discussion of the uncertain future of area studies.

THE SHAPE OF THE PROGRAM

At most liberal arts colleges, international study is a three-legged stool. Curricular offerings in the humanities and the social sciences are central. Study-abroad programs provide opportunities to deepen formal academic knowledge and to complement it with on-the-ground experience in a foreign culture. The presence of international students, faculty, and speakers on the college's campus is a third, sometimes neglected, resource.

Instruction in foreign languages and literatures is by far the largest curricular investment most liberal arts colleges make in international education. The classic argument for compelling students to learn a foreign language is that this will deparochialize them. Knowing a foreign language, we have been told for generations, is part of the armamentarium of a liberally educated person. There are also practical considerations. Although English has become the *lingua franca* of business, scholarship, and tourism the world over, it remains difficult if not impossible to understand another society (or conduct business in it) without reading and speaking its language. To depend on the willingness of someone from another culture to communicate in English is to make oneself vulnerable to everything from misunderstanding to manipulation.

Historically, foreign-language study has played a larger role in undergraduate education at liberal arts colleges than at universities. A study by Richard D. Lambert in the late 1980s found college students half again as likely as undergraduates at universities to persevere to advanced levels of foreign-language acquisition.[1] This is much to their credit, for throughout American higher education language enrollments are driven principally by institutional requirements. Since these requirements are modest—usually no more than two years of "seat time"—many students graduate with only a rudimentary capacity actually to use a foreign language. Acknowledging this, language faculty are quick to point out the other benefits of their courses, such as their introduction to other cultures and ways of think-ing. Still, with foreign languages housing the largest concentra-tion of faculty in many of our colleges, there are substantial opportunity costs for the institution and its students if they settle for mediocrity as an outcome in language instruction. It is worth asking whether a modest language requirement for all students is as powerful an investment in international studies as it would be to focus resources on deepening linguistic capacity in the smaller number of students who are actually interested.

Reflecting students' shifting interests and their assessments of the world around them, recent years have seen dramatic changes in the popularity of individual languages. Spanish, not wholly a foreign language in many parts of the United States, is now overwhelmingly the most popular language in most liberal arts colleges. Enrollments in other European languages have declined to one degree or another. This reflects a pattern affecting all of American higher education. In 1968, French accounted for 34 percent of all foreign-language enrollments in American higher education, Spanish for 32 percent, and Ger-man for 19 percent. By 1995, Spanish's share had risen to 53 percent, while French and German had fallen to 18 percent and 8.5 percent, respectively. By contrast, enrollments in Chinese and Japanese have grown, often surpassing those in German, Russian, and Italian. Between 1990 and 1995, enrollments in Chinese and Spanish grew 36 percent and 13.5 percent, respec-tively, while those in French, German, and Russian declined by 25 percent, 28 percent, and 45 percent.[2]

Apart from Chinese, Japanese, and Russian, the so-called truly foreign languages are seldom taught in small colleges, because enrollments cannot justify the expense. But collabora-tive approaches—such as the Southeast Asian Studies Summer Institute (SEASSI), taught each summer at the Southeast Asian Studies Center of one of the major universities—offer intensive study programs in regional languages to students who want or need them.

Languages aside, the growth stocks in international and area studies at liberal arts colleges appear to be in the social sci-ences, including history. This differs from the pattern a decade or two ago, when analysts such as Lambert often identified international study principally with the humanities. Today, trade, investment, development, public policy, immigration, gender and ethnic issues, the environment, human rights, and strategic issues provide more and more of our students with their point of entry to the study of other societies. Subjects such as these invite and reward comparative and interdisciplinary study, which liberal arts colleges find it relatively easy to integrate into their curricula. As Stephen Lewis, president of Carleton College, has observed, our colleges "do not have to face the demands of field specialties and sub-specialties that are imposed on graduate institutions (and, generally, on their undergraduate divisions as well)."[3] One of the great curricular challenges before us, however, is to improve the integration of social-science courses with foreign language and study-abroad programs. The use of foreign-language materials and case studies in mainstream social-science courses, and the provision of social-science programs or tracks in study abroad, is still relatively rare. One interesting exception is the group of programs being established in cities abroad by Trinity College to complement its growing urban programs at home in Hartford.

Study abroad is one of the most popular programs in residential liberal arts colleges. Its prominence in admissions materials and the high marks it receives on seniors' exit surveys testify to this. Practice differs from institution to institution, but on average liberal arts college students are far more likely than other undergraduates to study abroad. Although only about 5 percent of all American undergraduates study abroad, the percentage at four-year baccalaureate institutions is at least four times higher than this. At a number of liberal arts colleges, half or more of all students enjoy this experience. In the class of 1998, for example, 43 percent of graduating seniors at the eight coeducational liberal arts colleges belonging to the Consortium on Financing Higher Education (COFHE)—Amherst, Carleton, Oberlin, Pomona, Swarthmore, Trinity, Wesleyan, and Williams—had participated in study-abroad programs, and an additional 10 percent had experienced a foreign internship. Lambert's decade-old conclusion still rings true: "It seems clear that in most universities, undergraduate study abroad remains marginal to the undergraduate education for most students. . . .

Among four-year institutions, it is in the highly-selective, private liberal arts colleges that study abroad participation flourishes."[4]

For most, this proves to be experiential learning at its best: The experience of living in another country, developing the skills and the confidence to succeed on unfamiliar ground, causes students notably to mature and to broaden their perspective. How rich the experience is and how much students are challenged by it depend, in part, on how deeply immersed the student is in the host culture. Programs vary greatly in this respect. To suggest the range of this diversity, a number of years ago Craufurd D. Goodwin and Michael Nacht developed an aquatic typology, characterizing study-abroad programs' relationship to their host culture as one of "total immersion," or enrolling in a foreign institution just as one would at home in the United States; "swimming in the eddies," or registering at a foreign institution that caters to visitors; "staying by the pool," choosing a program based in an "enclave" or foreign campus created by one's own home institution; "paddling in the shallows," or taking part in programs that are simply overseas extensions of one's home institution's own curriculum and faculty; and "wind sprints to the raft," special missions to accomplish some specific purpose, such as an archaeological dig.[5] The Goodwin and Nacht typology need not be seen as a hierarchy of excellence. It is, however, a reminder that institutions and students alike need to be clear about their goals and choose appropriate means to pursue them.

The educational value of this experience increases to the degree that study abroad is integrated with language instruction and other courses on one's home campus. Ideally, students should choose a study-abroad program that will permit them to deepen and test what they have learned in traditional classrooms at home: in short, to treat study abroad as an educational laboratory, not just a new experience. Upon return from overseas study, moreover, students should be guided to courses and programs that will permit them to share and to build upon what they have learned in another country. Because of their small size and their ability to handcraft programs for individual students, liberal arts colleges have a good track record for integrating overseas study with the rest of their students' education. We could do even better, however, if we more tenaciously resisted the conventional piety that sees study abroad as simply "a good thing," like regular exercise, a sound diet, and an occasional trip to the opera.

At liberal arts colleges, as at other institutions, the profile of students who study abroad is likely to be skewed in favor of those majoring in the humanities and the social sciences. A recent study of seniors at COFHE institutions reported that 40 percent of humanities majors, 31 percent of social science majors, 21 percent of natural science majors, and 7 percent of applied science majors had studied abroad. One of the reasons for this disparity is the difficulty students encounter articulating the sequences and requirements of a science major with the possibilities available for study abroad. Other elements of the profile are equally notable. Women, whites, multiracial students, and those with high GPAs are more likely to study abroad than other students; though more people than ever are taking part in non-Western programs, a disproportionately large share of study-abroad students still choose English-speaking countries. (One sign of change, however, was that Asians proved more likely than whites to have held an internship abroad.) Most good colleges are working hard to diversify this profile in all respects, including creating opportunities for science majors. If study abroad is an educationally powerful experience, it should be accessible to all.

The presence of international students, faculty, and visitors on an American residential campus is another form of international education. Though some foreign students and visitors participate formally in the educational program—as, for example, teachers, language tutors, or resource persons in a course—their principal contribution is informal. Through their participation in courses and residence-hall life, they bring a fresh perspective to academic subject matter, to the daily news, and to aspects of American life that students would otherwise take for granted: food, political activism, dating habits, career planning, and more. Upon graduation, those who return to their homeland typically become ambassadors both for their college and for American higher education. I have been deeply impressed, for example, by the generosity of Pomona's overseas alumni, who seem never to tire of hosting visitors from the college, arranging internships for today's students, helping us recruit and explain the college to potential applicants and their families, and astonishing their compatriots by putting Pomona stickers in the back windows of their cars. One can only conclude that this is an enduring form of intercultural communication.

Information technologies have affected the delivery of international programs on our campuses, without thus far substantially changing their configuration. The benefits of the new technologies are clear. Language laboratories are more sophisticated; access to authentic foreign language materials and sources is easier; datasets on foreign societies, economies, and cultures make available to everyone a breadth and depth of information that would have been the envy of specialists only a quarter of a century ago. For liberal arts colleges—most of which are small and many of which are at least relatively isolated from other centers of learning—technology has proven especially valuable in bridging distance, enabling campuses to collaborate with each other and to thicken the texture of their contact with other nations and societies. Students on a small campus in the United States can now collaborate in "real" time with their counterparts in another part of the world to pursue an inquiry or to debate an issue. One even hears it said that "virtual reality" may someday obviate the need for firsthand foreign study and travel. But a school, or a student, would need to have rather limited goals to settle for this in place of direct human exposure. In international study, as in so many other aspects of the curriculum, technology has expanded our reach and provided valuable new tools for instruction and research, often at great cost, without notably changing what we do. It has helped us to pursue familiar goals more effectively.

EFFECTIVENESS

These approaches to international education have been unusually effective in liberal arts colleges. If size is taken into account, the leading liberal arts colleges are America's most productive undergraduate training ground for those who go on to earn Ph.D.'s in international fields and to pursue what might be called international careers in government, business, the academy, or the independent sector. In 1991, a group of colleges that had been unusually successful in this respect banded together, calling themselves "The International 50." Although they produced only about 1.8 percent of all the baccalaureate degrees granted in the United States, these fifty liberal arts colleges played a disproportionately large role in educating people for international careers and international service. At the time the group was organized, its share of U.S. ambassadors and students enrolled in graduate schools of international affairs was roughly six times its share of undergraduate degrees; it produced five times as many U.S. foreign service officers, Ph.D.'s in international fields, and lawyers specializing in international law, and 2.5 times as many Peace Corps volunteers.[6]

Though gratifying, this measure of success is in some respects counterintuitive. After all, universities have at least the potential to offer a broader range of course work, deeper library collections, and equal or greater overseas linkages. What, then, accounts for the colleges' unusual effectiveness and productivity?

Part of the answer to this question is to be found in the colleges' intentionality and their students' self-selection. As a group, liberal arts colleges appear to have assigned higher priority to undergraduate international and intercultural study than many other institutions. An international orientation is part of their history, as we have already seen, and their emphasis upon liberal learning rather than vocational education leaves space in the curriculum to pursue international study. The more occupationally oriented an institution's curriculum, by contrast, the less likely its students are to study abroad. Students who enter college knowing that they are interested in international questions and planning to study abroad might, therefore, be disproportionately drawn to liberal arts colleges in the first place.

This having been said, the liberal arts colleges' effectiveness in international education seems very much akin to their disproportionate role in providing the undergraduate training for future scientists, the phenomenon described by Professor Cech elsewhere in this volume. Thirty of "The International 50" were also members of the so-called Oberlin Group, a collection of liberal arts colleges that had proven unusually productive in educating future scientists. By Cech's ranking, nine of America's twenty most productive undergraduate institutions in educating future Ph.D.'s in science and engineering are liberal arts colleges. (A tenth, Harvey Mudd College, is sometimes considered a liberal arts college, and its students have the option of majoring in liberal arts fields taught at other institutions in the Claremont Colleges consortium.) A 1998 report prepared for the Annapolis Group of liberal arts colleges by the Pennsylvania Independent College and University Research Center concluded that independent national liberal arts colleges are markedly more productive than any other group of higher-education institutions in providing the undergraduate education for future Ph.D.'s in all fields. Seen in this light, the colleges' success in international education is simply an example of their overall effectiveness as learning environments.

If this is so, the ultimate cause of the liberal arts colleges' success in international education is to be found in their institutional character: their selective admissions, the teaching orientation of their intellectually accomplished faculty, the commitment of students and faculty alike to liberal learning rather than narrower forms of education for career and work, and the purposefulness arising from a small institution's need to establish priorities and focus on what it thinks most important and what it can do best. A relatively small liberal arts college cannot be all things to all people, cannot realistically aspire even to teach all important subjects at the undergraduate level. Fortunately, this necessary limitation is consistent with the faith of liberal arts colleges that any developed field of study can be as useful as any other as a means to shape one's intellect. For the purposes of a liberal arts education, it makes little if any difference whether one majors in chemistry, economics, or English. When a college chooses to invest in one of these fields, or in a theme such as international education that cuts across several such fields, it can focus its energies there to a degree that is difficult to match in larger institutions that aspire to provide "coverage" everywhere.

The organization of undergraduate international study around different areas or regions of the world has proven durable. It is now more or less half a century old. Almost certainly, international study will continue to be an important curricular emphasis both in American higher education generally, and in liberal arts colleges, particularly. Still, change is in the air. The traditional focus upon the differences that distinguish other areas of the world from our own is being challenged by growing linkages to domestic American diversity and ethnic-studies programs. At the same time, area studies' emphasis upon geographic or cultural entities as the unit of study is being challenged by the rise of transnational studies focusing upon a topic or disciplinary optic applicable to many regions. Finally, a growing interest in "global competence"—i.e., "the skills and perspectives that enable people to thrive in cultural settings other than their own"[7]—proposes to make the cosmopolitanism and cultural resilience of the student learner, not the language and institutions of a foreign land, the focus of international study.

The field of international studies as we have known it is being enlarged, and its boundaries are now being challenged, by interactions with domestic ethnic-studies programs. Americans' growing recognition of their own pluralism has led to new interest in the Asian, African, and Latin American origins of those who already constitute a majority of the school-age population in many cities and states. In addition, seeking to understand themselves better and insisting upon respect for their heritage, Asian Americans, African-Americans, and Latinos are reframing the study of the non-Western world to address what are to some degree domestic American concerns—highlighting some aspects of international study (at the expense of others), emphasizing the origins of the values and organizational patterns most meaningful to the group's identity in America, and de-emphasizing those institutions and practices either irrelevant or repugnant to those who emigrated and left them behind.

The traditional international- and area-studies ideal of understanding a foreign culture *on its own terms* sometimes appears less relevant from this perspective. In its place, one sees a growing interest in subjects such as Diasporic studies and border studies that are inherently comparative or deal with the intersection of different societies, cultures, and traditions. Exemplifying this approach to international study, the Association of American Colleges and Universities has partly merged its international program with its work on domestic diversity. The benefits of this approach are likely to be considerable. The risk, on the other hand, is that the immediacy and emotional power of Americans' concern with diversity at home may lead us to see foreign cultures through an American lens, and appropriate them to meet our own needs.

Transnational studies reassert the primacy of academic disciplines over the regional or cultural setting as the object of study. As Kenneth Prewitt, president of the Social Science Research Council, once put it, "Area studies holds area constant and invites the participation of multiple disciplines, in contrast to traditional comparative studies which held discipline constant and involved multiple areas."[8] Describing area studies as a field of scholarship rooted in the no-longer relevant world of the Cold War, the SSRC and the ACLS ended the Joint Committees that had for many years provided intellectual guidance to area studies at about the time Prewitt made this observation.

The sovereignty of the academic disciplines, and particularly the claim that their logic and application are the same everywhere, is a secular form of universal faith. The natural and physical sciences, which have always taken this view, have as a result subordinated not only international concerns but also those of gender and ethnicity. In the social sciences, economists have long claimed that an economic law is an economic law whatever one's literary tradition, religious faith, household ethics, or governmental institutions may be. It is notable that the growth area for transnational studies is in the interdisciplinary, thematic fields of the social sciences and the humanities that are becoming, as I mentioned above, the principal entry point to international studies in undergraduate colleges.

The need and the desire to understand other parts of the world will not go away on this account, but their place in the academic firmament may change. A different angle of vision leads to different academic priorities. A student who wishes to understand Southeast Asia will sooner or later interest herself in environmental questions, without necessarily needing to understand that field deeply. In much the same way, students of the environment, migration, or comparative institutional structures may turn to Southeast Asia for examples or case studies without needing to develop a substantial and independent knowledge of the region. It is possible, however, that deep and rigorous real knowledge may reassert itself as the quality control upon universal theories. One of the "laws" of the social sciences may rest upon impeccable mathematical modeling, and may correspond to experience in the United States or Western Europe, but its claim to be true everywhere must render a hypothesis testable in India or Brazil.

The somewhat elusive pursuit of "global competence" also has a role in configuring the future of international study.[9] Though the term is quite widely used, global competence means different things to different people. Knowledge of other parts of the world is an important ingredient for most commentators, but the heart of global competence appears to be a set of values and attitudes: the ability to put oneself in another person's shoes, a favorable disposition toward other and different cultures, the ability to function effectively on unfamiliar terrain. Globally competent people are said to be not ethnocentric, but "ethnorelative."

In these characterizations, one sees a powerful shift of focus from the subject matter to the learner. As in much contemporary talk about educational reform, the point of education for global competence becomes the empowerment of the student, not just mastery of the subject matter. Taking a positive attitude toward ethnic and cultural difference and learning how to work effectively outside one's own society matters more, from this perspective, than deep formal knowledge: understanding the societies of, say, the Southern Cone becomes principally a means to the end of fostering in students a positive outlook towards others and a capacity to work and live effectively on their terms. This view of global competence relates to area studies in defining international education as the aspiration to intellectual resilience does to mastery of canonical content in modern definitions of liberal learning.

Having backed into international studies myself, without any area training as a student and with no more than a courtesy membership in area studies centers as a professor, I take a more optimistic view of these challenges than some others do. It seems clear that the world is not going to become a single, English-speaking pond; that people wishing to transact business, implement government policies, or communicate about the environment, art, or ethics will continue to need knowledge of each other's society, institutions, and customs; and that in the long run our domestic concern with ethnic diversity will enlarge, not contract or confine, the scope of international or intercultural study. But the shape of the curricular landscape in our colleges may well differ in the years ahead from what we have known since roughly 1950, and this may in turn affect everything from hiring patterns for new faculty to the location and academic emphasis of study-abroad programs.

Institutions attempting to negotiate these currents of change must inevitably take into account the substantial cost of international study. With its requirements for foreign travel and networking, specialized course work, and expensive library collections, international education has far higher unit costs than, say, English or history. Ambitious programs can easily absorb resources needed elsewhere in the curriculum or for student financial aid or faculty research. If debate over changing patterns of international study breaks the momentum that has characterized the growth of the field, competitors for these resources will question how deep a need there really is for "globalmindedness" in colleges whose highest purpose is to develop the capacity for critical inquiry through disciplined learning. This is a fair question that each institution will have to answer in light of its own mission and values. For now, however, it appears that most liberal arts colleges believe that the game is worth the candle, that wise planning can magnify the impact of our means, and that improving global knowledge and understanding is a responsibility we owe to our students.

THE CAMPUS AS A METAPHOR FOR THE WORLD

The thread running through these growing interests in ethnic identity, transnational comparison and theory, and the cultivation of cosmopolitan attitudes in student learners is a turn away from inter*national* education (the study of nation-states, their policies, institutions, and paraphernalia of governance) to inter*cultural* education oriented toward the study of people-in-society. Even if theorists are right about the universality of the academic disciplines and their laws, people from different societies will still need to learn how to talk to one another, allow for different assumptions, values, and habits, acknowledge differing historical legacies, and find ways to learn from one another. In this branch of liberal learning, as in others, self-knowledge, the ability to live and work successfully on unfamiliar ground, and the capacity to communicate effectively with others remain worthy educational goals.

The residential liberal arts college is well suited to this emerging field of intercultural study, for its pursuit of academic rigor is grounded in a set of social commitments both to members of our campus commonwealths and to the society beyond the campus. The gates of Pomona College bear a quotation from one of my predecessors, urging Pomona graduates to "bear their added riches in trust" for humankind. Although the rhetoric is old fashioned, the spirit animates not only this college but many others as well. It is a modern expression of the missionary faith of our founders. Although infected to some degree by the careerism and preprofessionalism of our times, these campuses remain communities characterized by social conscience and by the aspiration to lead a good life in society with others. This explains, in part, the eagerness with which most liberal arts colleges have embraced diversity and service learning as goals, and doubtless contributes to the special interest accorded to study abroad.

If the new orientation of this field turns out to be intercultural and *supra*national, concerned with issues that cut across national boundaries, liberal arts colleges may prove once again to be a highly effective educational venue. Compared with larger universities, liberal arts colleges can more easily achieve a shared sense of purpose and of institutional commitments. Departmental boundaries are more permeable, opportunities for collaboration across existing disciplines are easier to realize, bureaucratic rigidities are less likely to set in place when people share common space and common aspirations. The weakening of departmental cultures and hierarchies that is sometimes lamented in our colleges is, in truth, a sign of their intellectual resilience. Interdisciplinary and comparative studies flourish in this sort of environment.

As our emphasis shifts towards comparative and interdisciplinary study of supranational themes, the affinity between what is loosely called international study and liberal learning will deepen and grow. In this field, as in others, it is helpful that the cul-de-sacs of specialization that small institutions find it difficult to sustain need no longer be the principal concern of undergraduate educators. A disciplined but generous-spirited cosmopolitanism has always been the heart of our enterprise.

ACKNOWLEDGMENT

I wish to thank my colleague Hans C. Palmer, Pomona College's vice president for academic affairs and dean of the college, for his help in preparing this essay.

ENDNOTES

[1]Richard D. Lambert, *International Studies and the Undergraduate* (Washington, D.C.: American Council on Education, 1989), 66.

[2]The foreign language enrollment data in this paragraph are drawn from Richard Brod and Bettina J. Huber, "Foreign Language Enrollments in United States Institutions of Higher Education, Fall 1995," *ADFL Bulletin* 28 (Winter 1997): 55, 58.

[3]Stephen R. Lewis, Jr., "'Internationalizing' the Liberal Arts College," in Katharine H. Hansen and Joel W. Meyerson, *International Challenges to American Colleges and Universities: Looking Ahead* (Washington, D.C.: American Council on Education, 1995), 100–101.

[4]Lambert, *International Studies and the Undergraduate*, 16–17.

[5]Craufurd D. Goodwin and Michael Nacht, *Abroad and Beyond: Patterns in American Overseas Education* (Cambridge: Cambridge University Press, 1988).

[6]"In the International Interest: The Contributions and Needs of America's International Liberal Arts Colleges" (Beloit, Wisc.: International Liberal Arts Colleges, 1992).

[7]Richard D. Lambert, "The External Frame for International Studies," *International Education Forum* 15 (Fall 1995): 76.

[8]Kenneth Prewitt, "Presidential Items," *Items* (Social Science Research Council, March 1996).

[9]The concept and pursuit of global competence are exhaustively examined in Richard D. Lambert, ed., *Educational Exchange and Global Competence* (Council on International Educational Exchange, 1994).

Born and raised in America, the discipline of international relations is, so to speak, too close to the fire. It needs triple distance: it should move away from the contemporary, toward the past; from the perspective of a superpower (and a highly conservative one), toward that of the weak and the revolutionary—away from the impossible quest for stability; from the glide into policy science, back to the steep ascent toward the peaks which the questions raised by traditional political philosophy represent. This would also be a way of putting the fragments into which the discipline explodes, if not together, at least in perspective. But where, in the social sciences, are the scientific priorities the decisive ones? Without the possibilities that exist in this country, the discipline might well have avoided being stunted, only by avoiding being born. The French say that if one does not have what one would like, one must be content with what one has got. Resigned, perhaps. But content? A state of dissatisfaction is a goad to research. Scholars in international relations have two good reasons to be dissatisfied: the state of the world, the state of their discipline. If only those two reasons always converged!

—Stanley Hoffmann
"An American Social Science:
International Relations"

from *Dædalus*, Summer 1977
"Discoveries and Interpretations:
Studies in Contemporary Scholarship"

Diane P. Balestri

Stability and Transformation: Information Technology in Liberal Arts Colleges

BOUT TWO YEARS AGO, a senior faculty member at Vassar College introduced his colleagues to me in the following way: "With a *certain* recent retirement"—pausing to cast a significant glance at those in the know—"every member of this department is computer literate." They all chuckled among themselves, and the conversation moved on to other matters. But underneath the humor lies the unavoidable truth: the transition is over, the commitment is absolute. For better or worse, no one living at or working for a small liberal arts college is untouched by the presence of digital technologies. As Richard Katz has recently put it, we are all "dancing with the devil."[1]

Information technologies have indeed become a pervasive presence on the campus of every small liberal arts college. As are all other sectors of higher education today, these institutions are increasingly dependent on complex combinations of technology for every routine function—from running the payroll and controlling the thermostats to pursuing the core mission of teaching and learning. If we have learned nothing else from the recent spate of Y2K prophecies, investigations, and remediations, we have come to realize that digital technologies also intensify relationships and vastly complicate interactions

Diane P. Balestri is director of Computing and Information Services at Vassar College.

293

between our colleges and the "real" world outside their physical perimeters.

But what has been the fundamental impact of these technologies on the nature of the liberal arts college? The issue is examined by Richard Hersh elsewhere in this volume when he asserts, "While most colleges need some of what modern technology offers, it is not so true that what technology can offer has anything that approaches the transformative power of a genuine liberal arts education." The careful qualifications that Hersh embeds in his statement suggest well the profound ambiguity with which the leaders of small liberal arts colleges have eyed the accelerating integration of technology into the infrastructure, the organization, the methods of instruction, and the carefully nurtured culture of their institutions. Below the surface of Hersh's statement, and other statements like it, lurk two even deeper concerns: first, that technology has the potential to vitiate the transforming power of liberal learning as we have always understood it, and second, that, despite huge expenditures, technology will have little or nothing positive to contribute to that transformative mission in the future.

The impact of these highly complex and volatile technologies on a set of stable institutions, place-centered and value-centered, is the topic of this essay. In the following pages, we will examine some of the perceived threats that have led Hersh to conclude that the impact of technology will at best be limited, and have led others to fear that the only "transformative" power of technology will be to upset and perhaps to destroy the small liberal arts college altogether. In response to these concerns, we will explore the possibility that, if properly conceived and managed as a set of tools and resources, technology can indeed become transformative in a most positive way: as a catalyst for creative teaching and for organizational renovations that will help small liberal arts colleges assure their own survival and their effectiveness in delivering "transformative" education beyond the short-term perils of Y2K and well into the next century.

THREATS POSED BY INFORMATION TECHNOLOGY:
PERCEPTIONS AND REALITIES

The practice of teaching and learning in residence is central to the concept of liberal education in America. Knowledge grows over time, we believe, and is fostered by serendipitous encounters with peers and faculty as well as by regular, structured work in groups; the growth of knowledge thus benefits from physical proximity to teachers, to fellow learners, to books, to laboratories. Knowledge is forged by building connections that are social and cultural as well as intellectual; such connections, again, require proximity.

It has been frequently suggested in the popular press and elsewhere, however, that rapidly expanding opportunities for "distributed learning" will call into question the fundamental concept of residential education. Powerful institutions, from the University of Phoenix to the University of Michigan, from Stanford to Harvard, are getting into the business of offering technology-mediated courses and course credits. Their offerings will become both attractive and highly competitive with those of residential institutions once they are staffed with famous professors and provide a high degree of on-line interaction in settings that are time- and location-free. Most small colleges will initially encounter these "virtual" courses as a form of direct competition when enrolled students present them for transfer credit. Will accepting these courses for credit be a tacit admission that presence and direct interaction are not essential components of liberal learning? What percentage of a degree program can a student pursue on-line and still be considered "liberally" educated in the traditional sense of the word?

It is not yet known how extensive this national trend toward distributing the availability of courses and degrees is going to become. The commercial market is providing a good deal of the connective infrastructure, as competition reduces the cost of computers and access to the Internet. But the economics of distributed learning for the colleges and universities themselves is only now being tested; the value of remote learning, particularly for the eighteen- to twenty-one-year-old students who are the primary applicants to small residential colleges, is by no means clear.

Only a few of the most affluent liberal arts colleges will be able to ignore this threat entirely, however; others are already attempting to adopt the strategies of distributed learning and turn them into opportunities. In an effort to save costs and rescue major programs with tiny enrollments, for instance, some colleges are banding together in consortia to use technologies such as videoconferencing, web pages, and interactive chat rooms for sharing courses. The benefits of such a strategy, particularly for a small liberal arts college that is financially insecure and physically isolated, appear great: the collaboration itself can be stimulating to students and faculty, and the ability to offer the full spectrum of the traditional liberal arts curriculum may be perceived as critical to the institution's survival. But start-up expenses are great, for installation and maintenance of the technologies themselves, for faculty training in the effective use of the technologies as vehicles for teaching, and for development of specific course materials. More important, the ongoing expenses and the ongoing appeal to students are largely unknown factors. Will such technology-dependent collaborative courses be sustainable beyond the period of the grants that are initially funding them?

It will be important for leadership at all small liberal arts colleges to keep a close eye on these experiments. Indeed, it could be argued that in "preparing its students for life-long learning" (a common component of many of our mission statements), small liberal arts colleges should be consciously equipping their undergraduates to take future advantage of the anytime/anywhere learning that institutions such as the University of Phoenix may one day be offering them. Short of actually sharing on-line course materials and course registrations among a consortium of institutions, a college might consider gradually making a subset of its courses available virtually to members of its community residing at a distance—to alumni/ae, for instance, or to students studying abroad.

Besides this broad challenge to the concept of residential education, information technologies clearly pose several other, very real threats to the security of small liberal arts colleges.

These threats take the form of unrelenting and nearly incomprehensible demand for rapid change, and they have the effect of destabilizing many core functions of the institution. This demand can seem intolerable to the essential culture of liberal arts institutions, which have valued tradition and continuity very highly and have embraced change deliberately and slowly.

Technological Change and Fiscal Stability

Several forces are driving the rate of technological change forward at a breakneck pace, and there is, unfortunately, no suggestion that this rate will slow down anytime soon. Some of these forces include:

· Trends in industry. Enormous wealth of intellect and even greater wealth of venture capital are currently feeding rapid development and deployment of new technologies. The "new" Powerbook on which I am writing this essay is preconfigured for wireless connectivity to the Internet, while my campus is in the process of committing many thousands of dollars to upgrading its wired infrastructure. The "instant messaging" system of America Online, I am told, is beginning to consume noticeable bandwidth on the college's already strained Internet connection. And that is only today. By the time you read this essay, several new technologies that I barely can imagine will have changed the virtual landscape even further and will be slouching toward our campuses with an apocalyptic energy of their own.

· The continuously rising expectations of entering students. Many of our entering students have had years of access to technologies that outshine those of most liberal arts colleges, whether in their homes, their schools, or their public libraries.[2] These students are discovering and judging the quality of colleges on the World Wide Web, and they enter expecting convenient access to computing equipment and connectivity to an Internet Service Provider. Many of them have used basic productivity tools and Internet materials in their schoolwork, and some of them are already generating significant income with their technical skills.

· The emergence of new research tools and new sources of knowledge. Many digital tools now used in teaching—including both hardware and software applications—were originally adapted or devised for advanced analysis and research in specific disciplines. They are "trickling down" to our campuses at an accelerating rate through the research interests of faculty, especially new faculty members recruited from prestigious research universities. With improvements to methods for storage, retrieval, and transmission, as well as better models for access and cost, electronic resources for learning have also proliferated, including: digitized texts of books and journals; data sets of information on topics ranging from the human genome to the census to the weather; enormous and well-conceived collections of sounds, video, and images. Needless to say, the pressure to acquire these electronic resources is putting yet another strain on the budget for library acquisitions.

These new tools and resources can be both expensive to acquire and highly specialized. They are changing the nature of laboratories and libraries as these facilities have been designed and funded in the past. New tools and resources have enabled faculty to introduce new methodologies for teaching; in turn, the evolution in teaching has fueled the demand for universal student access to many of the tools and resources formerly required only by a few seniors and their faculty mentors. Provosts and presidents at liberal arts colleges have experience solving the problem of providing rich environments for research in the sciences; but only with the emergence of digital hardware and software as research tools in the humanities, fine arts, and social sciences has the issue become generalized across the whole spectrum of the curriculum.

· Competition among liberal arts colleges. Most small liberal arts colleges are already using information technologies for recruiting new students. They are proudly, and wisely, advertising their technology-rich facilities in publications, and they are providing web pages for on-line applications. As each college improves its services to enrolled and prospective students, the stakes are raised for all others. The recent spate of advertisements for the position of "Webmaster" at these institutions suggests the sudden urgency being felt at the highest levels of administration to excel in communicating through a medium less than a decade old. Similarly, there has been great consternation on many campuses as a result of the rankings published in the three-year-old Yahoo survey of "wired" colleges and universities, even though that survey defines "wiredness" with a set of secretive criteria that may be largely unrelated to the goals of liberal education.

Technological Change and Organizational Stability

Information technologies also challenge the stability of management and organization in small liberal arts colleges. Selecting and funding these new technologies, maintaining them, and using them productively have often been exceedingly time-consuming endeavors, distracting leadership and diverting resources away from other mission-critical activities. The problems posed by the introduction of information technologies into college administration have been particularly frustrating, because the realities of implementation have so vastly differed from original expectations.

Many administrators in higher education initially believed that the benefit—indeed the primary purpose—of investing in technology for administrative functions was to eliminate labor costs through "automation." This promise came from information-technology managers themselves, in part to justify the high initial (and ongoing) costs for advanced administrative systems. As these new systems have come on line, usually with great pain and disruption, some job functions have indeed become obsolete (there are generally fewer secretaries, for instance—not necessarily a benefit, as it turns out), the time required to complete many tedious manual tasks has been substantially reduced, and sometimes analysis of complex institutional data for financial planning has become possible for the first time. But for every job eliminated, another one, or several, has been created, and a whole new branch of administration—technology experts and their managers—has emerged. These new jobs usually require more skill than the old. Filling them can be difficult and is certainly more expensive. For continuing staff, new technologies have changed the way they do their work, and the college must find time and resources for continuous technical training.

Along with new jobs, new tasks, and new skills in administrative offices have come additional headaches: institutional leaders are now called on to undertake broad reorganization around new needs and to determine how to find new resources or reallocate existing funding to support these new functions. Old organizational models that completely isolate technical expertise in a central Office of Computing, for instance, are increasingly inadequate. Polley McClure, John Smith, and Toby Sitko point this out in a seminal article on the current crisis in support services for information technology in higher education. They argue that central technology organizations, which originated as the custodians of wires, mainframes, and home-grown systems, have subsequently evolved into overburdened "service" organizations within the institution. Because of the pervasiveness of information technology and the depth of institutional reliance on it, as well as its cost, however, institutions must now consider information technology to be a strategic resource, requiring new thinking about how the institution is organized to implement and support it.[3] Acknowledging a mission-critical role for technology, and incorporating technology effectively into all aspects of institutional organization and planning, will thus be essential though particularly difficult for small colleges, where continuity and stability within the administration have helped to contain costs. New conceptual and organizational models can also be deeply disruptive at small institutions in which strong personal loyalties and bonds of trust within the institution have compensated for low salaries and minimal prospect of career advancement.

In addition, technology will inevitably call on many administrative managers working at liberal arts colleges to acquire new technical skills themselves, as well as new expertise about how to hire, educate, and compensate staff across the institution. Often the senior officials at these small institutions have no experience or expertise in evaluating the very skills that may be critical to the institution's future or even to its survival. For some colleges, outsourcing those aspects of information technology not considered to be at the core of the institution's mission is already being considered. For others, bringing the chief technology or information officer into a closer working relationship with senior officers, or even into the president's cabinet, will be a more effective solution.

Technological Change and the Future of Liberal Learning

But the deepest threat that technology appears to pose is erosion of the intensely interpersonal and reflective nature of liberal learning itself and devaluation of the methodologies for teaching and research that have sustained that kind of learning for hundreds of years. Technology is often assumed to promote characteristics of teaching and learning that are diametrically opposed to the values espoused by small residential liberal arts colleges: "asynchronous," or remote, relationships rather than face-to-face discussion; automated rather than personalized transactions; the amassing of undifferentiated data rather than the patient construction of knowledge; rapid quantitative analysis rather than qualitative reflection. Technology seems more effective when marshaled for the acquisition of skills than for the enhancement of liberal learning. There is quite understandable fear that insinuating too much technology into the process of liberal learning may reduce the experience to training and ultimately undermine its value.

The extensive introduction of technology into the process of teaching also has significant implications for the nature of the faculty, for the definition of their work, and ultimately for the established protocols surrounding tenure and promotion. Faculty reward has traditionally been based on a combination of teaching, research, and community service. In the recent experience of many faculty members at small colleges (and elsewhere), the use of technology for teaching and research is considered apart from all of these categories as a decorative addition to the portfolio, but hardly an integrated or decisive element. Departments and tenure/promotion review committees simply do not know how to evaluate the use of technology for teaching and have not yet given the subject the fresh thought that it requires.

QUESTIONS OF ASSESSMENT AND VALUE

Finally, and inevitably, looking at all the challenges to business as usual posed by technology, looking at the costs and disruption that technology has already caused on small liberal arts campuses—with no end in sight—college leaders find themselves asking, "How do I assess the benefits of these new technologies? Has there been a meaningful impact on student learning? On the quality of teaching? On the efficiency of administration? And even if that is the case, how do I measure these outcomes in order to chart a future course? How do I know what is the most effective and cost-efficient set of choices among competing technologies for my campus? And how do I balance the claims of technology on the institutional budget against all the other demands?" There have been no satisfactory answers to these questions.

Even the apparently simple question of "How are we doing with our information technology investments compared to other institutions of similar mission, size, and resources?" has proved immensely difficult to answer. According to Martin Ringle, while selective liberal arts colleges typically know (and track) the percentage of their operating budgets devoted to the library, they tend not to do likewise with their computing budgets. This is unfortunate, he notes, since it keeps the institution in the dark as to its real investment in technology and thus prevents decision makers from dealing with the investment in a strategic way. Ringle's analysis of recent data from a cross-section of selective liberal arts colleges, for example, shows that while some institutions who consider themselves to be technology leaders are spending roughly 6 percent of their budgets on computing, others who also consider themselves to be leaders are spending considerably less than 4 percent.[4] The value of these percentages as a basis for significant comparison is dubious, however, given that the financial data, as noted above, is not collected thoroughly or by any standard means. Nor does the number of dollars spent offer us adequate detail about how the dollars are being spent or what is being obtained.

Looking for the measurable "benefits" of technology for student learning has been even more vexing. Administrators and faculty at liberal arts colleges have not routinely tended to ask systematic questions about the merit of various teaching methods or materials. The "amount" or measurable "quantity" of learning achieved by individual students at a liberal arts college is seldom assessed beyond a small number of introductory courses—most commonly language, math, and science courses—in which well-defined bodies of information must be committed to memory, and in which it is thus possible to test for right and wrong answers. Instead, the quality or excellence of a student's learning is typically assessed by the judgment of an expert. Most often the expert is the faculty member leading the course; sometimes, as in the case of Swarthmore College's Honors Program, external faculty experts are called in; sometimes student-to-student peer review is invoked as an additional audience. These assessments are almost always narrative, qualitative, and private. They are not easily aggregated and studied for patterns or trends in learning as teaching methods and the students' resources for learning change over time.

Courses and whole academic programs, as opposed to specific students' performances, are judged, of course, but again more often by qualitative than by quantitative measures. Individual courses build their reputations as stimulating or boring through student course evaluations, for instance, or self-reports between faculty members over lunch. A colleague's success as a teacher may be inferred by the quality of his or her research and professional presentations, by the enrollments in courses, or (in the increasingly rare case of sequenced courses) by the degree of preparation students appear to have received in one course for the next. The quality of a major may be judged by the number of students who choose it, by the reputation or scholarly productivity of faculty, or by external review committees, who must also rely primarily on expert opinion rather than on quantifiable data. Ultimately the value of the liberal arts education is judged over a long period of time, with a retrospective view of alumni/ae, their characters, their contributions to family, to work, and to community—and, of course, their contributions to their alma mater as well. Relatively little research on the long-term benefits of liberal arts education has been done that differentiates among the specific components of that education, and it is hard to imagine how the long-term impact of a particular methodology, tool, or learning resource could be effectively "measured."

But the questions remain pressing because, as I have suggested, the concerns behind the questions are fundamental. These concerns are about cost, yes, but also about the possibility that the nature of the enterprise is being gradually eroded from within as well as from without by the very technologies that we are so fervently though often fearfully embracing.

TURNING THREATS INTO OPPORTUNITIES FOR EXCELLENCE

In confronting this tendency to regard information technologies as a threat, small liberal arts colleges should neither retreat nor submit. Instead, they must learn to deploy and manage information technologies as strategic tools and enabling resources that provide opportunity for each sector of the college to examine and improve upon accepted methods and processes. In this vision, information technologies become a catalyst to reassert commitment to excellence at every level of the institution from the daily work habits of each employee to the fulfillment of the academic mission. The challenge is twofold. The first challenge is to determine how information technologies will be positioned by strategic planning as agents of institutional excellence, on the one hand undergirding and stabilizing the institution's core and on the other hand enabling necessary and appropriate transformation. The second challenge is to turn that strategic vision into an operating plan for information technology that effectively balances the maintenance of a sound and stable working environment with projects that manage and enable change by adopting, adapting, rejecting, even inventing information technologies as they suit the mission of the institution.

Each liberal arts college has developed its own unique characteristics and priorities, and so each will choose differently among the vast array of technologies available to it, the uses to which those technologies are put, and the rate at which they are deployed on campus. But all liberal arts colleges in common should undertake campus-wide discussions about information technology that are both strategic and operational. From information about strategic planning for technology gathered at over 150 institutions, Martin Ringle and Daniel Updegrove have constructed a general ten-step model that is broken into two closely related phases, the first developing socioeconomic objectives (shared vision and strategy), and the second focusing on technical objectives (agreed-upon operational goals). The key to success in their model is continuous iteration, gathering and sharing information among planners and users.[5] This means engaging faculty, administrators, students, and trustees as well as the campus technologists in an ongoing discussion about the relationship between the mission of the institution and the vision for using information technologies strategically to implement it. Strategic planning of this sort does not focus exclusively on building a financial model, though ultimately the rate at which visions are implemented depends on the resources available to do so.

Ringle and Updegrove recommend that thorough strategic planning for information technology should take place on a five-year cycle, with annual updates to the operational plan. Planning, in their view, should be guided, but not owned, by the college's chief technology or information officer. It can also be very effective, however, to embed components of strategic planning into institution-wide planning initiatives, such as accreditation self-studies, curricular reviews, and master planning. A year-long master planning process for classroom renovation at Vassar College, for instance, provided the opportunity to survey faculty extensively and to develop a long-range plan for the instructional technologies in classrooms that is congruent with faculty's expressed teaching goals.

The outcome of an institution-wide strategic review might yield statements such as the following:

· *The mission of our institution is to provide distinctively excellent undergraduate education. Information technologies serve that mission most effectively when they provide:*
   · Tools that enable students and faculty to communicate with one another and to interact effectively;

- Tools that are fundamental to learning and independent work in each of the disciplines we offer;
- Resources that enable students to undertake independent learning and research;
- Resources that enrich students' cultural and social awareness.

- *All members of the campus community, be they students, faculty, senior administrators, or staff, are able to use information technologies productively in their work. Generally speaking, information technologies serve this purpose best when they are both as ubiquitous as necessary and as unobtrusive as possible. Thus:*
  - The campus technology infrastructure should be robust, reliable, and capable of serving the mission as described above;
  - Sufficient staff should be assigned to assure that the infrastructure is maintained and that all members of the community have the assistance they need to make excellent use of it;
  - Research into emerging technologies and planning for technological change are critical to the future of the institution, and should be fully supported.

- *We serve the college's mission by attracting a talented and diverse student body. Information technologies help us to enroll students most effectively when they provide:*
  - Vehicles for communicating our message widely;
  - Easy channels for prospective students to communicate with us;
  - Databases for managing student information that also help us understand and improve all aspects of this process.

- *We serve the college's mission by being fiscally sound. Information technologies help us meet that goal when they provide:*
  - Vehicles for communicating with our constituents, including alumni/ae and other potential donors;
  - Information databases and financial systems for tracking income and reporting about it accurately and in timely ways;

· Financial systems and processes for effectively managing resources and expenses.[6]

This brief and hypothetical sketch of a strategic plan is ambitious, and, of course, it ought to be. There are a number of possible ways to prioritize among the goals that follow from a strategic vision for information technologies; prioritizing ultimately will help small colleges merge vision with fiscal reality. In sorting out priorities, it is tempting but not adequate for the purposes of planning simply to order priorities by an exercise that sets up arbitrary alternatives: is it more important to expand basic infrastructure or to support instructional projects? To develop database structures that manage on-line applications or to train office staff in using existing productivity tools? To install new classroom technologies or to update the residential hall wiring? Here is an exercise in frustration—surely all of the above are high on our priority list (we tell ourselves). How is it possible to choose?

Instead of trying to choose, planners need help from the campus computing experts in understanding the basic interconnectedness of the technical infrastructure. Inevitably even a small adjustment in one component—a decision to introduce a new desktop application for clerical staff, to extend remote access capabilities for faculty, or to provide a mechanism for students to share their work more easily, for example—has a successive effect on every other aspect of the computing environment. So prioritizing involves not simply making choices, but also determining sets of interacting sequences: On the one hand, how does undertaking each initiative help us accomplish the others? On the other hand, to what extent does each require prior attention to others as a condition of its success?

For small liberal arts colleges, the primary challenge of information technology lies in articulating as clearly and specifically as can be imagined the relationship between the institutional mission and the capabilities of technology to support progress toward fulfilling the mission. Effective planning will enable small liberal arts colleges to control costs better by managing information technology through strategic decision making rather than by succumbing to information technology as an incessant and undifferentiated driver of change. In this way the rate of change can be better managed, and intelligent decisions can be made about when to select the evolutionary integration of a new technology, when to opt for a highly focused, or revolutionary, change, and when to reject a technology altogether.

A strategic approach will also help to focus the mission and the priorities of the central computing organization. Their functions should be to maintain the robust core services, or what might be called the "production environment" for technology, at the college, including both the infrastructure and the support of users; to study and recommend emerging technologies; to participate fully in institutional strategic and operational planning; and to build multiple partnerships with other campus offices to assure that users are supported effectively.

Small colleges cannot and indeed do not need to compete with major research universities for leadership in bringing the latest technologies to campus. The earliest adopters must be willing to bear enormous cost for their status as technical innovators. On the other hand, small colleges have much to learn by keeping an eye on the national leaders as test beds for new technologies and as the source of information about trends and new ideas relevant to higher education. Institutions in the Research Universities I category of *A Classification of Institutions of Higher Education*, published by the Carnegie Foundation for the Advancement of Teaching, in particular have been very willing to share their experiences and even to help their colleagues at smaller institutions interpret and develop strategies that suit their smaller scale and more limited budgets.

Finally, all technology planning must have an element of flexibility built into it.[7] Sometimes serendipity will bring an idea and a technology together with spectacular results, and sometimes a new technology will appear with stunning speed, as did the World Wide Web well within this past decade. Even a small college should be able to assess and, when the impact or benefit is congruent with its mission, act quickly.

EXPLORING CURRICULAR OPPORTUNITIES

While information technologies can and should be strategic instruments for small liberal arts colleges in recruiting students, raising money, and managing administrative functions, the greatest opportunities lie just where these technologies have sometimes been perceived as posing the greatest threat to the traditional values and methods of liberal education: in the realms of teaching and learning. I would not have said this fifteen or even ten years ago with such conviction. At that time desktop technologies were just beginning to penetrate the market, and only a handful of faculty members were developing projects that demonstrated the potential for information technologies to enable "transformative" liberal learning. These projects, though sometimes powerful and even enduring, tended to be isolated and seldom had an immediate impact beyond the students of a particular instructor.[8] With the exception of certain fields in the sciences and quantitative social sciences, digital technologies as instruments for learning seemed in those early days to be answers in the proverbial search for their defining questions.

In the past decade, however, the tables have turned: significant numbers of faculty members in all disciplines and at every sort of institution, including most small liberal arts colleges, have been using whatever information technologies are available to them to supplement, to develop, and—most of them report—to improve their teaching and their students' learning. Suddenly, the questions that faculty members are posing of technology, and their desire to implement advanced and multiple technologies in courses, are actually outstripping the solutions that available technologies can provide.

Each liberal arts college has its own distinctive curriculum and pedagogy, and each must begin with a clear vision of what these are in order to understand the role that technology is best suited to play. To one degree or another, however, all wrestle with the same general questions. What do we value as the outcome of the education we provide? Do we expect to prepare our students for professional careers? Do we expect instead to develop experts in what we might call "amateur learning" or "learning to learn"? Do we promote collaborative learning or independent research—or both? How do we expect faculty and students to interact? How do we judge their accomplishments, and are we satisfied with our assessments?

A brief look at the evolution of computer-based communication technologies as tools for learning provides just one example of the way in which digital tools penetrate and, yes, transform the learning process. Computers first became everyday tools for students at liberal arts institutions in the late 1980s. Suddenly personal computers were affordable for many students to own and for colleges to place in public clusters; but, more important, teachers of writing were recognizing that their new, process-oriented pedagogy for teaching composition was perfectly matched to the power of word-processing software, which for the first time enabled their students to perform both easy and extensive revisions. In their hands, the computational machine became a machine for communication.

Next, electronic mail, that unique cross between written and interactive personal communication, enabled students to write more extensively and less formally, sustaining academic dialogue with faculty members begun in the classroom and during office hours. Faculty members also reported that students too shy to seek them out regularly in their offices were willing to ask for help through on-line communication. Today digitized written communication is also extending and enriching the interaction among students outside of class hours in "chat" rooms that can be unmonitored opportunities for even more writing or organized by the professor for both controlled and informal discussion. At Allegheny College, for example, on-line discussions are bringing together students in several courses with a common theme but very different intellectual foundations to exchange ideas in writing outside the boundaries of their separate classrooms. Facing a new and very real peer audience for their thoughts and for their writing, students are motivated to read more carefully, analyze more deeply, and express themselves more persuasively. From time to time, experts from outside the college join in the discussion, further enriching the process.

The digital technologies, it turns out, are actually enabling a time-honored vision: that the intellectual life of the student at a residential college is only initially shaped in the classroom, but continues to develop outside of it as well—in the library, the dorm room, the computer cluster, the student center, perhaps even on the grassy slopes of the campus and the sidelines of athletic events. At some institutions, faculty members are taking this now-ubiquitous tool of digital communication and expanding its value even further, by creating experiences that enable the kind of language learning that only direct immersion in a foreign culture can offer. In an electronic MOO—a web-based, multimedia space that promotes live discussion among participants—Vassar College students attempting to learn German communicate over the Internet in real time, about real topics, with fellow students in Münster, Germany, who are simultaneously building their command of English. The motivation to "talk" in writing so as to be understood by a native speaker is very powerful, and students find themselves becoming both teachers and learners in the process. In each case—whether it is revising a paper, creating expanded dialogue among students or between students and faculty, or building an immersion experience for language learners—a simple, ubiquitous technology has been the vehicle for realizing the goals of liberal learning.

Similar stories could be constructed about the way uses of many other digital technologies have evolved and matured as tools and resources for learning. I have already noted how discipline-specific tools, such as digital instruments for data capture and analysis, have moved from the research lab to the classroom. We are also witnessing the evolution of image collections from the personal slide trays of an art historian, an anthropologist, or a biologist into virtual museums and libraries, available free or by license on web sites. These new resources are enabling faculty to reconceive their teaching and their students' learning around the availability of an incomparably greater store of evidence and example. As standards for digitizing images become widely accepted and copyright issues are resolved, these collections will proliferate even further, and new teaching methods that utilize them will follow.

Whether in the use of general-purpose tools, discipline-specific tools, or digital resources, the characteristics of the learning are exactly those that liberal arts institutions have always highly valued: learning that is not limited to lecture and text-book; learning that is based on the engagement of the student with original materials; learning that is both active and inter-active; learning that involves developing the capability for independent research using the fundamental tools of the disci-pline; learning that involves rich participation in collaborative projects; and learning that does not take place in isolation from significant cultural and social contexts.

PURSUING STRATEGIC GOALS

If information technologies demonstrably contribute in so many ways to the "transformative power" of a liberal education, how can a small, residential college of inevitably limited re-sources introduce these new opportunities for faculty and stu-dents while at the same time managing the demand? Put an-other way, how is it possible to incorporate these ever-changing information technologies into the stable structures of teaching and learning at the small liberal arts college? The answer is straightforward: in a planned and coherent way that corre-sponds to the broader institutional mission. This observation seems no more than common sense—until we acknowledge how often decision making about technology on small college cam-puses continues to be driven by rising threats, internal or exter-nal, such as those described above, or by unexpected but short-lived opportunities, particularly in the form of grants or dona-tions.

There are many possible models for introducing and manag-ing change. Models for managing technical change based on iterative or spiraling patterns of experiment and gradual, delib-erate integration are the most realistic.[9] More important than choosing the model, however, is managing the rate at which a small college chooses to incorporate change; the appropriate rate of change should depend on its culture as much as on the forces in the marketplace or even the depth of its resources.

Whatever the rate, there are a number of practical steps every small college should consider in moving from planning for information technology to implementation.

Regularize Budgeting for Information Technology

Liberal arts colleges have become much more savvy in recent years about building and maintaining their physical plants—as residential institutions, they know the value that lies in a strong sense of "place." Where possible, they are even providing endowment for buildings, so that maintenance is guaranteed. Similarly, strategic planners need to conceptualize the entire information infrastructure as an essential physical asset that equally requires its own guaranteed funding, or endowment. Some expenses, for instance to replace software and desktop hardware, may become so routine that they can be literally folded into the operating budget. On the other hand, staffing levels and salaries may be the most difficult to regularize, as technologies become more sophisticated, user needs more intense, and the marketplace continues to draw off experienced personnel.

Build an Infrastructure and a Teaching Environment based on Standards

It is easier and much more cost-effective to expand support for desktop computing technology based on commonly accepted standards than it is to customize idiosyncratic pieces of equipment for every user. The same principle applies to uses of technology for teaching. Most colleges, to one degree or another, are already fostering exemplary curricular uses of technology on campus. The single most important criterion for selecting these projects should be their strong relationship to the core of the institution's teaching program —whether the project be implemented in a core discipline or a core course, enhance a core methodology, or demonstrate the instructional use of a core technology (i.e., a technology that is widely distributed and supported on campus). General purpose classrooms or laboratories will not always be able to accommodate sophisticated "core" projects that require dedicated equipment or expensive software—examples might include laboratories for scientific visualization, for film production, for gathering data about brain functions. The decision to implement too many dedicated labs at small colleges should be carefully weighed, however. Sometimes the need may be acute but temporary, as even very complex and initially expensive technologies are quickly becoming available in the commercial market and can be distributed to personal desktops.

This principle of standards should also be applied to as many aspects of student computing as possible. A periodic, systematic review of student computing, with an eye to developing a standard environment for all students, might include issues such as: student access to college-owned technology; student ownership of personal technology; the locus and quality of support for students' use of technology; the level of technical expertise that students should acquire; and how the college should plan for teaching those skills.

Make Information Technology a Routine Part of all Institutional Policy-Making

The institutional policies that will be required range from the practical to the abstruse, from the establishment of campus-wide standards for hardware and software to the interpretation of copyright law and guidelines. As they review proposals for new courses, the faculty members of the curriculum committee should be asking, "What technologies will this course require? What are the purposes and the proposed benefits of using those technologies? How will they be made available? Are there new costs, and if so, what is the source of funding?" Working groups that convene to plan and implement upgrades to classroom, laboratory, and library facilities should include faculty members, librarians, and technologists as well as facilities managers. College handbooks for staff, faculty, and students should incorporate consistent, institutionally-approved policies about appropriate use of the computing resources provided by the college. Finally, a few institutions will try to figure out how to integrate the use of technology into their system of promotion and tenure for faculty. Only when this problem has been addressed will an institutional strategy for information technology be fully in place.

ASSESSMENT AND QUALITY, REVISITED

Small liberal arts colleges will cease to feel threatened by information technologies as their ability to manage the technologies they have chosen to incorporate grows, as they begin to put technologies to effective and varied use for teaching and learning, and as they plan for their routine maintenance and support. Even so, the questions of "how are we doing?" and "how do we know how we are doing?" will inevitably remain.

As Gregory C. Farrington, president of Lehigh University, correctly notes: "It will take quite some time and a great deal more research before the best uses of the new technologies in education are sorted out."[10] In the interim, liberal arts colleges can take a number of steps that will help shape immediate institutional practice, and will also contribute in useful ways to the slowly growing body of research on the uses of technology in higher education, in particular teaching and learning with technology. For instance:

1. Do a better institutional job of gathering information and data. Many small liberal arts colleges have ignored or underestimated the value of institutional research to identify useful trends and provide internal benchmarks for improved planning. When new, large, and continuing expenses are involved, as is the case with information technologies, having the expertise of an institutional researcher to plan and execute good quantitative and qualitative studies is invaluable. It is unlikely that the central computing organization will have skills necessary for this task, though they may provide or support tools that can do some of the initial data collection.

2. When examining the impact of technology, assess excellence in use and outcome as defined by the mission of the individual institution—as liberal arts colleges have always done. The characteristics defining "excellence" in use and outcome will vary from college to college, and should be specified clearly as the focus of study. Excellence can be assessed in several different ways. Formative evaluation, or examination of work in process, records progress along a timeline toward the original goal, notes deviations, and may suggest adjustments in either the goal or the process as a result. Distributing surveys,

collecting verbal reports, conducting focus groups, and then telling stories based on that information, rather than simply listing dates, events, and dollars spent, provides a multi-faceted perspective that is often more compelling than aggregated data alone. Building a "balanced scorecard" for assessing information technology that includes multiple perspectives (financial, user, business process, and staff development) is a useful strategy drawn from the corporate sector.[11] Looking to other institutions for benchmarks of excellence or models for "best practice" against which the home institution's practice is compared can be useful, but only where there is first a shared view of the excellence being sought.

3. When it comes to assessing the success of technology specifically for teaching, it is a common mistake to use scores on common tests for comparing old teaching practices with new, and then to judge the merit of the new against the standard of the old. Instead, we must begin our assessment of technology and teaching with the observation of faculty in many disciplines that thoughtful incorporation of technology into the learning process has actually changed both what is learned and how it is learned. New kinds of learning and new ways of learning, sometimes planned and sometimes unexpected, have become possible. Assessment should focus on ascertaining the benefits to students in both of these areas.[12]

4. The technology itself can be effectively used as a medium for carrying out certain aspects of good evaluation. All kinds of quantitative data can be generated about the use of a web site, for instance, given the proper tools. Surveys can be compiled, and even conducted, electronically. A college that wishes to assess the overall impact of computing technologies on student learning might consider developing a Digital Student Portfolio project. A rich combination of digital tools and storage space would enable students to build personal electronic portfolios over the course of their college careers. At the time of their graduation, selective study of those portfolios, with appropriate permission, could provide a much deeper insight into the intellectual careers of a college's students than has ordinarily been possible in the past.

5. Assessment may be a less overwhelming task, and therefore more likely to be undertaken systematically, if the process is shared among consortia of small liberal arts colleges with similar definitions of "excellence," as well as similar organizations and teaching methods. Building a body of common methodologies and describing the outcomes of assessment in a common vocabulary would help validate the conclusions and actually give planners and teachers a richer body of information for future planning.

Small liberal arts colleges have recognized that information technologies are agents of change and bring onto campuses all the risks inherent in change. The greatest risk, however, comes from failing to accept the challenge of managing these technologies effectively. The opportunity, and perhaps even the future viability of small liberal arts colleges, lies in realizing the potential for shaping technological change to serve the mission of liberal learning.

The message coming from other sectors of higher education is that the chief benefit of information technology for students is its functionality as a vehicle for convenient learning—"anytime, anywhere, any topic, from any provider." The message that the small liberal arts colleges must send back in reply is that the real power of information technology lies far beyond convenience, useful as that may be. Information technologies instead are challenging tools and resources that enable the sort of complex investigation and rich communication in pursuit of knowledge that are the very hallmarks of our distinctively American liberal learning.

ENDNOTES

[1]Richard N. Katz and Associates, *Dancing with the Devil: Information Technology and the New Competition in Higher Education* (San Francisco: Jossey-Bass Publishers, 1999).

[2]Microsoft chairman Bill Gates and his wife, Melinda, are heavily underwriting a national effort to bring computers, Internet access, and technology training to libraries in low-income communities.

318   *Diane P. Balestri*

[3]Polley A. McClure, John W. Smith, and Toby D. Sitko, "The Crisis in Information Technology Support: Has our Current Model Reached its Limit?" CAUSE Professional Paper Series, no. 16, 1997.

[4]See Ringle's forthcoming article, "Taming Technology Costs: A Primer for Presidents, Provosts, and other Key Decision-Makers," in preparation.

[5]Martin Ringle and Daniel Updegrove, "Is Strategic Planning for Technology a Oxymoron?" *CAUSE/EFFECT* 21 (1) (1998): 18–23.

[6]One good example of an actual strategic plan that is both brief and clear can by found on the web site of Mt. Holyoke College: <http://www.mtholyoke.edu/lits/about/plan/index.shtml>.

[7]Ringle and Updegrove advocate identifying a portion of the annual technology budget as "fungible," for capitalizing, literally, on unexpected opportunities.

[8]For those interested in examples of these early projects, many of which are the parents and godparents of what are now routine uses of technology for teaching and learning, see the FIPSE Technology Study Group, *Ivory Towers, Silicon Basements: Learner-Centered Computing in Postsecondary Education* (McKinney, Tex.: Academic Computing Publications, Inc., 1988) and Judith V. Boettcher, ed., *101 Success Stories of Information Technology in Higher Education: The Joe Wyatt Challenge* (New York: McGraw-Hill, Inc., 1993).

[9]For example, William H. Graves describes a useful four-stage "life-cycle" model in "Developing and Using Technology as a Strategic Asset," in Katz and Associates, *Dancing with the Devil*, 95–118.

[10]"The New Technologies and the Future of Residential Undergraduate Education," in Katz and Associates, *Dancing with the Devil*, 79.

[11]Christopher Spalding Peebles, Laurie G. Antolovic, Norma B. Holland, Karen Hoeve Adams, Debby Allmayer, and Phyllis H. Davidson, "Modeling and Managing the Cost and Quality of Information Technology Services at Indiana University: A Case Study," in Richard N. Katz and Julia A. Rudy, eds., *Information Technology in Higher Education: Assessing its Impact and Planning for the Future* (San Francisco: Jossey-Bass Publishers, 1999), 39, 49–50.

[12]For useful insight into conducting evaluations of technology and learning, see Stephen C. Ehrmann and Robin Etter Zúñiga, *The Flashlight Evaluation Handbook* (Washington, D.C.: TLT Group, 1997).

The Liberal Arts College

What follows is the list of colleges found in the "Baccalaureate (Liberal Arts) I" category of *A Classification of Institutions of Higher Education*, published by the Carnegie Foundation for the Advancement of Teaching (1994). Institutions falling within this category are defined as those that "are primarily undergraduate colleges with major emphasis on baccalaureate degree programs. They award 40 percent or more of their baccalaureate degrees in liberal arts fields and are restrictive in admissions." The liberal arts disciplines include English language and literature, foreign languages, letters, liberal and general studies, life sciences, mathematics, philosophy and religion, physical sciences, psychology, social sciences, the visual and performing arts, area and ethnic studies, and multi- and interdisciplinary studies.

PUBLIC INSTITUTIONS

Maryland
St. Mary's College of Maryland

Minnesota
University of Minnesota, Morris

New Jersey
Stockton State College

North Carolina
University of North Carolina at Asheville

Virginia
Virginia Military Institute

West Virginia
Shepherd College

Puerto Rico
University of Puerto Rico,
   Cayey University College

PRIVATE INSTITUTIONS

Alabama
Birmingham Southern College ·
Huntingdon College · Judson College

Arkansas
Hendrix College

California
Claremont McKenna College · Mills College ·
Occidental College · Pitzer College ·
Pomona College · Scripps College · Thomas
Aquinas College · University of Judaism ·
Westmont College · Whittier College

Colorado
Colorado College

Connecticut
Connecticut College · Trinity College ·
Wesleyan University

Florida
Eckerd College

Georgia
Agnes Scott College · Morehouse College ·
Oglethorpe University · Spelman College ·
Wesleyan College

Illinois
Augustana College · Illinois College ·
Illinois Wesleyan University · Knox College ·
Lake Forest College · Monmouth College ·
Wheaton College

Indiana
DePauw University · Earlham College ·
Franklin College of Indiana · Goshen
College · Hanover College · Wabash College

Iowa
Central College · Coe College · Cornell
College · Grinnell College · Luther College ·
Wartburg College

Kentucky
Berea College · Centre College · Georgetown
College · Transylvania University

Maine
Bates College · Bowdoin College · Colby College · College of the Atlantic

Maryland
Goucher College · St. John's College · Washington College · Western Maryland College

Massachusetts
Amherst College · College of the Holy Cross · Gordon College · Hampshire College · Mount Holyoke College · Radcliffe College · Simon's Rock College of Bard · Smith College · Wellesley College · Wheaton College · Williams College

Michigan
Albion College · Alma College · Hope College · Kalamazoo College

Minnesota
Carleton College · College of Saint Benedict · Concordia College at Moorhead · Gustavus Adolphus College · Hamline University · Macalester College · Saint John's University · Saint Olaf College

Mississippi
Millsaps College

Missouri
Westminster College · William Jewell College

Nebraska
Hastings College · Nebraska Wesleyan University

New Jersey
Drew University

New Mexico
St. John's College

New York
Bard College · Barnard College · Colgate University · Hamilton College · Hartwick College · Hobart and William Smith Colleges · Houghton College · Manhattanville College · Sarah Lawrence College · Siena College · Skidmore College · St. Lawrence University · Union College · Vassar College · Wells College

North Carolina
Davidson College · Guilford College · Salem College · St. Andrews Presbyterian College

Ohio
Antioch University · College of Wooster · Denison University · Hiram College · Kenyon College · Oberlin College · Ohio Wesleyan University · Wittenberg University

Oregon
Lewis and Clark College · Reed College · Willamette University

Pennsylvania
Albright College · Allegheny College · Bryn Mawr College · Bucknell University · Chatham College · Dickinson College · Franklin & Marshall College · Gettysburg College · Haverford College · Juniata College · Lafayette College · Moravian College · Muhlenberg College · Swarthmore College · Ursinus College · Washington and Jefferson College · Westminster College

Rhode Island
Providence College

South Carolina
Erskine College · Furman University · Presbyterian College · Wofford College

Tennessee
Rhodes College · University of the South

Texas
Austin College · Southwestern University · University of Dallas

Vermont
Bennington College · Marlboro College · Middlebury College

Virginia
Christendom College · Hampden-Sydney College · Hollins College · Randolph-Macon College · Randolph-Macon Woman's College · Sweet Briar College · Virginia Wesleyan College · Washington and Lee University

Washington
University of Puget Sound · Whitman College

West Virginia
Bethany College

Wisconsin
Beloit College · Lawrence University · Ripon College